FRAGILE GIANTS

A Bur Oak Original

FRAGILE GIANTS

A NATURAL HISTORY OF THE
L O E S S   H I L L S

Cornelia F. Mutel

UNIVERSITY OF IOWA PRESS
IOWA CITY

University of Iowa Press, Iowa City 52242
Copyright © 1989 by the University of Iowa
All rights reserved
Printed in the United States of America

Publication of this book was assisted by a grant from
the Iowa Science Foundation.

Figures 50, 52, 56, and 58 are reprinted from
The Wild Mammals of Missouri with the permission of
the University of Missouri Press.

Library of Congress
Cataloging-in-Publication Data

Mutel, Cornelia Fleischer.
Fragile giants: a natural history of the Loess Hills/by
Cornelia F. Mutel. — 1st ed.
p.   cm. — (A Bur oak original)
Bibliography: p.
Includes index.
ISBN 0-87745-256-3 (alk. paper)
ISBN 0-87745-257-1 (pbk.: alk. paper)
1. Natural history—Iowa.   2. Natural history—
Missouri.   3. Natural history—Nebraska.
4. Ecology—Iowa.   5. Ecology—Missouri.
6. Ecology—Nebraska.   I. Title.   II. Title:
Loess Hills.   III. Series.
QH105.I8M87   1989   89-35497
    508.777—dc20   CIP

10 9 8 7 6 5 4 3 2

96 95 94 93 92

*For my young and tender creatures
—Chris, Andy, and Matthew—
and for the young and tender of earth's
millions of other species*

CONTENTS

MAPS

TABLES

ACKNOWLEDGMENTS

Much of the work on a book such as this is done in solitude. But always, in the shadows, the contributions of others nudge the author forward.

Now, at last, I can pull these others out of the corners and formally acknowledge them as they deserve. I can express my thanks to researchers, both modern and of earlier times, who provided the basic information on which this book is based. To the artists and photographers who turned the manuscript into a work of beauty and who were unusually generous in sharing their time and talent. To the Iowa Science Foundation, administered through the Iowa Academy of Science, which funded a portion of my fieldwork and virtually all of the book's graphics. To the Institute of Agricultural Medicine and Occupational Health, the University of Iowa, which granted me sufficient leave time to complete the manuscript

To my husband, Robert, and young sons, who cared for each other during the many long weekends and late nights when I was away writing. To my father, Herb Fleischer, who patiently read and criticized the entire manuscript. To Nancy Jones and other friends who allowed me to use their homes as writing retreats. To the residents of the Loess Hills, who from the start welcomed me to the region. And, of course, to the native species and natural features themselves, which are easy to love and, once loved, would inspire anyone to keep writing.

To specify every person who has contributed to this book would require a long list of names, and the book already has enough of those. But several special contributions must be noted. Dean Roosa, Iowa's State Ecologist, first inspired the book. He and Jean Prior, research geologist with the Iowa Department of Natural Resources, encouraged its completion by patiently providing information, explaining processes in the field, reviewing portions of the manuscript, and never failing to express their belief in the project's worth.

Duane C. Anderson, Iowa's previous State Archaeologist, now executive director of the Dayton Museum of Natural History; Richard G. Baker, Department of Geology, the University of Iowa; John Fleckenstein, Iowa Department of Natural Resources; Douglas Ladd, Director of Stewardship, the Nature Conservancy, Missouri Field Office; Paul Waite, Iowa's previous State Climatologist; and Virginia K. Wallace, Missouri Department of Conservation, were especially generous in providing information in their fields of expertise and also reviewed portions of the manuscript. The contributions of Art Bettis, Iowa Department of Natural Resources; Thomas B. Bragg, Department of Biology, the University of Nebraska at Omaha; Shirley Schermer and others at Iowa's Office of the State Archaeologist; lepidopterist Dennis Schlicht; and Scott Sorensen and others at the Sioux City Public Museum also deserve commendation.

Dianne and Bill Blankenship, prairie enthusiasts in Sioux City, welcomed me from the start. They were two of the many residents and public employees of the Loess Hills region who provided me with information, shared their valuable insights in the field, and in some instances opened their homes to me. Some of the others included Barbara Cochran, Bob Dolan, Gary Garabrandt, Kirk Payne, Jim Perley, Don and Pam Poggensee, Don and Luella Reese, Otha Wearin, and Barb Wilson. Getting to know these people and many others in the region enriched both me and the book.

To all of these persons, and to many others unnamed here but not forgotten, I extend my warmest thanks.

PART ONE

NATURAL HISTORY OF
THE LOESS HILLS

ONE

INTRODUCTION

"These Bluffs are a great Curiosity." So stated railroad entrepreneur John Insley Blair during his 1863 expedition to survey a route west to the Missouri River. Thirteen years earlier, missionary Thaddeus Culbertson had described the Loess Hills in his travel journal in this way: "The term Mountains in Miniature is the most expressive one to describe these Bluffs. They have all the irregularity in shape, and in valleys that mountains have, they have no rocks and rarely timber."

In 1832, the artist George Catlin spoke of the Loess Hills far more eloquently: "the prairie, whose enamelled plains that lie beneath me in distance soften into sweetness, like an essence; whose thousand thousand velvet-covered hills . . . go tossing and leaping down with steep or graceful declivities to the river's edge, as if to grace its pictured shores . . . this prairie, where Heaven sheds its purest light and lends its richest tints."

Modern-day visitors are rarely that effusive, but they too comment on the special characteristics of the Loess Hills. "They look like they don't belong here," say some; others state that they seem to have just stepped into the Appalachian Mountains. Like the earlier travelers, today's visitors seem to recognize that they have entered a land apart, far different from other landscapes they know. Suddenly, the roads cut and curve through near-vertical walls of silt. Quaint farmsteads, tucked into hollows, nestle among forests and brownish red grasslands. Steep slopes are bathed by the sun and combed by the winds, which never seem to cease. Most of today's visitors to the Loess Hills have probably grown up on farms or in cities, landscapes shaped for human use. But regardless of background or training, they sense that in the Loess Hills, nature is still in control.

The sense of specialness is well entrusted in the Loess Hills, for this landscape is one of North America's gems, possessing natural features rarely duplicated elsewhere on the planet. The most obvious of those features are the substance and shape of the hills. They consist of exceptionally large, homogeneous piles of fine-grained, cohesive quartz silt. Depths of loess deposits in general exceed 60 feet, and well drillers have reported depths of more than 200 feet. The word "loess" denotes the silt's origin. The tiny particles were light enough to be lifted into place by the wind.

Loess is not in itself a rarity. The parent material for many of the world's richest agricultural soils, loess deposits are associated with major river valleys throughout the world. Deep loess deposits characterize sections of the Rhine Valley in Germany, where the word "loess" was coined. Deep loess dominates parts of the southern Soviet Union. The Yellow River, one of China's major drainages, is named for the large quantities of loess that color the river as they wash into it from adjacent highlands. Notable North American loess deposits occur along the Missouri, lower Mississippi, and Platte rivers and in eastern Washington. Loess covers tens of thousands of square miles of the Midwest, with depths varying greatly from place to place.

All of Iowa, excluding the tongue-shaped section in the north-central part of the state that was most recently covered by glaciers, is coated with several feet or more of loess. Nearly 40 percent of the state's prime soils are loess-derived. A good-sized piece of Nebraska and nearly all of Missouri are loess-mantled. However, the Loess Hills are unique in North America, for only here is loess deep enough and extensive enough to create new landforms—to give form and substance to the land surface.

Today's corrugated, angular, intricate Loess Hills landscape is the result of running water's reshaping of the deep loess primarily during the past 12,000 years. Undisturbed deep, dry loess is highly cohesive, able to stand in near-vertical cliffs. Loess is also extremely prone to erosion. Water has produced the characteristic shapes that caught the eye of the earliest explorers. Steep-sided knobs, narrow undulating ridges with abundant side spurs, numerous interconnected drainages, gullies cutting deeply into the valleys, and small terraces called catsteps give an impression of a giant's massive but delicately sculptured carving (fig. 1).

Hidden within this deep loess is a rich collection of fossils and archaeological artifacts. In addition, the native inhabitants of the Loess Hills have to some degree been protected by the rugged loess topography. While lands on all sides have been converted to cropland, extensive areas of the

Figure 1. *The Loess Hills: knobby, irregular, intricately carved piles of deep wind-deposited silt, covered with plants and animals typical of grasslands found much farther to the west. Note the eroding, sharply cut gully in the center foreground and the catsteps crossing the hillsides, both typical of the Hills. State Historical Society of Iowa, Iowa City.*

Loess Hills have remained in prairie and woodland, communities that contain rich and unusual mixtures of native species. Some species are rare or endangered; many are at the fringes of their ranges of distribution.

The prairies command the greatest attention of biologists, for Loess Hills prairies contain many plants and animals typical of hot, dry areas far to the west. Yucca, tumbleweed, the Great Plains toad, cowboy's delight, and the plains pocket mouse (to name a few) reside in the Loess Hills because the well-drained loess and its steep, sun- and wind-exposed slopes create a desertlike local climate. The Hills' assemblage of western species is not found elsewhere in Iowa, Missouri, or eastern Nebraska.

The wild, untrammeled character of this landscape, its relatively large remaining prairies, and its unusual and rare species have attracted national attention in recent years. The Loess Hills have become the focus of scientific research, education, and conservation. Such efforts are not misplaced, any more than efforts to preserve Rembrandt's paintings or Bach's music would be misplaced. The Loess Hills can feed our spiritual hunger and our intellectual curiosity as richly as the highest products of human civilization would feed them. We are now coming to realize that maintenance of biological diversity and healthy natural systems, such as those in the Loess Hills, is necessary for the perpetuation of human life as well. Wisely used and managed, the Loess Hills can continue to satisfy the needs of both humans and native species indefinitely.

SCOPE AND PURPOSE OF THIS BOOK

This book is intended to be a resource for the many types of people attracted to the Loess Hills, from the reader with no special training in natural history to the educator and research scientist. Readers with an interest in one specific topic may read appropriate sections. The book may also serve as a field reference.

Three car tours and a listing of Loess Hills public use areas and educational resources lead the casual visitor to points of interest and promote a general understanding of the region's natural features. Details of natural features are explained in chapters 2 through 6. Those chapters are useful as a field reference, study guide, and armchair exploration of the region. Because the book summarizes the majority of biological, geological, and archaeological research recently completed in the Loess Hills, it also is a useful scientific reference and educational tool and can serve as a text for students in environmental and ecological fields of study. Last, the book can provide guidance and useful background information to land-use managers, land-use planners, and private landowners involved in the Loess Hills.

This book is a comprehensive natural history. A broad spectrum of information is covered, including geology, climate, native plant and animal species, and communities formed by those species. Human cultures of the last 12,000 years and their environmental effects have also been considered. Instead of looking at features individually, as separate entities, the book attempts to integrate information and explain the interrelationships of all elements—that is, to discuss the ecological systems, or ecosystems, of the Loess Hills.

Chapters are arranged chronologically, beginning with the earliest times, long before the Loess Hills were formed, and proceeding through management issues that will determine the future of the landscape and its native

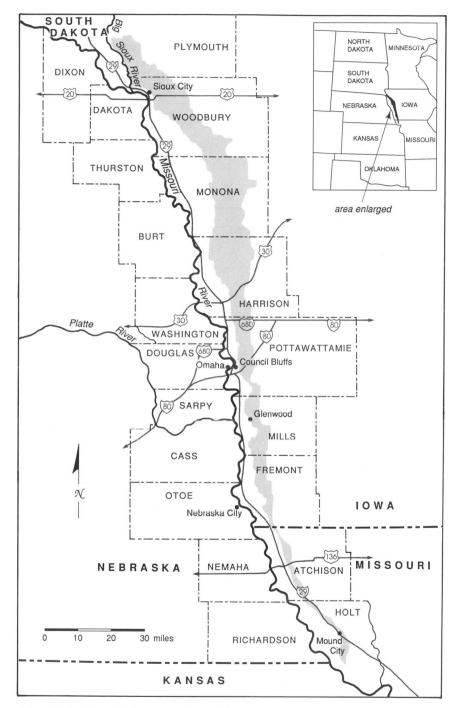

Map 1. The Loess Hills region. Heidi Perry.

species. Sidebars throughout the text give in-depth information on specific points.

Discussions concentrate on features of the Loess Hills as defined in following paragraphs and outlined in map 1. The book can also be used to understand a larger surrounding area, where prairies, woodlands, and loess deposits share some similarities with the Loess Hills. In addition, numerous references are made to sites and characteristics of the Missouri River floodplain, adjacent to the Loess Hills on their western side.

Throughout the book, comparisons have been made with the bluffs in Nebraska, which border the Missouri River valley on its western side. Loess has accumulated on both sides of the Missouri River valley. However, riverside bluffs in Nebraska and Kansas are not included in the formal definition of the Loess Hills because loess deposits west of the river are thinner and less extensive than in Iowa and because they do not constitute a distinctive regional topography. As a result, the rugged, angular topography typical of the deep loess can be found only sporadically. In addition, native communities differ significantly from those in Iowa and Missouri.

DEFINING THE BOUNDARIES OF THE LOESS HILLS

The Loess Hills, as defined in this book, stretch from the town of Westfield in central Plymouth County, Iowa, to just south of the Squaw Creek National Wildlife Refuge in central Holt County, Missouri (map 1). Between those two points, the Loess Hills form a north-south band of varying width approximately 200 miles long. Deep loess landforms are best developed in a strip between 3 and 10 miles wide along the edge of the Missouri River valley. In general, the band of deep loess landforms is greatest to the north, in Harrison, Monona, Woodbury, and Plymouth counties, Iowa. It narrows to the south, in places becoming extremely thin. For much of their extent in Missouri, the Loess Hills are reduced to a sliver that barely extends east of the westernmost bluffs.

The western boundary of the Loess Hills is clearly defined and easily recognized (fig. 2). Here the Hills border the Missouri River alluvial plain, a flat lowland shaped in the past by the river's shifting waters. The boundary between the level plain and rugged Hills is razor-sharp. Elsewhere the boundary of the Loess Hills is less obvious, and its definition is somewhat arbitrary. For example, to the east, the depth and dominance of loess gradually decrease, and the Loess Hills merge with a more rolling land-

Figure 2. The boundary between the rugged western edge of the Loess Hills and the level Missouri River floodplain is razor sharp. Prairies with drought-tolerant plants and animals cover these near-vertical bluff faces. Carl Kurtz.

scape, an eroded glacial plain. Loess mantles the plain but is not deep enough to mask or reshape the basic form of the land.

Loess Hills boundaries correspond approximately with a loess depth of 64 feet or greater, as mapped by R. V. Ruhe (1969). The landform region in Iowa is that defined by J. C. Prior (1976), which was mapped primarily on the basis of geological traits. In the field and on large-scale topographic maps, she identified those high-relief areas where loess was known to be deep and where loess obviously controlled the landscape. More specifically, she mapped the Loess Hills as a region of steep, finely dissected terrain with numerous interrelated drainages, shown by irregular, closely spaced contour lines, frequently indicating isolated knobs of loess. She also considered ecological characteristics and maps of soil types, since soils forming in deep loess and on steep slopes are distinctive.

The map of Missouri's Loess Hills, also drawn by Prior for use in this book, was based on examination of much smaller scale topographic maps. In addition, it took into account the author's field identification of bedrock features, loess depth, and ecological characteristics (primarily prairie distribution). The southern terminus corresponds with the most southerly significant, characteristic dry prairies found on loess-dominated terrain that remain today. Isolated patches of loess-dominated terrain are found south of there, but they are not significant enough to be mapped at the scale utilized here.

The southern boundary of the Loess Hills is perhaps the most arbitrary, and it is more restrictive here than in other publications. In the far southern Loess Hills, the loess becomes increasingly discontinuous and the influence of bedrock increases. Rugged loess terrain can be observed south of St. Joseph, in Bluffwoods State Forest. Sporadic, isolated patches of fairly deep loess extent eastward along the Missouri River nearly to its confluence with the Mississippi River (Beveridge, 1980). R. H. Thom and J. H. Wilson (1980) state that loess dominates the topography of the western section of their Glaciated Plains Natural Division of Missouri. Their boundaries include a large section of northwestern Missouri, extending east and south to where the original loess was only approximately 10 feet thick. They also point attention to the steep loess mounds along the Missouri River.

In the past, a southern boundary based on the location of dry loess bluff prairies may have differed because of the shrinking range of the prairies. B. F. Bush wrote in 1895 that such prairies extended to a few miles south of St. Joseph. Today small bluff prairies can still be seen in Riverbreaks State Forest, south of our southern terminus of the Loess Hills but 20 miles northwest of St. Joseph. Future studies taking all of those factors and additional fieldwork into account may redefine the boundaries of the southernmost Loess Hills.

 **TWO**

ANCIENT LANDSCAPES
AND COMMUNITIES

The history of the Loess Hills began when extraordinarily deep blankets of silt were first deposited in this region. Much can be told of how the silt was lifted by wind and then shaped by water; of the gigantic mammals that wandered the region's valleys and climbed its slopes; of the plant communities that migrated to and from the Hills, broad-leaved and needled trees from the north and east, grasses from the south and west. The Loess Hills' history is one of climate, inhabitants, and landscapes constantly responding to one another.

Long before the loess was blown skyward, a series of other landscapes existed in the region, landscapes far different from those of today. Their varied histories lie recorded within the fossils and rock layers that for the most part are today hidden beneath the Loess Hills, a mute testimony to slowly but constantly changing landscapes, climates, and communities. At least six times the region was smoothed by advancing glaciers, which as they receded left piles of loose debris to be carved by rivers and rain. Long before that, warm, carbonate-rich seas cyclically covered the region, leaving deposits that were compressed into bedrock over still more ancient solid rock.

Those early periods, preceding the Holocene (the last 10,000 years), are the focus of this chapter. (The standard geological terms used to outline the chronology are listed in table 1.)

TABLE 1. Timetable of Geological Processes

Era	Period	Years before Present	Geological Processes and Formations
Cenozoic	*Quaternary Holocene,* or modern, epoch	10,000 to present	shaping of Loess Hills through erosion
	Pleistocene, or Ice Age, epoch	2.5 million to 10,000	deposition of loess, preceded by glaciation of region and deposition of till
	Tertiary	65 to 2.5 million	
Mesozoic	*Cretaceous*	130 to 65 million	age of dinosaurs; marine and nonmarine deposition of bedrock visible today in northern Loess Hills
	Jurassic	185 to 130 million	
	Triassic	230 to 185 million	
Paleozoic	Permian	265 to 230 million	
	Pennsylvanian	310 to 265 million	coal swamps and coastal seas; marine and non-marine deposition of bed-rock visible today, from Harrison and Monona counties, Iowa, through Missouri's Hills

TABLE 1 (*continued*)

Era	Period	Years before Present	Geological Processes and Formations
Paleozoic	*Mississippian*	355 to 310 million	deposits of shallow, carbonate-rich seas
	Devonian	413 to 355 million	
	Silurian	425 to 413 million	
	Ordovician	475 to 425 million	deposits of shallow, carbonate-rich seas
	Cambrian	570 to 475 million	
Cryptozoic	*Precambrian*	4.5 billion to 570 million	deposition of oldest, deepest bedrock

Note: Periods known to have left deposits in the Loess Hills region are italicized. During other periods, either no deposits were made or deposits were later washed away through erosion.

EARLIEST TIMES: LAYING DOWN THE ANCIENT BEDROCK

If one were able to cut through the Loess Hills deep into the earth, the knife would slide easily through the unconsolidated earth nearly to the base of the hills and then would saw with difficulty through several horizontal layers of successively older solid rock. Eventually, the knife would dig deep enough to hit Precambrian bedrock one billion to two billion years old, a part of the same rock system that forms today's Rocky Mountains. However, although the younger layered rocks were later uplifted and then washed away in western mountainous states, they have remained as cover over much of the Midwest. Thus Precambrian rocks can be seen at ground surface in Iowa only in one place, the extreme northwestern corner of the state at Gitchee Manitou State Preserve. They also are evident aboveground farther to the north in central Minnesota, Wisconsin, and Canada.

Lying on top of that ancient rock are layers upon layers of rocks deposited at successively younger times, each under somewhat different conditions. Fossils embedded within the layers portray life from its earliest beginnings through the evolving complexity of marine and nonmarine life. If the lowest of the deeply buried layered rocks were exposed, it would tell of late Cambrian times approximately 500 million years ago, when a shallow inland sea periodically covered the Loess Hills region, leaving shoreline, inner shelf, and offshore deposits. Fossils in the sandstone and other Cambrian rocks would reveal that life then was limited to primitive forms: trilobites, algae, brachiopods, burrowing wormlike organisms.

During the Ordovician Period 450 or so million years ago, a shallow, warm inland sea once again flooded the region. The sea's sediments formed a diversity of rock types, reflecting the emergence of a far greater diversity of life. Algae and all major invertebrate groups including corals, mollusks, echinoderms such as the beautifully delicate crinoid "sea lilies," and annelid worms were abundantly present.

When seas were absent, erosion undoubtedly shaped the land and removed some marine sediments. Complete removal by erosion may have been the fate of Silurian deposits, left a bit more than 400 million years ago. Or perhaps no deposits were left on the Loess Hills region during that period. In any case, Silurian deposits are not present underneath Iowa's Loess Hills, although they are found in central and eastern Iowa. But the following period, the Devonian, left an extremely fossiliferous rock record (fig. 3). Once again, limestone, dolomite, and other rock types were formed from sediments of ancient seas and coastline environments. Organisms living within the seas included the invertebrate groups present earlier, although some were by now more advanced. Brachiopods, for example, were dominated by articulated forms. In addition, animals with backbones had made their debut. Fish fossils are abundant and include placoderms (primitive fish with a framework of cartilage), sharks, and bony fish. Spores, the reproductive bodies of primitive plants, are common in some shales.

The Mississippian Period, from 310 to 355 million years ago, saw the last of the widespread carbonate-rich seas spread across the interior of the continent. The layers, primarily limestones, of this period contain immense quantities of fossils. The Mississippian is well known for its crinoids,

Figure 3. *In ancient times, the present area of the Loess Hills region was periodically covered by shallow seas with a variety of evolving plant and animal life. In this Devonian seascape, invertebrates such as brachiopods, crinoids, cephalopods, corals, and bryozoans are joined by larger vertebrates, including sharks and joint-necked armored fish. Will Thomson.*

but other types of organisms described in previous paragraphs also left their remains. Following recession of the sea, the Loess Hills region and surrounding lands were part of a large emergent land mass that experienced weathering and erosion.

All of the rock systems just described can be seen east of the Loess Hills in Iowa and Missouri, and drilling has shown that they all lie deep underneath the Hills, although none is visible there. The oldest bedrock visible in the Loess Hills region is from the Pennsylvanian Period, the time when great coal-forming swamps covered much of the eastern United States, beginning approximately 310 million years ago. Pennsylvanian bedrock can be seen in certain road cuts and streambeds from the middle of Monona County, Iowa, south through Iowa's and Missouri's Loess Hills, and in limestone quarries along the bluffs such as those near Council Bluffs and Thurman in the southern Loess Hills. It underlies Nebraska's floodplain and Missouri River bluffs along the edge of Burt and Washington counties, becoming more widespread to the west from Douglas County and Omaha to the state's southern boundary. Pennsylvanian bedrock consists of complex sequences of limestone, shale, sandstone, siltstone, and coal, deposited cyclically in marine and nonmarine environments. A great shallow sea reached well into today's Iowa about 275 million years ago, its shoreline advancing and regressing a number of times across the low, flat Loess Hills region. When seas were high, marine sediments were deposited in the region. When seas receded, sediments were deposited by coastal streams. All the deposits later were compressed into solid rock.

Nonmarine deposits also consisted of accumulated plant materials from the junglelike growth of coal swamps. Such coastal swamps were massive. One reached across today's southern Iowa and extended down into Missouri. Their plant material, which was buried and altered faster than it could decompose, was the source of coal beds high in ash and sulfur content that may extend from central Iowa into the Loess Hills region.

Marine fossils in Iowa's Pennsylvanian rocks demonstrate that life forms were becoming more varied and complex. Representatives of all major common marine invertebrates, as well as sharks and other fish, are included. Calcareous algae are abundant. Fossil hunters searching in the right place may find remains of brachiopods, corals, crinoids, bryozoans, and any of a number of other ancient marine dwellers. A real treasure, however, would be a fossil from the coal swamps (fig. 4). Such a find would provide a glimpse of early terrestrial plant life in the Loess Hills region. Scale trees, or lycopods, grew to 100 feet in height. Lycopods are represented in the modern-day flora by small club mosses that dot the floor of northern coniferous forests. Scouring rushes, or sphenopsids, relatives of today's much smaller scouring rushes, were also present. Ferns and seed ferns grew as tall as today's trees and provided a dense understory. Lack of growth rings in all those plants is interpreted to mean that distinct seasonal changes were absent. The prolific plants grew in a perpetual summer of warm, moist subtropical or tropical conditions. Many of them, more primitive than our modern-day seed-bearing plants (angiosperms), reproduced by spores.

Following the Pennsylvanian Period, during the late Paleozoic and early Mesozoic eras, the Loess Hills area was probably above sea level. Either no sediments were deposited during that long interval or deposits were later removed by erosion. In any case, the Loess Hills region contains no rock record of the Permian and Triassic periods (excluding Permian deposits in central portions of Nemaha and Richardson counties in extreme

Figure 4. *Huge coal swamps covered much of southern Iowa during the Pennsylvanian period. These swamps were home to scale trees, club mosses, seed ferns, dragonflies, cockroaches, snakes, and large amphibians. Will Thomson.*

southeastern Nebraska). Although Jurassic rocks are exposed near Fort Dodge, Iowa, none are demonstrated in the Loess Hills. During that stretch of time, from approximately 265 million to 130 million years ago, the region is thought to have been a low plain with an arid or semiarid climate.

Then at the end of the Mesozoic Era, during the Cretaceous Period

Figure 5. Outcrops of Cretaceous bedrock can be seen underlying the loess in the Sioux City area. This bedrock, composed of sandstone, shale, lignite, conglomerate, and limestone, is formed of sediments deposited in and along the coast of shallow seas during the age of dinosaurs. Photo by the author.

about 100 million years ago, the Loess Hills region once again was invaded by shallow seas. The advancing seas laid down sediments both in and along the coast, as marine shelf, coastal delta and lagoon, and alluvial deposits. Today, ripple marks from water movement of those ancient seas can be seen in regional sandstone deposits. Deposits of shale, lignite, conglomerate, and limestone also constitute the Cretaceous bedrock, which underlies the Loess Hills from the middle of Monona County, Iowa, to the north, with a small isolated segment also found on the border of Harrison and Pottawattamie counties. It underlies Nebraska's bluff areas approximately from Washington County on to the north, although Pennsylvanian bedrock borders the eastern edges of Burt and Washington counties. Outcrops of Cretaceous rocks are quite evident along the Missouri River in northeastern Nebraska and in the Sioux City area, in particular in the numerous shale quarries, in Stone State Park, and north of Sioux City along the Big Sioux River (fig. 5). Because those rocks are less resistant to erosion than Pennsylvanian bedrock to the south, the Missouri River has been able to cut a broad valley near the northern Loess Hills.

Plant and animal life had changed greatly by the time of the Cretaceous seas. Primitive coal-swamp plants had been replaced first by gymnosperms, commonly thought of as conifers or plants with needles, and then by angiosperms, the plants with true flowers and broad leaves that today dominate the earth. The dominance of flowering plants during the Cretaceous is demonstrated by the diverse and locally abundant angiosperm leaf fossils (forerunners of magnolia, poplar, sassafras, willow, and other trees) as well as casts of tree trunks and petrified wood found in the Loess Hills region. The Sioux City area has proven to be good hunting ground for those and other Cretaceous fossils.

Dinosaurs ruled the earth during the Cretaceous. Reptiles diversified and dominated on land, in air, and in the sea, but the traces of their dominance are not abundant in the Loess Hills. Along the Missouri River a bit downstream from Sioux City, embedded in Nebraska's sandstone, a portion of an ornithopod dinosaur's femur has been found. No dinosaur fossils have been found in Iowa's Loess Hills or, indeed, in all of Iowa. However, in the late 1800s, a series of vertebrae of a large marine reptile, a plesiosaur, were excavated north of Stone State Park. The vertebrae are now on display in the Sioux City Public Museum. A partial skeleton of a large marine turtle was discovered in southeastern Nebraska, near Fairbury, about the same time. Fragments of plesiosaurs and mosasaurs, gigantic marine flesh-eating reptiles, and of giant turtles and crocodiles are present in regions surrounding the Loess Hills. They correspond to more complete fossil records found farther to the west.

Other marine fossils are present in Loess Hills Cretaceous deposits. Fossils of sharks; mollusks including oysters, cephalopods, clams, and snails; and a diversity of bony fish including the giant predatory ichthyodectids have been found. Fossil remains of mammals and birds are unknown from this region, although those creatures first appeared on earth during the Cretaceous. From study of fossil remains elsewhere, we know that following the Cretaceous, after the demise of the dinosaurs, mammals and birds diversified rapidly.

The Cretaceous seas were the last massive bodies of water to cover much of the continent. During the following period, the Tertiary, lands previously covered by water were above sea level and exposed to processes of weathering and erosion. Tertiary deposits do not exist in the Loess Hills region or across Iowa, although they cover much of Nebraska west of the loess bluffs and a bit of southeastern Missouri.

The Tertiary saw the arrival of climate and communities resembling those of modern times. Before the Tertiary, the climate of the Loess Hills region had been generally tropical or subtropical, without annual fluctuations. Its stable climate began to deteriorate during the Tertiary, in part because the land mass forming today's United States, which had previously been located near the equator, was slowly drifting northward into its present-day position. Although remaining milder and moister than today, the climate became cooler and less stable than it had been previously. Cyclical climatic fluctuations heralded the Ice Age that was destined to follow.

As climate changed, plant communities evolved from humid subtropical forests to savannas or savanna-parklands. Several bits of information from areas farther to the west point to the establishment of open grasslands in today's Great Plains since the middle Tertiary. One of the more fascinating bits is the discovery of seeds and other plant parts stuck between the teeth of a Tertiary-aged rhinoceros, whose fossils were found in Nebraska. The plant parts, which are more than ten million years old, are the earliest records of modern grass families, the predecessors of today's prairie grasses. Other plant fossils and vertebrate remains, for example those of small horses adapted for savanna life, also support the theory of early grassland establishment.

Mammals diversified and assumed dominance of the earth during the Tertiary. Although only a few vertebrate fossils have been found in streambeds of western Iowa, diverse mammalian fossils occur in more-western states. They tell of a strange collection of mammals: minute horses, ancient rhinoceroses, ancestors of the cat family, peccaries, a variety of forms of camels, a number of horned ruminants, and many additional forms of archaic animals. Their ancient landscape may well have resembled today's African savanna, the only place on earth where such a richness of large mammals can still be found.

THE ICE AGE

Glaciation of the Loess Hills Region

Toward the end of the Tertiary, an increase in precipitation and a shift in the world's climatic heat balance, causing a decrease in the Midwest's mean annual temperature of perhaps six to eight degrees centigrade, resulted in the accumulation of great sheets of snow and ice in the Canadian Arctic. The massive sheets moved south under their own weight, covering today's United States from the Atlantic Seaboard to the plains east of the northern Rocky Mountains, and then receded as the climate returned to warmer temperatures similar to those of today. Once again the climate would cool and glaciers would move southward, only to melt and recede. This was the Ice Age, more formally termed the Pleistocene Epoch of the Quaternary Period. It began approximately 2.5 million years ago and ended formally only 10,000 years ago. Many scientists consider our present climate to be merely a warm interval preceding another period of colder temperatures.

Traditionally, four great glacial advances were thought to have covered the midwestern states. Two, the Nebraskan and Kansan stages, covered the Loess Hills region. However, recent studies of rock sequences in western Iowa and eastern Nebraska have demonstrated the presence of at least six tills (materials transported and deposited by glacial ice), deposited between approximately 0.5 and 2.1 million years ago. The tills now are collectively called Pre-Illinoian, that is, preceding the Illinoian glacial advance of 160,000 years or so ago.

Following glacial advances, the tills were left to weather and erode into new landscape forms for tens of thousands of years. Ideally the tills—unsorted sediments with rocks in a matrix of firmer sand, clay, and pebbles—are easily differentiated from the older solid rock below and the younger, finer-grained loess above. But the sequence of deposits may be far more complex, since ancient soils and other windblown or waterborne deposits may lie between and over the ancient tills. Sand and gravel sequences, deposited by water running over the till, often contain vertebrate and invertebrate fossils. Layers of ash, blown into western Iowa from major eruptions of now-extinct volcanoes in today's Yellowstone National Park, can be seen in widely scattered roadcuts (fig. 6). The ashes have been dated at 610,000 to 2 million years old. One such ash layer is visible along the road at the base of the bluffs on the border between Harrison and Monona counties, Iowa. Similar ash deposits from those massive eruptions are present in eastern Nebraska, across the Great Plains, and even along the West Coast and in Pacific Ocean bottom deposits.

Formation of the Loess Hills

The last two glacial advances, the Illinoian (approximately 130,000 to 150,000 years ago) and Wisconsinan (with coldest temperatures approxi-

Figure 6. *Volcanic ash, which blew into the region from now-extinct volcanoes in today's Yellowstone National Park, is recognized as a light-colored layer underlying the loess. Here the ash is seen as a light band about a third of the way down from the top of the photograph. Don Poggensee.*

mately 18,000 years ago), are of major significance to the Hills. For although advancing glaciers stopped north of the Hills region, they were responsible for the formation of the Loess Hills through the following mechanisms. Moving, massive glaciers have the force to grind rock into powder, or glacial "flour." As melting water flows from the margins of the sheets of ice, the ground rock is carried downstream to new regions. Today's visitors to glaciated mountain ranges are familiar with rivers of glacial milk, colored grayish white by the powdered rock.

Streams, flowing from the Illinoian and Wisconsinan glaciers that lay to the north of today's Loess Hills, fed tremendous volumes of water and sediment into river valleys throughout the Midwest. Waters covered miles-wide floodplains during the warmer summers but slowed to a trickle when winter temperatures halted the glaciers' recession. Then the finely ground rock, left exposed on expansive floodplains, was free to be picked up by the strong winter winds. Clouds of silt, clay, and fine sand rose into the sky, to be dropped on some leeward upland surface. The process can still be observed in certain glaciated Alaskan valleys.

The north-south section of the broad Missouri River floodplain, from today's Sioux City, Iowa, to Kansas City, Missouri, provided an especially
rich source of particulates for the prevailing westerly winds. Great moving
clouds of dust were abruptly checked by the uplands on the eastern side of
the river valley. Typically the winds moved material from west to east, but
sometimes the winds would shift and material would be carried to the west
side of the Missouri River, into today's Nebraska. As the turbulent air left
the floodplain, sediments dropped quickly to blanket broad river terrace,
glacial till, knobby protrusion of limestone, river bottom sand and gravel,
whatever material formed the irregular preexisting land surface. Some entire valleys were filled with loess. The Loess Hills were created.

That process may seem to be obvious today, but it was not evident to
nineteenth-century natural historians, who hotly debated theories regarding the formation of the Loess Hills. (The story of the modern theory's development is told in sidebar 1.)

Because of the depth of the loess, the land's shape before loess deposition remains a mystery. Also unknown are the hills' shapes at the zenith of
their creation, for running waters have had 12,000 years to reshape the
loess since major deposition ended. However, several aspects of Loess
Hills formation are well understood. The landscape was created during the
last two glacial periods. The oldest and bottommost loess, Loveland loess,
is presumed to have originated during the Illinoian glaciation. It forms the
base of the bluffs of Iowa and extends a relatively short distance, only 19 to
37 miles eastward, although it is more extensive in the Great Plains and
elsewhere. Wisconsinan loess, deposited between approximately 31,000
and 12,000 years ago, forms the bulk of the Loess Hills and is divided geo-
logically into two formations. The earliest, or basal, Wisconsinan loess is
also called the Gilman Canyon Formation and Roxana loess in other locations, and the upper Wisconsinan loess has been named Peoria loess
elsewhere.

Although the bulk of the loess was deposited during those two glacial
periods, the process did not start and stop abruptly. The natural historian
Bohumil Shimek, who did much of the early research in the Hills, described
watching great dust clouds lift from sandbars in the then-unchannelized
Missouri River and drift toward the Hills, confirming his wind-centered theory of formation. In addition, loess deposition was periodic rather than
constant. Periods of little deposition were long enough to allow local formation of soils, seen today as dark bands within loess. When loess was not
being deposited, particles from other sources were laid down on one loess

SIDEBAR 1. Debating the Deposition of Loess

The mechanisms of formation of the Loess Hills were hotly debated for many years around the turn of the century. Persons who first studied the Hills concluded that they were somehow deposited by or in water. From the start, the deposits were correctly associated with waters and sediments from glaciers, but natural historians incorrectly theorized that the sediments were deposited directly by water, either during violent floods or by settling to the bottom of bodies of water.

Charles White, the state geologist, gave his theory of bluff formation in one of the first reports of Iowa's Geological Survey (1870). He stated that the extremely muddy Missouri River, heavily laden with sediments produced by the grinding action of glaciers ("the mills of the gods"), flowed into a broad lake. The sediments dropped to the bottom, quickly filling the lake to the height of the tallest bluffs. The Missouri River then cut a channel in the deposits, which remained first as a broad, undrained marshland and later as dry uplands. Following shaping by erosion, the modern bluffs are essentially, White stated, "miniature mountain ranges of dried mud."

Bohumil Shimek, one of the state's early and all-time great natural historians, studied and wrote much about the geology, plant communities, and large mammal fossils of the Loess Hills. Although he first commended the fluvial formation theory, stating in 1895 that the loess had been deposited "by quiet overflows of the sluggish prairie streams" and also in ponds and lakes similar to prairie potholes, he later retracted those statements. Instead, he stated, the loess had been carried and deposited slowly by wind. Shimek supported his new theory with several pieces of evidence, a major one being the predominance of land-dwelling snail fossils throughout the loess. Snail fossils typically are found within loess where the snails originally lived. Shimek's terrestrial snails obviously had lived on uplands rather than in lakes. Therefore, the bluffs could not have been deposited by water. Shimek went on to use the identification of those fossils to theorize about the types of plant communities and climate present during loess deposition.

layer, later to be covered by a second. Because of the interbedded formations, and because the loess buried a preexisting landscape of hills and valleys, the Loess Hills are not as uniform in thickness or composition as one might first think.

Changing Communities and Climate

Iowa's Loess Hills contain some of the richest fossil assemblages in the state. From fossils, we can describe the animals that lived here during parts of the Ice Age and in the Holocene. However, little is known of the animals, plants, and climate of the early Ice Age beyond the obvious: the climate alternated cyclically from cooler to warmer as glaciers advanced and receded. Fossil records show that the southern Great Plains were extensive grasslands with forests along streams, but no such records exist for the Loess Hills region.

(A note on fossils: The community and climatic reconstructions suggested here have been the result of studying traditional fossils such as rock-embedded invertebrates and large, ancient bones. Other types of fossils are also used to decipher prehistoric ecosystems. Pollen has been preserved in lakes and bogs near the Loess Hills, where researchers extract it with long hollow drills. They can identify the microscopic pollen and date other organic materials found along with it. The relative abundance of certain types of pollen pinpoints not only vegetation types but also climate, since certain plants grow only in given climates. Larger remains of plants from archaeological digs, alluvial deposits, and other sources are similarly useful, as are the bones of small mammals and even shells of snails. Some fossils have been washed, blown, or weathered away. Because fossils are not available everywhere, gaps in the fossil record are inevitable. Thus the picture of prehistoric communities of the Hills region is discontinuous and has been extrapolated from a variety of locations, many of which are near but not in the Loess Hills.)

The first clue to areas surrounding the Loess Hills dates from the Wisconsinan stage. More than 40,000 years ago, today's Iowa north of the Loess Hills was a spruce forest. States to the west and south also have evidence of conifer presence during that cooler, moister period. As the Wisconsinan progressed, eastern Iowa became home to an open spruce-pine forest that became denser around 28,000 years ago. Areas to the south and west of the Loess Hills were pine parklands either with spruce (northeastern Kansas) or without spruce (Missouri). Farther to the south and west, only grasslands appear to have been present.

The first records allowing climatic interpretation specifically of the Loess Hills region date from 23,000 years ago, when the Wisconsinan glaciation was dropping temperatures to their lowest levels. At that time, Mills County was primarily grassland, probably moist meadows, with some coniferous and deciduous trees presumably in favorable valley or slope sites. Deciduous trees were not abundant.

Small mammals included species that still are residents today: the plains pocket gopher, the extremely abundant meadow vole, the prairie vole, and ground squirrels. Numerous fossils of open-ground species support the theory that grasslands were extensive. Fossils of tree-dependent mammals are scarce. Other small mammals that were present—the arctic shrew, heather vole, northern bog lemming, northern pocket gopher, and others—indicate that the climate was significantly cooler then than now. Today those mammals live far to the north and northwest of Iowa.

Fossil snails, which were deposited within the loess throughout its deposition and are much more abundant than any other fossils, present a more general picture of the Hills. They support the idea that plant communities were more diverse than at present. The fossil snail fauna, in addition to being more diverse than today's snail fauna, contains species that are typical both of coniferous and tundra ecosystems and of deciduous woodlands. Species present then, if not extinct, are found today in the colder northern tundra and subarctic coniferous forests, in the Rocky Mountains, as glacial relicts on cool rocky slopes in northeastern Iowa, and in deciduous forests now dominant in the eastern United States. The fossil snail fauna changes from the northern to southern Loess Hills: deciduous forest elements are more abundant in southern counties, while northern and Rocky Mountain elements dominate northern counties.

Around 20,000 years ago, plant communities now typical of more northerly climates appeared on the plains. Tundra covered parts of present-day Minnesota and eastern Iowa. West-central Missouri and northeastern Kansas were spruce forests. Conditions in the Loess Hills are unknown. Western Iowa is thought to have been more open (less densely forested) than eastern Iowa throughout the earlier periods, but whether Loess Hills plant communities were tundra or dryish grasslands is unknown. Coniferous forests prevailed in places, for around 14,500 years ago, in Mills County, trees were locally dense enough to support the chickaree, now a species of northern coniferous forests, and also the yellow-cheeked vole, today a species of northern tundra-forest borderlands. Deciduous trees were locally present. Grazing rodents, and therefore open grasslands, were still present but in decreased concentrations. The environment may have been similar to the borderlands between prairie and forest in northern Minnesota today, with a mosaic of grassland, coniferous forest, and deciduous tree groves. The cooler climatic conditions once again are demonstrated by the presence of many small mammal species that now live well to the northwest or north of the Loess Hills.

Studies of mammalian assemblages such as this are perplexing in a sense, for today no site can be found where such a diversity of mammals lives together. The fossil fauna is "disharmonious." Instead, the mammals living in Mills County 14,500 years ago are today found separately in several different areas, each with its own climate. Thus although climates in general were certainly colder than those of today, they were unlike any climatic regime found on the earth today.

When glaciers started to retreat, forest groves became larger and more dense than during the preceding full glacial period. Closed spruce forests covered parts of eastern Iowa, and spruce-dominated woodlands also were the successors to Minnesota's tundra. But soon afterward, toward the end of the Ice Age, deciduous trees (especially oak and elm) mixed with the conifers of the eastern plains and elsewhere. With time, the conifers disappeared to leave a forest of deciduous trees, which was well established by the end of the Ice Age. Grasslands probably persisted on central and southwestern plains. Tree species in the Loess Hills area also shifted from conifers to deciduous species, and the Hills likely had elements of both deciduous forest and grassland ecosystems.

The Megafauna

Perhaps the most spectacular element of communities remains to be described. The megafauna, an assemblage of giant mammals, roamed the Loess Hills area for hundreds of thousands or even millions of years. Picturing today's Midwest covered by thousands of feet of ice, bordered by arctic tundra or coniferous forests, is difficult but possible since those communities still can be seen far to the north. Add to that scene herds of woolly elephants quietly grazing Great Plains grasslands and an ox-sized ground sloth reaching up to strip a tree of leaves and twigs and stuff them into its mouth; the largest rodent in North America, a giant beaver fully as large as a black bear, noisily feeding on swamp vegetation; grasslands dotted with herds of single-humped camels; the stag-moose with an antler spread of more than five feet; the caribou; barren-ground and woodland muskox; wild horses; the piglike flat-headed peccary; and an armadillo twice the size of the modern-day species. A picture of such an animal community may be beyond the imagination, but fossils of all of those animals have been collected throughout western Iowa and studied for more than 100 years.

The earliest fossil of the megafauna from the Loess Hills is one of the wonderful stegomastodon, an elephantlike grazer measuring nearly eight feet tall at the shoulder. Dating back into the Tertiary, the gigantic mammal roamed early Ice Age grasslands until driven into extinction more than a million years ago, possibly through competition with the newly arrived mammoths. Fossils of small three-toed horses also date from the early Ice Age, and could be much older. The large one-toed horse evolved from such early relatives. Although other Ice Age animals are known to have existed in pre-Pleistocene times, the remaining Loess Hills fossils are of a later date, representing animals known to have first lived here perhaps one half to one million years ago. The fossils typically have been washed downhill and today are found as fragments in reworked streambed deposits, not on upland sites where the bones were first deposited. For that reason, and because the fossils are too old to be dated by radiocarbon techniques, exact fossil ages usually cannot be determined.

Fossils have also been excavated from sand and gravel pits since the late 1800s. The Turin gravel pit, in Monona County, Iowa, has been quarried intermittently for many years, producing an outstanding fossil fauna for several decades. In those Ice Age gravel deposits that underlie loess, bones of mastodon and mammoth, dire wolf, musk-ox, river otter, jackrabbit, and fragments of a number of other animals, both large and small, have been found. Especially significant was the discovery of a nearly complete ground sloth cranium. Ground sloths otherwise are known in Iowa only from a scanty collection of isolated teeth, bones, and claws, which are impressive in their eight-inch length. The excavated cranium was that of a Jefferson's ground sloth, the terminal species in a lineage of ground sloths that first appeared in North America about five million years ago (fig. 7). Visitors to Iowa Hall, the University of Iowa's natural history museum, will remember the full-scale model of the species. Ground sloth fossils have been found in so many types of habitats, from peat bogs to caves, and over such a widespread area, from Alaska to central Mexico and coast to coast, that details of the sloth's environmental requirements remain poorly understood.

Both amateurs and professionals have discovered hundreds of fossils of proboscideans in western Iowa's streambeds and stream banks. The ani-

Figure 7. *Jefferson's ground sloth, one of the many very large mammals that roamed the Loess Hills region during the Ice Age. Will Thomson.*

mals were elephantlike giants with tusks and trunks, and included the American mastodon and species of true elephants or mammoths. Bones, teeth, and tusks have been found in all seven of Iowa's Loess Hills counties. In situ remains of one mammoth, including a tusk segment more than five feet long, were unearthed in a Pottawattamie County roadcut, along with fossils of a snowshoe hare and other smaller mammals. Proboscideans were some of the most impressive Ice Age herbivores.

Remains of mammoths are more numerous and more widespread than those of mastodons, supporting other evidence that grasslands were better developed than forests in western Iowa during the late Ice Age. The mammoths, with their flat, grinding teeth, were grazing animals; the mastodons used their pointed teeth to chew leaves pulled from trees with their trunks. In Missouri and farther to the east, where forests were better developed, fossils of mastodons far outnumber those of mammoths.

Although Ice Age and Holocene animals are generally well represented by fossils, a 4,000-year gap in the fossil record occurred between 12,400 and 8,400 years ago. Nothing is known of Loess Hills animals during that critical period. Before the gap, a rich assemblage of large and small mammals occupied the Hills. Most were grazers, but some used forested and wetland areas or preyed upon other species. Some species had widespread distributions. After the gap, the Loess Hills region had a relatively impoverished fauna consisting primarily of much smaller mammals. The ground sloth, giant armadillo, beaver, mammoth and mastodon, peccary, camel, stag-moose, stilt-legged deer, and woodland musk-ox all had become extinct, disappearing from the Loess Hills and from the earth. Why?

Although hotly debated for many years, the reasons for that sudden, widespread extinction of a large group of animals remain an enigma. The trigger may have been dramatic climatic change, which resulted in changes in vegetation and loss of habitat for the mammals. Perhaps the environment changed so dramatically and so rapidly that the animals, some of which were overspecialized, no longer could feed themselves or raise their young. Or the animals could have been weakened by the changing environment, and then become more susceptible to disease.

Competition from modern-day species also could have been important. Sudden storms, low reproductive rates, drought, and multiple other factors may have created a mosaic of adverse conditions. The reasons for the extinction were undoubtedly complex and may have varied from species to species and region to region.

Some researchers deny that environmental change was the primary cause of extinction, at least for certain members of the megafauna. They point to the small mammals that have survived from the Ice Age into modern times. Those mammals today either remain as residents of the Loess Hills or can be found in cooler, more northerly climes. Why didn't environmental change drive them into extinction as well? Those researchers favor the arrival of a new species as the decisive factor in megafauna extinction. During the Pleistocene, humans first arrived on the plains, migrating here with their spears and highly developed hunting techniques (fig. 8). The Paleo-Indian population could have undergone rapid population growth in response to a new and virtually unlimited food supply. The giant mammals,

Figure 8. *The first humans arrived in the Loess Hills toward the end of the Ice Age. Hunting pressures of these early people may have been responsible, at least in part, for the disappearance of the megafauna. Will Thomson.*

who before probably had faced attack only from the fangs and claws of sparse predators, would have had few defenses against such an onslaught.

Humans were to dominate the Hills for the next 12,000 years, throughout the Holocene. The evolution of human cultures in the Loess Hills, and the changes in the natural landscape brought about by humans and by natural forces, are the topics of the following chapter.

THREE

HUMANS COME
TO THE HILLS

Humans first migrated to North America in the late Pleistocene, during the formation of the Loess Hills. Both events were precipitated by the vast glaciers that then covered parts of North America and Eurasia. While meltwaters carried the silt that was lifted by the wind to form the Loess Hills, the glaciers tied up thousands of cubic miles of the earth's water, lowering ocean levels worldwide and exposing landmasses previously deep beneath the sea. One of those landmasses, Beringia, formed a bridge between present-day Siberia and Alaska. The bridge today lies submerged beneath the Bering Strait.

Humans migrated eastward across Beringia several times, along with plants and other animal species. The majority of human arrivals most probably occurred between 12,000 and 20,000 years ago. Once in North America, the immigrants fanned out to occupy locations throughout the continent, becoming progenitors to today's American Indians. Humans probably arrived in the Loess Hills region just as major loess deposition was ending, about 12,000 years ago. Thus human occupation of this region coincides fairly well with the Holocene, or modern period, which commenced 10,000 years ago and extends to the present. That period is the focus of this chapter.

Whether they recognized it or not, those first human immigrants were about to witness rapid and dramatic changes in their natural world. Only a few millennia before, the region had been borderland to glaciers, flooded by their sediment-laden meltwaters. With the Ice Age coming to a close, summer temperatures were becoming warmer. Coniferous forests were giving way to deciduous trees, which in turn were to be supplanted by modern prairies. The giant mammals, the early Indians' major food source, would soon become extinct, replaced by a relatively species-poor assemblage of smaller mammals. And the Loess Hills, newly cloaked in their final coatings of silt, were ready to enter an era when water rather than wind would determine their shape. In short, the Loess Hills were about to enter modern times, assuming an appearance and ambience akin to that found by Euro American settlers.

HUMAN CULTURES OF THE LOESS HILLS

Paleo-Indians

The first human inhabitants of the Loess Hills were the big-game hunters, highly nomadic Indians who traversed the region for approximately 3,500 years, between 12,000 and 8,500 years ago (fig. 9). The hunters banded into small groups to bring down large animals with spears tipped by leaf-shaped stone points several inches long. They worked together to drive herds of bison over cliffs or into marshes, where the animals were killed and butchered. Presumably the hides of the animals served as clothing and as coverings for temporary homes. In season, the Paleo-Indians may have gathered plant foodstuffs such as seeds, nuts, and berries. Even though they apparently specialized in hunting large game, those earliest Indians were able to weather tremendous changes in environment and climate, as midcontinental animal and plant communities transformed from woodland to grassland associations at the close of the Ice Age.

The earliest Paleo-Indians, classified as the Llano Culture, saw the last of many of the Pleistocene megafauna described in the previous chapter. The Indians used large (3- to 6-inch-long) Clovis spear points to bring down mammoths, horses, camels, and certain bison species upon which they depended for survival. Hunting pressures by the expanding Paleo-Indian population may have contributed to the giant mammals' extinctions. Their major food source gone, Paleo-Indians gradually turned to hunting other large game. The following Folsom Culture Indians hunted a second type of now-extinct bison with spears carrying smaller Folsom points. That culture was succeeded by the Plano Culture, which hunted modern species of game such as bison with a diversity of point types.

Figure 9. *Paleo-Indians, highly nomadic hunters and gatherers, were the first human residents of the Loess Hills region. Will Thomson.*

Paleo-Indians roamed most of today's United States but left few signs of their presence. Most of what we know of them has been deduced from campsites south and west of the Loess Hills, sites where game was killed and butchered. Spear points are the most common tools found, although campfire stones, charcoal, and game-processing tools (stone knives, scrapers, choppers, and some bone tools) sometimes are present. Only a single Paleo-Indian site has been excavated in western Iowa: it revealed a Plano Culture spear point with bison bones, located a bit east of the Loess Hills near Cherokee and dated at 8,500 years old. Occasional discoveries of isolated spear points, found on the ground surface in the uplands of Mills and Woodbury counties, Iowa, testify that Paleo-Indians did indeed hunt in the Hills.

Archaic Indians

A 6,000-year period, between 8,500 and 2,500 years ago, is known as the Archaic Period. Its beginning is marked by new types of projectile points—triangular stone points, some only a few inches long, often with notches at the base to assist in tying them to a shaft. The points likely tipped the shafts of darts or spears. The nomadic Archaic Indians, who resembled the Paleo-Indians in many ways, used such tools to hunt bison, depending on large game for much of their food and probably for clothing and shelter as well. They sometimes killed large numbers of bison by stampeding them into a V-shaped trap and thence over a cliff. Artifacts imply that unlike the Paleo-Indians, Archaic Indians underwent a veritable technological explosion, utilizing an increasing diversity of tools and making broader use of the environment. The atlatl, a throwing device that propelled spears and darts, was embellished with charms, including weights and bannerstones. The ground stone tool made its first appearance. Manufactured from harder rock than chipped tools, ground tools were used to grind, crush, and chop. The mano and metate, for example, allowed grinding of seeds and nuts. Ground stone axes were effective butchering tools and tree fellers. Archaic Indians throughout eastern North America traded for chunks of raw copper, procured from the Great Lakes region, which they hammered into artifacts. Bones became awls, scraping tools, and even musical instruments. A flute made of a hollow bird bone, excavated just east of the Hills near Cherokee, Iowa, is one of the earliest musical instruments known in North America. Bags and fabrics may have been woven from plant fibers.

The weight of some of those tools and the repeated use of some campsites imply that Archaic Indians were gradually becoming less nomadic. They also were increasing their reliance on plants (in the form of wild seeds and nuts) and on smaller animals as food sources. The remains of deer, fish, birds, turtles, shellfish, and other animals have been found in Archaic sites.

While Paleo-Indians throughout North America apparently followed similar ways of life, Archaic Indians started to show adaptations to regional environments. Archaic sites found in western Iowa, where they are especially numerous, show similarities to sites found across the Missouri River and throughout the western plains-prairie region.

Several Archaic sites have been located in the Loess Hills and their immediate surroundings. The oldest, the Hill site, just northwest of Glenwood, Iowa, was a small camp temporarily occupied by bison and deer hunters who brought their prey there to process and roast. Turtles and birds were also eaten. Tools were manufactured and repaired in the 7,300-year-old site. The nearby Lungren site, which is a bit younger, was also a small campsite. An isolated bison kill has been found six miles south of Pisgah, Iowa.

Human burials occurred at both the 4,700-year-old Turin site (in Monona County, Iowa) and the 2,800-year-old Lewis Central School site (near Council Bluffs, Iowa). The Turin site contained four shallowly buried skeletons lying in flexed positions on their sides. One had been buried with a necklace of shell beads and a projectile point and was covered with red ocher, a common prehistoric practice of unknown meaning. The burials indicated care and concern and were similar to European and Near Eastern burials dating from the same period. The Turin site became notorious when it was first discovered in 1955, since it was thought to contain the oldest known human remains in North America. Although that supposition has been disproved, the site remains significant as an example of Archaic burial practices. Its human skeletal remains are the oldest known in Iowa.

The Lewis Central School site also received greater-than-normal attention because of its role in resolving a conflict regarding reburial of excavated prehistoric human remains (see sidebar 2). Some of the 25 individuals buried there may have been wrapped in bundles and brought to the site for communal burial well after their deaths, perhaps after having lain for some time in trees or on platforms. If so, the burials would be an early example of societal integration, which was demonstrated much more strongly by the Woodland Culture that followed.

A few miles east of the Loess Hills lie the Cherokee Sewer and Simonsen sites, both in Cherokee County. All but the oldest, lowest layers were Archaic bison kill sites. At least 25 animals were killed, butchered, and partially eaten at the 8,400-year-old Simonsen site. Masses of bone, intermixed projectile points, other tools, hearths, and plant food remains have been found here. The Cherokee Sewer site, which was used intermittently over a 2,000-year period until approximately 6,300 years ago, was occupied in late winter as a bison processing site. Here, bison ambushed nearby were brought for butchering, cooking, and dressing of hides. Tools were made and repaired, and hides were sewn. The site was occupied for short periods by groups of families working together.

Sites such as the last two, where well-preserved artifacts lie deep within sediments accumulated at the junction of small and larger valleys, have led archaeologists to prophesy that a wealth of information concerning Archaic peoples and perhaps Paleo-Indians will be uncovered as excavations pry farther into the deep loess regions.

Woodland Indians

A bit before the time of Christ, approximately 2,500 years ago, the Woodland Culture emerged throughout the Loess Hills. It remained dominant until about 1,000 years ago. This culture has been defined primarily from traits of Indians farther east, where the Woodland period was more distinctive and better developed. Though widely distributed in western Iowa, the Woodland period there is marked by a lack of data, which confuses descriptions of the Indians' lives and culture as well as relationships to contemporaneous cultures to the east. In the west, the period may be best understood as one of transition. Changes were sparked by a steadily increasing human population density, which necessitated more social organization and more concentrated and reliable food production through plant cultivation. During that time, Indians went through several transformations—from being hunters and gatherers to becoming horticultural peoples; from living in small, local, usually autonomous bands to occupying large integrated communities; from living in egalitarian societies, apparently lacking in formal leadership, to forming ranked societies with specialized officials.

Despite the paucity of information about western Woodland Indians, they can be identified by the same three traits that identify the culture elsewhere: the development of pottery, creation of burial mounds, and the appearance of horticulture. Late Woodland Indians also were the first to use the bow and arrow, leaving behind small, triangular arrow points in

SIDEBAR 2. New Approaches to Ancient Burials

The sentiments of Native Americans regarding prehistoric burial grounds have focused on events in the Loess Hills. There the issue of rebury- ing excavated Indian skeletons was first raised, and there the issue was resolved, with actions leading to an Iowa law that received national attention.

In the late sixties and early seventies, Native Americans became in- creasingly vocal about the archaeological excavation of ancient ceme- teries, the treatment of their ancestors' bones as objects for scientific in- vestigation, and the display of prehistoric Indian skeletons as museum objects. Then, in 1971, a cemetery containing 26 Euro-American skele- tons and one Indian skeleton was unearthed during a highway project near Glenwood, Iowa. Although the 26 Euro-American skeletons were promptly reburied in a local cemetery, the Indian woman's bones were removed for scientific study. After considerable pressure from Indians, churches, and students, the Indian skeleton received equal treatment and was also reinterred.

In 1972, when numerous prehistoric individuals were unearthed at a Sioux City sand and gravel operation, violence and legal confusion re- sulted. Although historic cemeteries were protected by law, authorities had no guidelines for dealing with prehistoric burial grounds. With ar- chaeologists and Native Americans at odds for several years, the scien- tific investigation of human remains came to a standstill, even though numerous skeletons were accidentally discovered during that period.

addition to the larger chipped stone, ground stone, shell, and bone tools developed earlier. Late Woodland materials display regional and local di- versification, sometimes showing different traits from one valley to the next.

The appearance of pottery is the single most pronounced mark of the Loess Hills Woodland Indians. Those first potters produced vessels that were thick, coarse, and simple. The typical early pot was almost baglike, with a round or pointed bottom, fairly straight walls, and a slightly flared rim. The characteristic cord designs left in the pottery, and designs of fab- ric pressed into the pot while still moist and soft, today reveal weaving pat- terns and cord-making practices used by the Woodland Indians.

The simple burial mounds found in the Loess Hills demonstrate that these Indians were removed from the elaborate, hierarchical religious be- liefs and far-reaching trade networks displayed by the more sophisticated

In 1975, when an Archaic ossuary was unearthed at the Lewis Central School construction site in Council Bluffs, Iowa's state archaeologist worked with Indian activists to resolve the conflict. Indians and archaeologists conferred with legal authorities to formulate guidelines for hand excavation, limited scientific study, and reburial of Indian remains. The Indians believed that sequence was preferable to excavation of the skeletons by bulldozer and immediate reinterment. The jointly supported approach was incorporated into Iowa's law in 1976. The spirit of cooperation engendered in that effort has led to other joint projects by Iowa's scientists and Native Americans. One example has been the planning of an Indian mound preserve near Dubuque, Iowa.

Today state law grants identical legal protection to ancient burial grounds and modern cemeteries. Human remains older than 150 years, when subject to destruction through construction activities or natural processes such as erosion, may be excavated and investigated by professional archaeologists and physical anthropologists. The scientists must follow rigid guidelines adopted by the Office of the State Archaeologist and an Indian advisory committee. Scientific investigations reveal much about how the earliest Americans lived and died, the state of their health, and their burial customs. Once studied, the human remains are respectfully reburied in one of three state cemeteries established for the purpose. One cemetery fittingly covers a massive bluff in Iowa's Loess Hills, a bluff that prehistoric Indians likely considered sacred.

Indians farther to the east. There, conical earth mounds with elaborate contents were an expression of the widespread Hopewell burial cult. Log tombs, multiple burials and cremations, stone slabs over bodies, and elaborate gifts are typical of the Hopewellian cult. Grave gifts include animal figurines and finely carved stone pipes frequently incorporating obsidian, copper, mica, and shell from as far away as the Rocky Mountains or Gulf Coast. The Hopewellian cult extended into eastern Iowa, as did the Late Woodland practice of constructing effigy mounds. The bear-shaped, bird-shaped, and other massive earth mounds that now lie within Effigy Mounds National Monument in northeastern Iowa are examples of such effigies. Much simpler conical mounds have been found in the Loess Hills and nearby on the plains, primarily along the Missouri River and its major drainages. Many have been destroyed through cultivation or erosion.

SIDEBAR 3. Where Can the Past Be Found?

Until recently, archaeologists studying the Loess Hills either searched for artifacts lying on the ground surface or excavated sites of the most recent occupants—the horticultural Indians whose ruins and artifacts were still obvious on the land surface. The region was rich in late-pre-historic village sites, and archaeological activity proliferated in the Hills, especially near Glenwood, Iowa. Occasionally the buried remains of older cultures were found fortuitously. In general, however, the horticultural Indians became well studied while Indians of the previous 11,000 years were poorly studied because of the lack of sites. Presumably the bulk of the earlier remains had weathered away or been washed into oblivion.

Research techniques have changed dramatically since 1978. Archaeologists and geologists working together realized that the Loess Hills and nearby areas with deep coatings of loess contained a wealth of early archaeological remains, unsurpassed elsewhere. The remains had been buried in layers of loose valley sediments and in alluvial fans, triangular landforms constructed of water-washed sediments that are found where small valleys enter larger floodplains. The sediment layers are distinctive in color and texture. Boundaries between the layers represent old land surfaces, valley floors where prehistoric inhabitants of the Hills dwelled. Sometimes the sediments were later washed away, along with

Woodland Indians of the Loess Hills region are thought to have lived in seminomadic family bands. At times, small groups wandered in search of food. In the winter the bands gathered into camps that were repeatedly occupied. Remains of structures are scant and poorly preserved. The Indians probably occupied easily decomposed shelters framed by poles and covered with bark or other material. Longer-lasting underground food pits today indicate locations of winter villages in smaller protected valleys. One excavated site, the Rainbow site just northwest of Hinton in Plymouth County, Iowa, was occupied seasonally from A.D. 200 to 800. (The Rainbow site is especially significant because of its role in the development of new archaeological research techniques. See sidebar 3.) Toward the end of the Woodland period, occupations seem to have become more permanent, the Indians increasingly using resources close to camp and leaving only for periodic hunting and collecting forays.

Woodland Indians were hunters, gatherers, and to a limited degree horthe archaeological remains they contained, just as Indian artifacts left on the uplands were commonly destroyed through erosion. But elsewhere, the artifacts have remained buried and preserved in excellent condition to the present.

Today archaeologists know that remains of Late Archaic and Woodland Indian cultures should be sought deep under sediments that have filled small Loess Hills valleys during the last 3,500 years. The Rainbow site is one such valley site. Because episodes of gully cutting and filling have been dated by geologists and can be correlated from one valley to another, archaeological remains of a given age now can be systematically located in previously unexplored sediments. New sites also are identified when pot shards, points, or other artifacts are found along the walls of expanding gullies, where water has exposed the buried remains.

Older sites, dating from 8,000 to 3,500 years ago and belonging to the earlier Archaic Indian cultural period, can be systematically located in alluvial fans. The Cherokee Sewer site, described in the section on Archaic Indians, lies within such an alluvial fan.

Archaeologists hope that future studies of well-preserved sites will illuminate the lives of the poorly understood Woodland, Archaic, and possibly even Paleo-Indians of the Loess Hills and surrounding deep loess regions. The new research techniques are equally significant to paleo-ecologists who search for buried remains of animals and plants, using them to decipher the climate and ecosystems of ancient times.

---

ticulturists. The extreme diversity of food sources distinguishes their culture from its predecessors and successors. Much of the diet was deer, which probably substituted for bison in providing skins for clothes and bones for tools. But the Indians also took a remarkable variety of small animals: rabbit, squirrel, beaver, raccoon, badger, prairie and woodland birds, fish, mussels, turtles, even the pocket gopher. They gathered seeds, nuts, and berries. Thus they used all portions of the local environment— prairie, woodland, and river—a bit, without depleting any single food source. They grew crops requiring little attention, mostly members of the squash family, in dispersed plots. Maize (Indian corn) made its appearance during the Woodland period, and by A.D. 1000 it was prevalent on the plains.

An unusual burial site of seven Woodland Indians (the Hanging Valley site dated at A.D. 190 to 310) was excavated from the side of a Loess Hills gully in Harrison County, Iowa. All the skeletons were women and children, with bones and extremely worn teeth that demonstrated periods when growth had ceased, indications of severe environmental stress or disease. The people apparently had clung to the edge of existence, regularly facing malnutrition and episodes of extreme starvation. The site was a habitation or camp as well, for hearths and charcoal were found along with the remains of pots, plant foods, a diversity of animals, and a poorer collection of tools than would be expected. Such discoveries, along with skeletal traits, indicate that the people resembled Archaic hunters and gatherers with a thin overlay of Woodland traits.

Based on information from that burial site, some archaeologists have portrayed the Loess Hills Woodland Indians as a destitute, isolated group leading a harsh and tenuous existence. Their social organization and technology appear to have been far less complex than was previously assumed, a trait that may have been unique to the Loess Hills. Perhaps Woodland Indians here lived in smaller and more dispersed groupings in response to the rugged terrain, developing their distinctive style of pottery and cruder-than-normal stone tools because they lacked quality chert. Questions concerning the Woodland period in the Hills region may be answered in the future through excavation of sites that have been well preserved in the sediments of smaller valleys.

Toward the end of the Woodland period, the outline of the Plains Villagers was clearly emerging as Indians became more sedentary and increasingly reliant on cultivated crops. Drought and an insufficiency of resources were ever-present threats among the growing human population. Social cooperation and more highly organized social structures were needed to maintain and defend horticultural plots. The stage was set for the appearance of the permanent horticultural villages that followed. Some of the Woodland peoples may have lived alongside horticultural villages for many decades before the Woodland Culture completely disappeared from the Hills.

Village Horticulturists

The climate was moist and warm about a thousand years ago, ideal for cultivation of corn and other crops. The human population was growing, becoming denser and increasingly stressing wild food resources. Conditions were right for the emergence of more complex and integrated Indian cultures, ones in which larger groups joined in permanent communities and for the most part gave up their nomadic existence. In communities, Indians could cultivate, harvest, and protect a dependable food source rather than hunting and gathering what they might find in the wild.

Three such village farming cultures spread into the Loess Hills: the Great Oasis Culture (about A.D. 900), the Mill Creek Culture (about A.D. 900 or a bit later), and the Glenwood (about 1000 or perhaps later). All three remained until approximately 1300. Each was limited to certain sections of the Hills. The groups also lived outside the landform region.

The northernmost Loess Hills is a rich region for Great Oasis and Mill Creek sites, which were occupied contemporaneously. The Great Oasis Culture was the most widespread, with villages throughout most of northwestern Iowa, in southwestern Minnesota, and in northeastern Nebraska up along the Missouri River to Chamberlain, South Dakota. Sites are numerous in the Loess Hills of Plymouth County, Iowa.

The Mill Creek Culture is one member of the Middle Missouri tradition, a grouping of similar Indian cultures that were found from northwestern Iowa up along Missouri River tributaries into North and South Dakota. Mill Creek sites are located in Plymouth County, on terraces along the Big Sioux River and eastward into the Loess Hills along Broken Kettle Creek. They also occur northwest of the Hills along the Little Sioux River and certain of its tributaries.

About 100 miles to the south, the Glenwood people lived along the westernmost edges of the Loess Hills, which are considerably less rugged there than elsewhere. Sites are concentrated in a nine-mile stretch incorporating Pony Creek, Keg Creek, and smaller tributaries of the Missouri River near the modern-day city of Glenwood. A few sites have been found south of there. The Glenwood group is Iowa's member of the Nebraska Culture, which (as the name implies) was much more extensive in Nebraska, inhabiting sites along the Missouri River for much of the state's eastern border. The Nebraska Culture has broad similarities to other settled farming cultures in Kansas and farther west in Nebraska, and together they form the Central Plains tradition.

The origin of the three groups remains unproven. The Glenwood people (and other members of the Central Plains tradition) appear to have arrived in the region fully adapted to life in a forested environment along plains watercourses, with basic elements of their cultures already well developed. Their ancestral cultural roots probably lay in regions to the southeast and east. The Great Oasis people are thought to have been direct descendants of resident Woodland peoples. Considerable debate has focused on origins and taxonomic relationships of the Mill Creek Culture. One theory infers that the Great Oasis was ancestral to the Mill Creek. A second theory states that the Mill Creek people were a product of colonization by the expanding Mississippian people of Cahokia, a site in today's southern Illinois. The Mississippians were horticultural Indians who built large and densely populated urban centers, typically surrounded by a defensive ditch and sometimes by log stockades. Inside the villages were massive earthen temple mounds, structures of a highly organized religion. Cahokia's temple mound was 1,000 feet long. Cahokia was a major political and religious center, with considerable influence and wide-ranging trade networks. Today many scholars disagree with both theories and believe instead that the Mill Creek Culture developed locally, parallel with the Great Oasis, presumably from a Late Woodland base. Its development obviously was influenced strongly by its Mississippian neighbors, with whom the Mill Creek people had strong ties, and also by the Great Oasis.

The Glenwood, Great Oasis, and Mill Creek groups evolved independently and maintained their distinctive characteristics throughout their existence, but all three share certain broad traits. All constructed substantial and permanent homes partially underground, using both logs and mud in their structures. The earth lodges were clustered into village groups, a trait true for only some of the Glenwood houses. Villages in the Loess Hills were clustered at the region's western edge, on gentler terraces or ridges near river bottoms, where water, wood, and game all would have been abundant. In addition, those locations offered plenty of easily worked, fertile alluvial soil nearby to cultivate corn, squash, sunflowers, and sometimes beans. The Indians also were hunters, taking deer and bison with bows and arrows. Villages may have been abandoned at certain times of the year while inhabitants left on communal hunting forays. A variety of smaller game was taken as well, and fish were caught with hooks. Those animal foods, along with cultivated plants and smaller amounts of wild plant foods, provided a varied diet.

Foodstuffs and possibly household goods were stored in underground pits, which became trash pits once food spoiled or was invaded by rodents. Today the pits provide archaeologists with a wealth of concentrated artifacts—broken pots, damaged tools, and the like. Trade networks brought goods from other Indian cultures and distant locations into the artifact collections of all three cultures. The Indians appear to have led a fairly prosperous and secure existence, at least in their earlier years, using corn as a staple food source.

Yet, by 1300, all three groups had moved out of the region, leaving no clear signs as to where they went, or why, or what had become of them. Village peoples across the central plains similarly disappeared. A number of reasons for the apparent evacuation of the villages have been proposed. The truth may lie in some combination of factors, perhaps different for each of the three cultures.

One line of thought focuses on the environmental effects of climatic change. Beginning about 1200, the warm, moist climate so advantageous to corn apparently became drier. Corn crops may have failed repeatedly, leading to shortages of the staple food. Or the drying climate may have led to changes in natural communities that were devastating to the Indians. Perhaps rainfall was insufficient for tree regeneration, further shrinking woodlands already stretched thin by hundreds of years of cutting for construction and fuel. Or perhaps drought reduced the diversity of plant communities near Glenwood homes, to the point that the Indians no longer could harvest the variety of readily accessible plants and animals upon which they depended. The effects of climatic stress, which may have been working simultaneously to decimate crops and decrease the availability of local wild plants and game, may have been multiplied by natural increases in the human population.

A second line of thought stresses decimating cultural factors, namely the decline of Cahokia and increased pressures from other nearby Indian groups. Cahokia's unexplained decline around 1150 might have been especially stressful for the Mill Creek Indians, who would have been abruptly cut off from an influential trade partner. The fortifications that appeared around some Mill Creek villages about that time, probably through Cahokia's influence, suggest that indeed the Mill Creek were threatened, perhaps by raiding groups to whom they lost corn and lives (fig. 10).

The most likely raiders would have been Oneota, a culture that first appeared around 1,000 years ago and eventually became well represented throughout much of the Midwest, including today's Iowa, Missouri, Kansas, Nebraska, South Dakota, Minnesota, Wisconsin, and Illinois. Although Oneota groups may have occupied the Hills and must have wandered here at times, no Oneota sites are known from the Hills. Yet the Oneota were nearby, for their pottery artifacts have been found in excavations of a Glenwood village. Oneota sites have been found near the Hills, along

Figure 10. The Mill Creek Indians formed one of three horticultural, village-inhabiting cultures of the Hills a thousand years ago. Raiding by Oneota Indians may have been a reason for their disappearance. Will Thomson.

parts of the Little Sioux River. The sites were occupied contemporaneously with Great Oasis and Mill Creek sites nearby, but there are no indications of Oneota trade or contact with either village group.

Like their neighbors, the Oneota were horticultural Indians, growing squash and corn and perhaps beans and tobacco. But they seem to have been more nomadic than the village Indians; many Oneota sites reveal no permanent structures. Perhaps their greater ability to wander in search of food and to adjust to environmental change saved them from extinction. Indeed, the Oneota did decrease their reliance on horticulture and increase their reliance on game after the climatic change, as indicated by the increased abundance of hunting tools and bison bones in later Oneota sites. During the environmental change, the Oneota might have occasionally raided the villagers' corn supply and through their own hunting further stressed the villagers' supply of game. Those stresses on the food supply may have combined with environmental stresses to force the more sedentary, less adjustable village cultures out.

The Oneota expanded, and their successors survived to enter the historic era. Archaeologists think that the village dwellers probably moved westward and northward, where they blended with other Indian cultures. Their cultural identities reshaped, they supposedly passed through several centuries, of which little is known, and emerged with new and different identities in historic times. Some archaeologists have suggested relationships between the Mill Creek and Mandan, Glenwood and Pawnee, and Great Oasis and Omaha Indians.

The Great Oasis. Great Oasis and Mill Creek peoples inhabited the same area of the Loess Hills contemporaneously. In one site they occupied villages across the creek from each other. At Plymouth County's Larson site, toward the end of the villagers' existence, traits of the Mill Creek and Great Oasis blended to form a unique mixture; the two seem to have assimilated one another and perhaps even consolidated to live jointly in a single spot. The joining of cultures and peoples may have been a reaction to increasing stress from climatic change or from the Oneota. However, for the most part the two cultures apparently retained close contact and friendly relationships while maintaining distinct cultures and lifeways.

The life of the Great Oasis people was definitely less culturally complex than that of the Mill Creek. Great Oasis pottery was less elaborate, and both pottery and artifact inventories were much less varied for the Great Oasis. Their villages were smaller, their trade routes less well established, and they may have been more nomadic. Some scholars have suggested that the Great Oasis retained more of a primitive hunting and gathering culture, trading meat for vegetables with their farming-oriented Mill Creek neighbors.

Life-style patterns can be deduced from two Loess Hills excavations (fig. 11). The Broken Kettle West site was an open, unprotected village of 25 or more houses. The long rectangular structures, 25 by 40 feet in size, were sunk in a pit 1.5 feet deep. Walls were made of vertical posts, interwoven with sticks and plastered with mud, topped by domed roofs of grass thatching. A central fireplace and many subterranean pits dotted each floor. Animal remains indicate that the sites were occupied seasonally (in fall, winter, and spring) and that the majority of meat consumed was deer and elk. Many other animals and a variety of plants also were eaten. The village site appears to have been largely abandoned in the summer, while inhabitants left for communal hunts. The nearby Williams site may have been a small summer agricultural campsite. Garden seed and remains of a temporary shelter have been excavated there. A number of other small, short-term campsites have been found in the area.

Local prehistoric cemeteries of this era could have belonged either to

Figure 11. The Great Oasis Indians inhabited villages containing rectangular lodges, which may have been largely abandoned during the summer when inhabitants went out onto the plains to hunt. Will Thomson.

Great Oasis or Mill Creek peoples. Archaeologists have not been able to assign the cemeteries definitely to either culture. Burial sites contain single or multiple burials, cremations, and a variety of grave offerings. One of many such sites is the Siouxland Sand and Gravel site, high on a loess bluff in present-day Sioux City, which contained perhaps hundreds of burials. Many were covered by limestone slabs. Two particularly interesting artifacts found there are a wolf "mask" (modifed wolf jawbones that presumably served ornamental or ceremonial purposes) and a "long-nose God mask." They show affinities with the more sophisticated prehistoric Mississippian cultures that inhabited areas farther to the east. Any further disturbance of the large cemetery is prohibited by state law.

Loess Hills burial sites often were located on bluff tops, which likely were special sites to the Indians. High spots elsewhere on the plains were of ceremonial importance, being used as sacred calling sites. One story tells that the Indians called the west-facing loess bluffs a sun bridge, from which their souls would travel to the afterworld via the rays of the setting sun. Certainly the large number of bluff-top burials implies that the sites were important to prehistoric Indians. Of the 124 prehistoric burial sites known in Iowa's Loess Hills, 69 are atop bluffs or ridges.

Mill Creek. Of the three village groups, the Mill Creek Culture certainly was the most socially complex and structured, with the most elaborate and varied material goods. Villages were large and compact, demonstrating a high degree of social organization. In the Kimball site, at the edge of the Loess Hills along the Big Sioux River, houses were lined up in orderly rows. Elsewhere, fortified villages must have looked a bit like simple wooden versions of medieval castles. At the Wittrock site, along the Little Sioux River to the east of the Hills, a log stockade was surrounded on three sides by a ditch seven feet deep and by a river on the fourth side. Bastions were built at the entryway and elsewhere along the wall, and entrance was permitted by access ramps.

Village occupation was intensive and long-term. Materials found today at excavated sites are deep and concentrated. In some places new houses, large rectangular structures somewhat like those of the Great Oasis, were built on top of old collapsed structures. Even today such villages form mounds on the landscape, 10 to 12 feet deep and as much as an acre in area. Artifacts are abundant and varied. In addition to tools such as knives, sickles, bone fishhooks, long needles, and awls, bone hoes manufactured from bison scapulae are common. Decorative items—shell beads, shell pendants, bone pins, teeth, porcupine quills—are found along with ceremonial items. The Mill Creek people may have possessed medicine bundles (sacred objects wrapped in bird or animal skins) similar to those of historic Indians. Other items, possibly including feather headdresses, may have been made from wings, tails, and claws of raptors.

Although pottery showed a consistency of style from generation to generation, skilled potters turned out a variety of elaborate wares. Bowls, seed jars, bottles, pans, and other ceramic objects large and small were decorated with distinctive, often geometric designs. Human or animal effigies—small, finely shaped heads and tails of animals that protruded from rims of bowls or jars—sometimes served as handles.

Several artifacts are identical to those commonly found in Cahokia. Perhaps items such as earspools (ear ornaments), "chunky stones" used in games, elbow-shaped pipes, and shell pendants were obtained from Cahokia through trade. Perhaps they were copied by Mill Creek artisans following a diffusion of ideas along the Missouri River corridor or following personal contact or intermarriage with the distant Mississippian peoples. Whatever the case, the ties with Cahokia were evidently close. Shared items such as the long-nose God mask indicate Mill Creek acceptance of Mississippian ideology as well as material goods.

The Mill Creek villagers also had close contact with their neighbors, the

Great Oasis. Just across the creek from the Mill Creek Broken Kettle site, north of Sioux City, lay the Great Oasis village excavated as the Broken Kettle West site.

The Mill Creek were successful horticulturists. Hunting, also important, provided the bison, elk, deer, and antelope upon which they depended heavily. Smaller game, fish, birds, mollusks, and wild berries, seeds, and nuts supplemented their diets.

Although excavated village sites give every indication of continuous and extended inhabitation, several occupation patterns may have been the reality. Possibly some villages housed stable long-term populations, while others were occupied for a time, abandoned when local resources became stressed, and then reoccupied. Perhaps favorable environmental conditions, resulting in population growth, spurred the formation of new villages elsewhere. Such colonies may have been abandoned later, when threats from raiding Oneota forced consolidation into defensible sites. Reuse of housing sites may have been required once fortifications restricted village expansion. Some Mill Creek and Great Oasis villages may have even coalesced later in their cultures' histories, a possibility implied by the Larson site, discussed in the preceding section on the Great Oasis.

Glenwood. The Glenwood people appear to have lived a peaceful and stable existence, which changed little during their occupancy (fig. 12). Lodges were open and unprotected, lacking any indication of fortification. Only one village of any size (the Kullbom Village, a cluster of approximately 15 lodges on a valley floor) has been found. Although other lodge sites are numerous in the Glenwood region, their irregular and often widely spaced placement does not portray a highly centralized, structured village life.

About 80 lodge sites have been found in the Glenwood region. Lodge sites, recognized as depressions in the soil surface, were obvious and commonly seen in the late 1800s. Since then, construction of roads and buildings has destroyed many sites, and farming has filled in many of the depressions.

The Glenwood were active horticulturists, a trait revealed by the abundant charred remains of cultivated plants and by artifacts such as shell and bone hoes and crop-processing tools. In addition, they hunted deer and elk, caught large Missouri River fish with hooks and harpoons, collected mussels, and took many smaller animals. The surrounding woodlands, wetlands, and prairies provided a rich variety of wild game and plant foods. Those nearby environments appear to have been intensively uti-

Figure 12. *The Glenwood Indians constructed earth lodges in which they appear to have lived peaceful, stable lives, growing crops, hunting, and fishing. Will Thomson.*

lized, while the Glenwood people seem to have forgone the longer-ranging communal hunts typical of other village cultures.

One interesting inhabitant of the Glenwood lodges, present in unusually large proportions, was the marsh rice rat (*Oryzomys palustris*), a species now limited to more southerly regions. It apparently was a residential pest of the Glenwood villages, much like the house mouse in modern-day homes. The rat may have been tolerated in lodges. One hypothesis even states that the rat's presence was encouraged, either because it was exploited as a food source or used as a burial offering.

A diversity of bone, stone, antler, and wooden tools were used by the Glenwood people, including meat- and skin-processing tools, many types of knives and scrapers, drills, needles, anvils, and the like. Some ornaments have been found, as have distinctive clay pipes. Ceramics also display variety, including several types distinguished on the basis of decoration and rim formation, and a number of different forms (large pots, beads, miniature vessels, scoops). Although in general Glenwood sites show little evidence of contact with other Indian cultures, and foreign trade items are rare, certain features of their pottery resemble those of the Mississippian peoples of Cahokia. The Glenwood also apparently had contact with the Oneota, perhaps through intermarriage. Shell-tempered pottery found in the Kullbom site is similar to that of certain Oneota excavations.

Lodges were constructed in a square or slightly rectangular shape with rounded corners. Walls were formed of closely spaced vertical posts, sometimes plastered with clay. The floor was sprinkled with cache pits. A central hearth was sometimes bordered by a wide bench. Four vertical poles inside the house helped support the roof, which is thought to have been sod. A covered entryway often opened toward the south.

Although construction techniques are similar from site to site, the size and settlement patterns of lodges show considerable variation. Larger lodges (more than 900 square feet) are found as single isolated structures on uplands along ridges or, less commonly, on flat stream terraces. More commonly, lodges are found strung out irregularly, in a linear pattern, along ridge spurs or the bases of slopes. Clusters of up to five lodges, possibly forming loosely organized villages, have been located on low sites at the mouths of streams. Kullbom Village, the largest cluster of Glenwood lodges, also fits that category. Lodges clustered into hamlets typically are smaller than isolated lodges; the majority of Glenwood lodges are small (less than 700 square feet).

What accounts for the variability in size, organization, and location of lodges? Certainly topographic constraints were important: larger lodges were built where flat, wide ridges or terraces permitted, but the hilly Loess Hills terrain dictated that most lodges must be small, strung out on more rugged, steeply sloping sites at the base or top of a hill. Several other theories, often contradictory, have attempted to explain the variations. Perhaps the people moved from large to small lodges when changing climate started to stress their resources. Or, perhaps they moved from small to large lodges at that time. Perhaps large and small lodges were occupied contemporaneously but in different seasons, with patterns of social aggregation changing from winter to summer rather than over the years.

Archaeologists question how long the Glenwood people occupied the area, and again hypothesized answers show considerable variation. Radiocarbon dating done in the 1970s implied that various types of lodges were simultaneously occupied, representing a community that flourished perhaps for only 100 or 150 years. The Glenwood then may have moved on before changing climate or other stressors forced evacuation. In contrast, earlier archaeologists had stated that the area was occupied for as long as 800 years. Clearly much remains to be discovered about the occupancy period, settlement patterns, and social organization of the Glenwood.

The richness of archaeological research on the Glenwood Indians deserves mention. Research reports of excavations were appearing in major journals as early as 1881. Activity then waned until the Great Depression, when intensive surveys were performed by archaeologists and a Works Progress Administration crew. Since the century's midpoint, a number of studies have been completed through universities and as archaeological salvage operations preceding construction projects. Studies also have been completed by two amateur archaeologists from Glenwood, Paul Rowe and D. D. Davis. Rowe's extensive collections and displays of Glenwood Indians are now on display in the Mills County Historical Museum. Depressions indicating lodge sites of the Nebraska Culture can be seen at Fontenelle Forest Nature Center, just south of Omaha.

The Interim Period

After the disappearance of the Plains Villagers around 1300, human use and occupation of the Loess Hills is poorly understood. For the 500-year period until 1804, when the Lewis and Clark expedition created the first recorded descriptions of the Loess Hills, one can only speculate about what might have occurred there. Although Indian tribes may have occupied the Hills, no archaeological sites for that period have been located. Indians must have journeyed through the region and possibly hunted there, but if so they left no definite record of their passage. Certainly the Hills do not appear to have been heavily used by humans, as portions of the landscape had been by earlier Indians.

Fragmentary documentation of scattered events in areas surrounding the Loess Hills—a few archaeological sites, terse eighteenth-century records—allows a rough sketch to be drawn for the region as a whole. The semisedentary Oneota remained after the Plains Villagers had left. Oneota probably were the only Indians to roam the Loess Hills region for several hundred years. Their culture and cultures evolving from the Oneota were distinguished by the use of red pipestone catlinite, which was made into ceremonial pipes and plaques. Sacred to the Indians, the rock today can be seen at Pipestone National Monument in southwestern Minnesota.

Oneota sites have been found close to the Loess Hills, along the Little Sioux River east and northeast of the northern Loess Hills; along the banks of the Missouri River in Woodbury County, Iowa, west of the town of Sloan; possibly in the St. Joseph, Missouri, area; and in the far northwestern corner of Iowa. There, along the banks of the Big Sioux River, the 600-acre Blood Run site was occupied from roughly 1200 to 1700. The site appears to have been a major ceremonial or trade center for the Oneota and their successors. The period was one of movement and change for the Oneota. During those 500 years, they diversified into a variety of Siouan-speaking peoples, which entered historic times as the Ioway, Oto, Omaha, Missouri, Osage, and other tribes.

Even before history recorded the existence of those groups, they were being influenced by the westward wave of Euro-American settlement. The first imports arrived indirectly, through Oneota contact with other Indians who traded with the whites. Then direct contact was made with early trappers and traders. Some of the "gifts" of the Euro-Americans, trade goods such as glass beads, cooking utensils, and brass and copper jewelry, were seen as beneficial. Others—especially infectious diseases such as smallpox that were imported from Europe—were devastating. Infectious diseases to which the Indians had no immunity are thought to have wiped out entire tribes before their existence was recorded. If some members of the tribe survived, disease often broke their health and vigor.

The earliest written records for the region surrounding the Hills predate the Lewis and Clark expedition journals by about a century. The French trader and explorer Le Sueur left diaries dated 1701. Writing from his southern Minnesota camp, Le Sueur recorded the reports of his scouts and of the Dakota Sioux, who described an Ioway village in the Spirit Lake area northeast of the Loess Hills.

Subsequent early journals and maps, which often were inaccurately drawn and thus of questionable authenticity, indicate one or a succession of Ioway villages on the Big Sioux River in the early 1700s. Later the Ioway inhabited a village on the Missouri River, which probably corresponds to the site described in the Lewis and Clark journals on July 28, 1804, as the "spot where the Ayauway Indians formerly lived." It lay just south of present-day Council Bluffs and was presumably occupied in the mid-1700s. The Ioway then moved eastward. By 1777, they were located along the Des Moines River, and from there they continued to roam freely over Iowa and parts of adjoining states. A series of nineteenth-century treaties with the United States government increasingly restricted their movement. In 1836, a reservation just west of the Missouri River on the border between Kansas and Nebraska was established for the Ioway. They subsequently were moved to Oklahoma. Today, although two small Indian groups still identify themselves as Ioways, most of the culture of the Indians that gave Iowa its name has been lost.

Other Indian tribes inhabited prehistoric Iowa for shorter periods than the Ioway. The Oto, who were closely related to the Ioway, appear to have shadowed the Ioway across Iowa to the Missouri River, establishing their villages only a short distance from the Ioway. Several records suggest that they crossed to the west side of the Missouri River around 1700, establishing their main village on the Platte River in Nebraska. Because they continued to come back across the river to hunt, the Oto were sometimes encountered in western Iowa.

The Omaha had a large settlement on the Big Sioux River and were joined by the Ioway and Oto there around 1700 or a bit later. Like the Oto, the Omaha seem to have found the western side of the Missouri River more attractive than its eastern shores, and they too apparently crossed the Missouri River to the Nebraska side, where they resided in historic times. The Omaha still live just across the Missouri River, on a reservation in Thurston County, Nebraska. Today the Omaha are extremely interested in their tribal history and are returning to their tribal customs to the great est degree possible.

Northern Missouri was roamed first by the Oneota, then by the Missouri and Ioway. In the late 1700s, the Missouri traveled westward across the Missouri River to the Platte River, where they joined the Oto with whom they subsequently lived. They held council with Lewis and Clark on August 3, 1804, a meeting that later gave the city of Council Bluffs its name.

The Dakota Sioux were well established in southern Minnesota by the late 1600s, when their nomadic hunting habits were described by Le Sueur. From there they regularly wandered southward into the Loess Hills region. Their forays into the Loess Hills were well recorded in the nineteenth century. Such forays presumably occurred earlier as well, perhaps for centuries before, as the Sioux traveled up and down the Missouri River and roved both sides of its shores.

Thus neither the Loess Hills proper nor their immediate surroundings appear to have had many if any permanent or long-term residents in late prehistoric and early historic times, although Indians may have used the region as a hunting ground. The Sioux and the Potawatomi (who will be described in the following section) were the only Indians with a major presence in the Loess Hills in historic times.

The Missouri River has been a major travel corridor for at least 1,000 years. In the early 1700s, French fur traders came upstream to establish trade with the Indians in the Loess Hills region but then concentrated their efforts on the more numerous Sioux beyond the Hills in South Dakota and southern Minnesota. Harassment from unfriendly tribes prevented the establishment of trading posts or forts, and the French finally withdrew. However the Sioux, Ioway, and other tribes reportedly continued to travel downstream to Fort Leavenworth and farther to the south and east, bringing their pelts to French markets. Other attempts to establish trade continued. Lewis and Clark met a trading boat from St. Louis bound for trade with the Yankton Sioux. Those early trade relationships laid the basis for the thriving fur trade that developed along the upper Missouri River in the nineteenth century.

Euro-American Settlement

On May 21, 1804, three boats commanded by Captains Meriwether Lewis and William Clark set out from St. Charles, Missouri, a bit upriver from the Missouri River's junction with the Mississippi. Their party of 45 men would be the first to explore the Louisiana Purchase, just acquired from Napoleon and France. Their orders, received from President Jefferson, were to ascend the Missouri River to its source. From there, they were to find a northwest water passageway to the Pacific Ocean. Their journey would last nearly two and a half years.

For much of July 1804, the expedition traveled past the Loess Hills, stopping to camp and hunt nearby several times. Their journals for that period are the first historical documents we have of the Loess Hills, the first written descriptions of this landscape.

Two events of major importance to the expedition occurred near the Loess Hills. Lewis and Clark had their first meeting with Indians. They held council with the Oto and Missouri Indians of the west side of the Missouri River at the present-day site of Fort Atkinson State Historical Park. Second, the only fatality of the expedition occurred in the Hills. Sergeant Charles Floyd died of "bilious colic," probably a ruptured appendix. Floyd was buried on the summit of a loess bluff, today marked by the Floyd Monument in southern Sioux City.

The shift in ownership of the enormous western region from France to the United States, along with Lewis and Clark's reports of the rich wildlife to be found there, precipitated a movement of explorers, fur traders, missionaries, and government agents into the upper Missouri River region. A thriving fur trade developed with the Indians. Fur trade dominated activities until the middle of the nineteenth century, when agriculture and permanent settlement took precedence. The first American firm to enter the fur trade on the upper Missouri River did so in 1809. Fort Lisa, across from present-day Council Bluffs, became an early but important trading post. A number of other forts were later established in the region in an effort to keep peace among Indian tribes. Fort Atkinson, just north of present-day Omaha, was built in 1819 to protect the burgeoning western fur trade and remained operational until 1827. During that time the post of 1,000 men was the nation's largest and remotest military post, a gateway to the opening of the West.

The first steamboat traveled the Missouri River in 1831. Steamboat passengers frequently commented on the Loess Hills. Much descriptive information appears in journals of trade and military expeditions, naturalists' records, surveyors' reports, and artists' sketches and notes. Among those to sketch or comment on the landscape were Dr. Edwin James, George Catlin, Karl Bodmer, and John James Audubon.

One of the least honorable segments of Loess Hills history occurred between 1837 and 1846, when the Potawatomi Indians (accompanied by a few Ottawas and Chippewas) inhabited an approximately 5,000-acre reserve in southwestern Iowa. Originally from the lower peninsula of Michigan, the Potawatomi had been relentlessly pushed westward as their homes were seized by settlers. In 1833, they had signed a treaty ceding all of their lands east of the Mississippi River in exchange for the reserve in southwestern Iowa. They consistently maintained pleasant relations with whites. By 1867, they had signed at least 53 treaties with the United States government, gradually ceding all of their lands.

The approximately 2,000 Potawatomi survived in the southern Loess Hills mostly by hunting and gathering. They also had some small garden plots. They resided in two main villages, one of which was near present-day Council Bluffs, and in other smaller villages and hunting camps around the reserve. The tribe suffered at times from lack of game, attacks by the

Sioux from the north, and debilitating drunkenness encouraged by white traders. The United States government provided little help. It focused scant time, attention, and money on the Indians and refused to recognize their request for a school.

With statehood imminent and white settlers already moving onto Indian land, the federal government took possession by treaty of all Indian lands in the territory of Iowa in 1846. The Potawatomi were to leave for Kansas within two years. Most moved within a year, although periodic hunting expeditions back to the Hills were common for the next several years. The Potawatomi later were moved one last time, to Oklahoma. Chief Wahbonsey (for whom Iowa's Waubonsie State Park is named) remained in Iowa, where he died, probably in 1848. He reportedly was secretly buried in an unknown location in Mills County.

Before 1843, the few settlers of the southern Loess Hills had arrived by boat. Then the great overland migration started, and immigrants began to cross Iowa in unexpected numbers. A new trail was blazed through southern Iowa to the Loess Hills. Settlement there remained slow, however, until 1846, when the Mormons started their migration toward the Great Salt Lake Valley (fig. 13).

In the previous few decades, the Mormons, with their leader Joseph Smith, had fled first Ohio, then Missouri, and then the town of Nauvoo. Since Nauvoo's founding in 1839, the Mormons had built it to be the largest town in Illinois and the showplace of the Mississippi. Because of negative sentiments regarding religious practices and polygamy, Smith was murdered in 1844, and the Mormons were driven from Nauvoo. The route they followed, and the trail they established through western Iowa and the Loess Hills, became in the 1850s a major road between the Mississippi and Missouri rivers. West of the Missouri River, the trail led up the Platte River valley.

The Mormons differed from other pioneers in that their migration amounted to villages on the march. As Mormons moved westward, they constructed trails and set up mileposts, built bridges or rafts for use by later parties, and planted garden plots. They established permanent towns and farms for the benefit of those who could go no farther and others still to come.

The first Mormons stopped temporarily near the Missouri River, where they camped with the Potawatomi Indians near the present site of Council Bluffs. Then permanent camps were set up on both sides of the Missouri

Figure 13. *The Mormon Trail passed through Iowa's southern Loess Hills. Here, Mormons cross the Missouri River at Florence, Nebraska, on their way to the Great Salt Lake Valley. Nebraska State Historical Society, Lincoln.*

River. Several settlements sprang up in the southern Loess Hills region to serve as staging places that would provide food, supplies, and repair services to following Mormons. Other towns were established by Mormons who broke with the church and by Mormons who decided to stay in Iowa as permanent residents when the last of the trail parties left for the Salt Lake Valley in 1852. The Mormon religion dominated the area now in Mills and Monona counties for several years. The influence of Mormon settlers was strong in that section of the Loess Hills. A handful of towns founded by Mormons, such as Glenwood, are still in existence.

In the 1850s, the availability of cheap government land attracted many new settlers to the wooded creeks that cut through the Loess Hills. Steamboat transportation was supplanted by overland transport. Stagecoach lines traversed the hills and ran along the base of the bluffs.

The earliest settlers (fig. 14) in the region found the Missouri River floodplain treacherous and fearsome. Difficult to travel because of tall wetland grasses, the valley became especially dangerous when flooded in spring and early summer. The insect-ridden lowlands were the source of malaria and other diseases. In contrast, the wooded creek bottoms at the base of the bluffs, as well as lower hills farther to the east, provided settlers easy

Figure 14. Early Loess Hills immigrants. Sioux City Public Museum.

access to wood and water, dry cropland, and protection from floods. There they settled and established their farms. They plowed prairies on all but the steepest hills and mowed valley grasslands for hay. Early settlers' houses still can be seen tucked into the bluffs' hollows that border the Missouri River floodplain, sometimes shaded by a few ancient apple trees. From early on, the region was recognized for its fine fruit-growing properties, a trait respected by apple orchardists to the present day.

As soon as the Missouri River valley floor was drained, agricultural emphasis switched away from the Hills. Farmers flip-flopped land uses, plowing up the valley hayfields for cropland and, in the Hills, converting all but the flattest cropland to cattle pasture. Transportation routes also moved from the Hills to the broad river valley.

The beauty of the Loess Hills and their prairies was lauded in settlers' journals and diaries and in immigrant guides. In spite of the praise, farmers as well as city folk regarded the rugged hills as obstacles to farming and urbanization and treated them accordingly. Rather than adjusting land use practices to the Loess Hills' strikingly different topography, settlers expected the Hills to adjust to human demands. Frontier work practices and patterns of development from less rugged areas in the East appear to have been applied without modification to the Loess Hills.

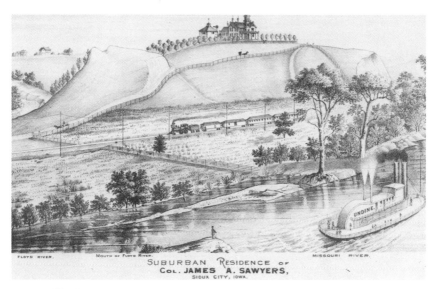

FLOYD RIVER.   MOUTH OF FLOYD RIVER.   MISSOURI   RIVER.
SUBURBAN RESIDENCE OF
COL. JAMES A. SAWYERS,
SIOUX CITY, IOWA.

Figure 15. Only thirty years after being a wilderness, the Loess Hills claimed
sophisticated transportation and communication networks and luxurious homes,
such as Colonel Sawyers' residence shown here. Andreas Atlas, Ninth
Congressional District, 1875.

The imposition of human land uses had a dramatic effect on natural features of the Loess Hills, resulting in changes that are described in the final
section of this chapter. However, aside from the recognition that prairies
were far more abundant than they are now, the nature of presettlement
native communities is poorly understood. (Their probable nature is described in sidebar 4.)

Permanent settlement of the Loess Hills region occurred extremely rapidly. A government land office was opened at Kanesville (now Council
Bluffs) in 1852, and the city soon became a leading commercial center.
Sioux City was surveyed in 1854, had a government land office by 1855,
and climbed to a population of 38,000 by 1890. In 1856, about 1,700
families resided in six of Iowa's Loess Hills counties. By the end of the Civil
War, that number had risen to 7,500 (fig. 15).

The Mississippi and Missouri rivers were first joined by railroad in 1867.
The transcontinental railroad was completed in 1869. Land sales boomed
with the great availability of unsettled land, the end of the Civil War, and
the expansion of rail traffic. Both cities and agricultural activities continued
to expand as the political, economic, and social life of the region took form
throughout the last half of the nineteenth century.

SIDEBAR 4. Plant Communities of Early Historic Times

Although our understanding of nineteenth-century plant communities remains incomplete, we know that the early settlers found a landscape far different from that of today. The communities of the early to mid-1800s can be outlined only broadly. Woodlands and prairies were both present. Prairies dominated the Hills, with forests snaking along streams and ravines. The most northerly prairies were treeless. Forested areas increased toward the south, where the increasingly moist climate became more conducive to tree growth. In the southern Hills, forests may have crept upslope on protected north- and east-facing slopes, but prairies likely maintained dominance, especially on the steepest, driest sites. Small clusters of trees must have dotted the prairie where natural windbreaks squelched the destructive force of prairie fires. Scattered bur oak speckled some prairies, forming communities called savannas.

That general picture is based on those historical records examined to date. However, a detailed examination of the records sometimes reveals conflicting pictures of early Loess Hills plant communities. Take, for example, our earliest written records, the 1804 journals of the Lewis and Clark expedition. They describe the "Bald Hills" and "round knobs devoid of timber" south of today's Council Bluffs but then mention the "high prairie and hills, with timber" farther to the north (July 17 and July 28). Early explorers deplored the lack of timber in some spots and proclaimed well-timbered hills to be prevalent elsewhere.

Sketches by early artists reveal a region impressive in its "bald" prairie attire. The uppermost, steepest knobs of loess are nearly universally free of trees. However, in Catlin's and Bodmer's 1830s sketches and in the work of other artists on through the late 1800s, good-sized trees dot many of the Loess Hills. Scattered open-grown trees, savannas, small woodland groves, and even mature extensive forests grace many of the sketches.

The best information now available on early Hills plant communities is contained in the United States government's land survey records completed in Iowa's Loess Hills between 1832 and 1858. Early land surveys of today's McCormack Natural Area, in Holt County, Missouri, indicate that rugged, steep bluffs were largely treeless and that extensive woody vegetation existed only in valley bottoms. Surveys of Iowa's Plymouth and Woodbury counties state that the northern Hills had many fewer forested acres than counties to the south. W. E. Loomis and A. L. McComb (1944) summarize land survey records for Iowa's Loess Hills by saying that scattered brushy groves were found in protected areas and on exposed slopes. Young bur oak were scattered throughout the grasslands in spite of regular fire. They were probably grubs, old trees that remained small and brushlike because they were repeatedly killed back by fire. The mixture of grubs and prairie plants may have formed "brush prairies," known to have been common elsewhere in the Prairie Province.

Recent work has called into question the accuracy of Iowa's early land surveys. G. W. Thomson (1987) states that an appreciable acreage of forest had probably been cleared before the surveys began. He also questions the surveyors' definition of "forest," stating that much of the land they identified as such would not be considered forest today. The possibility of change in the connotations of the words "forest," "timber," and "woodland" must be considered whenever examining early historical accounts of Loess Hills vegetation. Some researchers picture presettlement Loess Hills woodlands as much more open than those of today, with a well-developed ground cover, perhaps resembling what we now would call a savanna.

Our knowledge of Nebraska's presettlement bluffline plant associations also leaves many questions unanswered. It is thought that today's dense, nearly continuous bluffline forests were once less extensive and more open, and that there too forests have expanded at the cost of the prairies. Researchers point to the scattering of prairie plants found in today's woodlands and to the old open-growth bur oaks (presumably left from former savannas) now lost in a sea of younger trees. Perhaps upper bluff slopes were open savannas and lower slopes were forested. Since fires characteristically swept across eastern Nebraska from the southwest, denser forests could have survived on the protected northeast-facing bluffs, where fires would have slowed or stopped on the downslopes. Because the climate of those eastward bluffs is not so desertlike, Nebraska's bluffs probably always have been more heavily forested than the Loess Hills.

NATURAL CHANGES IN HOLOCENE NATIVE COMMUNITIES, CLIMATE, AND LANDFORMS

Once the cataclysmic fluctuations spurred by the retreat of the last glaciers were calmed, the Loess Hills seem to have slipped into the modern period fairly smoothly. Communities assumed the appearance and composition that they were to retain through much of the Holocene, or the following 10,000 years, at least until Euro-American settlement produced dramatic changes in the Hills.

With dates extrapolated from studies in nearby areas of small mammal fossils and prehistoric plant pollen, the beginning of modern prairie dominance of the Hills can be pegged at approximately 9,000 years before the present. Prairies probably maintained the upper hand from then until Euro-American settlement, although forests surely reached upward from ravines when brief increases in moisture permitted. Mammal fossils suggest that the large forested areas of the southern Loess Hills, so prominent today, were not as pronounced in the past.

Mammal populations of the Hills changed dramatically between 12,400 and 8,400 years ago, a period for which no fossils have been found there. Sometime during that fossil gap, nearly all of the giant mammals that had roamed the Hills during the Ice Age disappeared. Most became extinct. A few followed the retreating glaciers. Caribou and barren-ground musk-ox, along with several small mammals now residing in the Rocky Mountains or in the far north, fall into the latter category. Wild horses survived in Eurasia but not on this continent. Horses later were reintroduced to North America by the Spanish.

Bison remained, increasing in number until huge herds dominated the grasslands as mammoths and other large grazers had before. Elk, deer, black bear, gray wolf, and cougar also remained, as did badger, raccoon, fox, coyote, beaver, opossum, and many small mammals that had been residents during the Ice Age. That assemblage remained essentially unchanged through the Holocene, at least until Euro-American settlement and the accompanying elimination of many species from the region.

Small mammal fossils collected in and near the Loess Hills document the dominance of prairies for much of the period, with a small number of forest mammal fossils confirming the presence of low-lying woodlands along streambeds. Small mammals constantly adjusted their range in response to climatic change. Prairie species became more abundant during drought periods, when prairies expanded. Forest species increased when moisture increased. In general, prairies were more abundant than they are today.

The mid-Holocene witnessed a lengthy and intense drought that was crucial in shaping natural communities. Studies of nearby sites show that the region's climate slowly started to become drier about 9,000 years ago, with moisture dropping to a minimum 6,300 years before the present. Conditions then moderated until a moisture regime resembling today's was reached 3,000 years ago. That dry period, called the hypsithermal, was first felt in western states and slowly pushed eastward, pulling with it species of drought-tolerant plants and animals from the western plains. Prairies expanded as far as modern Ohio; forests shrank and receded from the Midwest. A number of western Great Plains reptiles, amphibians, mammals, and plants probably arrived in the Loess Hills during that time. The arrival of western species, during the hypsithermal or during other, less extended droughts, has been crucial in molding the unique assemblage of mixed-grass prairie species that today distinguish the Loess Hills.

Following that lengthy drought, increased moisture allowed oak forests to again expand and push westward, displacing many of the extremely drought-tolerant species from all but the driest sites. There they remained as hypsithermal relicts, sometimes separated from larger groupings of their kind by tens or even hundreds of miles. Cowboy's delight, the plains pocket mouse, and the ornate box turtle may be hypsithermal relicts in the Loess Hills.

Another dry period occurred relatively recently, around 1200, although its severity and effects are highly contentious. Before that time, the climate is thought to have been moist and mild, with abundant summer rainfall. Conditions were excellent for horticulture and for growth of maize, and indeed that was when horticultural Indians established villages in the region. The drought that followed may have been severe enough to decimate crops and force abandonment of the village sites, both in the Loess Hills region and throughout the central plains. Indians in Southwestern deserts also disappeared from their cliff dwellings during the period of drought. Some scholars hypothesize that the drought caused the abandonment of Aztalan, the far-northern outpost of the Mississippian Culture in today's southern Wisconsin. They also point to the Mill Creek Culture's switch from hunting deer to hunting bison as evidence that dry grasslands were expanding. Deer inhabit woodlands, but bison are animals of the drier grasslands. Studies of fossil pollen from the Loess Hills region do not necessarily support the occurrence of a drought of such magnitude. The climate moderated and moisture increased around 1550, about 250 years after the village peoples had disappeared.

The Holocene produced a dramatic reshaping of the Loess Hills landscape. If the Pleistocene in the Loess Hills had been dominated by wind, then the Holocene was dominated by water. Water carved the deep deposits of wind-driven silt into the undulating, angular, steep-sloped and narrow-ridged landscape that today characterizes the region. Water fed the plants that mixed with loess to form today's soils. Features such as loess kindchen, pipestems, and catsteps, which are described in the following chapter, were formed. The effects of water, although powerful, were not always consistent. Instead, periods of gully cutting alternated with periods of sedimentation. Tremendous quantities of sediments were stripped from hillsides. With deposits from the collapsed sides of gullies, the sediments filled valleys. The filled valleys then were eaten into in an episode of gully cutting, which was followed by another episode of deposition and erosion. Episodes varied in duration and intensity.

Sediments produced visually distinct layers in valleys, which today can be observed in gully walls throughout the Hills. The layers have been dated and named and can be traced from one drainage to another. At least six episodes of major gully growth and filling have been identified, the first one starting 25,000 years ago. Five occurred in the last 10,500 years. The present landscape, at least that of the lower Hills, is thought to be almost entirely the result of periods of erosion and deposition during the last 3,500 years. The most recent gully-cutting episode began between 1860 and 1900 and is still under way.

EFFECTS OF EURO-AMERICAN SETTLEMENT ON THE NATURAL LANDSCAPE

Each species that has come to the Loess Hills has left its mark on the ever-changing landscape, nudging it toward certain responses that have altered the land's form, its processes, and its communities' composition. Humans have been no different since their arrival approximately 12,000 years ago. Soon after the Paleo-Indians arrived, the assemblage of gigantic glacial-age mammals disappeared. Some may have become extinct because of hunting pressures exerted by the growing human tide. Later Indians used broadcast fire for a number of purposes and in doing so were a major influence on the nature and distribution of plant communities. However, the influence of prehistoric Indian cultures is no longer obvious. Today we must search for scattered artifacts left by those human inhabitants and for the few remaining surface depressions and mounds that indicate previous habitation.

The effects of the second major wave of human immigrants, Euro-American settlers, have been far more dramatic and continue to influence demonstrably the landscape and its native species (figs. 16 and 17). Settlers arrived with the goal of creating civilization as it was known in the eastern United States. The rugged Hills and adjacent floodplain wetlands were seen as obstacles to the formation of ordered cities and productive farm-lands. Archaeological sites were regarded as curiosities and either van-dalized or inadvertently destroyed. Although the beauty of the Hills was lauded in some pioneer journals, those sentiments did not slow the de-struction of natural features for amenities more to human use and liking.

Changes were rapid and dramatic, flowing both from the settlers' desire to purposefully transform nature and from their inadvertent alteration of natural processes. Within a few decades, diverse natural communities that had been self-sustaining for millennia were gone. Taking their place were simple associations of introduced plants and animals, completely depen-dent on humans for survival. The simple associations mingled with native species and natural communities that had survived, transforming the en-tire landscape into a newly formed mosaic. A wave of animal extinction once again swept the Hills, reminiscent of the megafauna extinction of 10,000 years earlier. The distribution and abundance of remaining native species often changed dramatically.

Species and communities favored by human-induced alterations in-creased in number and expanded their ranges. The quenching of prairie fires encouraged forests and shrublands to creep upward into the vast Loess Hills prairies, which were steadily pushed into smaller and more extreme sites. Valley floors and hills were reshaped to suit human needs. The forces of erosion and gully cutting were accelerated. In short, Euro-American settlement gave birth to many of the environmental problems that we are trying to solve today.

Perhaps the most obvious human alterations involved the physical re-shaping of the hills. At first, such reshaping was fairly small-scale. The hooves of settlers' horses cut trails into the loess. Trails became roads winding where passage was easiest—through lowlands or along the west-ern edge of the bluffs, just above the Missouri River's wet floodplain. Then, as now, passersby carved their names into banks of loess. Small dams pro-vided power for grist and saw mills. Settlers nestled homesteads into val-

Figure 16. *"Mouth of the Big Sioux River" by Karl Bodmer. Bodmer's 1833 sketch of the northern Loess Hills shows their prairie-dominated summits and slopes, native woodlands snaking along ravines, and bluffs freshly carved by the broad and free-flowing Missouri River. Joslyn Art Museum, Omaha, Nebraska.*

Figure 17. *Modern human use has covered the landscape with new patterns. Sioux City has replaced the prairies and woodlands that Bodmer sketched. Bluffline slumps now are intensified by human activities rather than by the undercutting of the Missouri River. The river has been restricted to a narrow, confined channel, freeing the floodplain for transportation routes. Sioux City Public Museum.*

Figure 18. *The cohesion and stability of loess allowed settlers to easily provide shelters and storage areas by digging into hillsides. Photo by the author.*

leys at the base of the bluffs. Realizing that undisturbed loess, when dry, would stand firm in nearly vertical exposures, they carved caves into hill sides to form small stables, wine cellars, and lime kilns. The caves provided shelter and storage areas without further construction of interior walls (fig. 18). In 1870, the geologist Charles White recommended construction of passageways under the Loess Hills for use as fortifications when needed. They would, he claimed, rival the catacombs of ancient Rome.

Small-scale disturbances gave way to more extensive reshaping as bluffs were mined for the limestone, shale, sand, and gravel that lay below them and as loess was hauled away for construction fill and for building roads across lowlands. Cities too were carved into the Loess Hills (fig. 19). In Sioux City, the only site in Iowa where the bluffs came to the river's edge, the imposing hills were described as "one of nature's freaks." Seventy feet of loess was scraped from hilltops into adjacent valleys by horse-drawn graders. Leveling of the hills allowed road construction and the use of cable and electric streetcars on sites once too steep for horse travel.

Such purposeful restructuring of the hills continued as cities expanded, as networks of roads increasingly webbed the countryside, and as agricultural operations were enlarged to include cattle feedlots and other more

Figure 19. Deep loess was terraced and hills were severed to allow home and road construction in Sioux City. Newspaper articles from 1889, when this photo was taken, document that major amounts of time and money were invested in cutting through the loess. Sioux City Public Museum.

intensive operations (fig. 20). Various types of terraces also were constructed to slow erosion on agricultural land. In recent years, roadways and construction sites have been built on previously inaccessible bluff tops to accommodate large suburban homes near Council Bluffs. Loess bluffs still are mined for fill dirt.

However dramatic and intensive, that reshaping of the hills did not match the reshaping of adjacent valleys. Tributaries of the Missouri River that flowed through the Hills were soon identified as being notoriously flood prone, threatening life and hindering intensive agricultural use of the valleys' fertile soils. In an attempt to drain the wetlands and control flooding, those tributaries and the Missouri River were taken from their meandering courses and relegated to straight channels designed to hasten runoff (fig. 21). Dikes bordered the ditches on either side to prevent overflow. Unfortunately, the practice also increased the erosive force of the rapidly running water. Later on, massive dams were built on the Missouri River upstream from the Hills to further control the mighty river's flow.

While purposefully reshaping the hills, settlers also were inadvertently

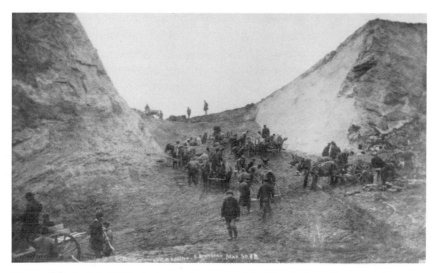

Figure 20. In this 1888 photograph, men assisted by donkey-drawn equipment cut through the loess, constructing the approach to the first bridge to span the Missouri River at Sioux City. Sioux City Public Museum.

Figure 21. The Missouri River and its tributaries have been transformed from meandering, free-flowing rivers bordered by wetlands to straightened drainage ditches crossing cropland. A river's previous course becomes obvious when runoff fills old oxbows, such as those to the right of the ditch. Don Poggensee.

intensifying natural processes that altered the form of the landscape. Hillside erosion, naturally high on the steep-sloped, fine-particled hills, has been accelerated by many activities: plowing of slopes for cropland, degradation of soil-holding prairies by grazing cattle, and baring of soil through construction and recreational uses (dirt biking, horseback riding, hang gliding, hiking). In addition to increasing erosion, those activities have increased the speed at which precipitation runs off the hills into drainages, which has increased flood potential.

Early settlers recounted slippage of great masses of bluff material downslope in very wet weather. Since settlement, cattle, dirt bikes, and construction have cut into bluff faces and steep slopes. Where human activities have increased infiltration of water into loess or have undercut the bases of slopes, the material's natural tendency to sheer off in vertical slabs has been increased.

Another natural process, the cutting of gullies into valleys and hillsides, has increased dramatically since settlement. Gully formation has been intensified by all the erosion-producing human activities listed above. However, examination of sediments in Loess Hills valleys reveals that over the centuries, gully cutting has occurred periodically in distinct episodes, the most recent episode beginning between 1860 and 1900. Thus, it appears that the erosion-intensifying activities of human settlement may have intensified a natural cyclical phenomenon rather than triggering the current bout of gully cutting.

Construction in the Hills has affected the land's topography in another, more subtle manner. When dry, loess is naturally strong, cohesive, and stable. In many cases, construction and land use practices have destroyed its stability and cohesion, leading to collapse. The land surface drops, damaging or destroying structures built on the loess. Collapse is common under pavement and under building foundations and has been a tremendous problem in suburban Council Bluffs. It can occur wherever construction increases the inflow of precipitation or surface water—where land is flattened, where construction blocks natural water drainage patterns, where roadside gutters leak, even where lawns are overwatered. In-flowing water increases soil moisture until the loess becomes saturated, at which point it loses its inherent cohesion and becomes what some geologists call loess mush. The saturated loess then settles or, if near a steep slope, runs out of the side of the hill, leaving a tunnel or chute (fig. 22). Collapse also can be initiated by the added weight of structures or fill dirt, which increases the pressure on loess that previously was stable. Although collapse is a natural

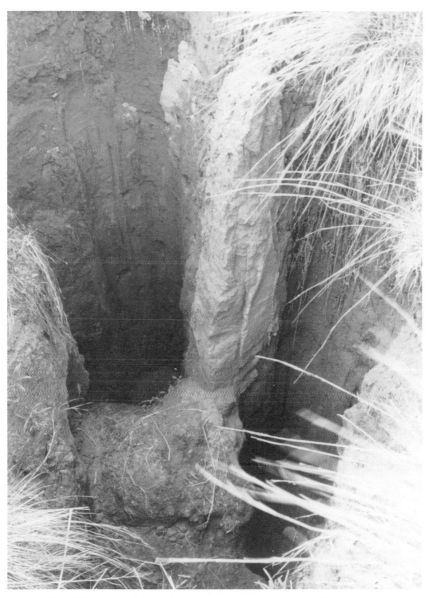

Figure 22. *Although stable and cohesive when dry, saturated loess becomes "loess mush." It may run out of the side of a hill, leaving a hilltop chute such as this one, a hazard to any person or structure perched on top of the bank. Don Poggensee.*

tendency of the Hills, it was a rarity before settlement. The well-drained and steep-sloped loess for the most part remained dry and stable. Increased infiltration and weight on the loess have multiplied the frequency of collapse.

In addition to physically reshaping the hills, settlers destroyed natural communities and replaced them with structures or with plant and animal associations deemed to be more useful. Wherever construction occurred or soil was moved for any purpose, native associations were demolished. In addition, many thousands of acres of native prairie were lost through purposeful conversion to agricultural land. Almost all of the Loess Hills has been affected by some form of agriculture at one time. Even steep slopes were plowed and used as cropland before flat river floodplains were drained and plowed. Some Loess Hills slopes have since naturally reverted to prairie, others to woodland, and others have been planted as pasture.

Native woodlands disappeared under the settler's arm, virgin timber being cut until some early residents feared that the firewood supply would disappear. Although today's naturalists are attempting to push invading trees out of prairies, in the 1870s planting of trees in the Loess Hills was encouraged. By the early twentieth century, shelter belts, windbreaks, and more extensive tree plantations were abundant. Fast-growing species such as cottonwood, soft maple, and box elder, several conifers (Scotch pine, white pine, Norway spruce), and several other species (e.g., black walnut, catalpa, and species of elm) were planted. Identifying those types of human-induced changes in plant communities requires a search of early historic records, a process discussed in sidebar 5.

The destruction of native communities was most dramatic in the valleys adjacent to the loess highlands. Once-bountiful aquatic marshlands, floodplain prairies, and streamside communities have been for the most part destroyed by the channelization of rivers, the heavy silt load carried by those rivers, and the conversion of valleys to cropland. The former richness of the valleys can best be imagined when observing the spring and autumn waterfowl migration along the Missouri River valley, a spectacle that now exhibits a fraction of the previous wildlife abundance.

Of course, an entire new set of species accompanied settlers to the Hills (fig. 23). The exotic species populated newly cleared sites and sometimes played havoc with the remaining natural communities. Some exotics were purposeful substitutions for former native species. Grasslands of corn and planted pasture species (such as brome and alfalfa) have replaced prairie

Figure 23. Early artists show the Loess Hills dominated by prairies and savannas rather than by the woodlands that today are prominent. Settlers superimposed their own land-use patterns on the Loess Hills, replacing diverse native communities with much simpler associations of domestic animals, crops, and fruit or decorative trees. Andreas Atlas, Eighth Congressional District, 1875.

grasslands. Cattle have replaced bison. Cats and to some extent dogs now feed on native species that formerly were prey to wild predators such as the mountain lion and black bear. Some exotic plants—Kentucky bluegrass and Russian olive for example, and a large number of garden plants, decorative trees and shrubs, and fruit-bearing trees—grace human-created lawns, parklands, and orchards. They sometimes spread into native plant communities.

Other exotic species, such as leafy spurge, sweet clover, common mullein, and dandelion, are now considered weeds. They have spread prolifically on disturbed sites. In places, they threaten the continued existence of native species. Still other species, in particular the house mouse and Norway rat, were uninvited guests that today thrive in Loess Hills farmsteads and cities, as they have thrived for centuries wherever humans have congregated.

In nearly all cases, creation of human-controlled communities has meant replacing diverse native ecosystems with simple associations (ones with few species). That in itself is a situation of concern, since communities with a large number of species naturally maintain their health and integrity,

---

SIDEBAR 5. Plant Community Changes:
Searching the Historic Record

From early on, natural changes in Loess Hills ecosystems were amplified by human activities. Thus the Loess Hills ecosystems of the early 1800s may have been as different from those of the late 1800s as they are from those of today. In the early nineteenth century, the woodlands were possibly still being shaped by routine fire. Local intrusions into woodlands were undoubtedly made by traders, federal militia, and the 2,000 Potawatomi who were moved into southwestern Iowa in the 1830s. Settlers plowed prairies, planted and then abandoned cropland, imported prairie-grazing cattle, and built and heated their homes with wood. They put an end to the grassland fires that had maintained the prairies. All of those activities affected existing woodlands and altered any tree and shrub reproduction that might have been occurring in the woodlands or prairies.

The ecological effects of human activities can be partially deciphered by comparing historical records. The Andreas Atlas presents a fairly detailed picture of tree distribution in 1875. The map of Fremont County portrays forest groves stretching along much of the blufline, being especially wide from today's town of Thurman to what is now the southern boundary of Waubonsie State Park. The Mills County map shows a nearly solidly wooded blufline, with forests extending eastward three miles near Glenwood. To the north, tree groves in Pottawattamie and Harrison counties' Loess Hills are still sizable, although smaller than those to the south and interrupted by large chunks of treeless bluffs and hills. Not until Monona County are treeless bluffs evident on the Andreas maps. They extend northward through Plymouth County, which by that time in history had only 375 forested acres remaining. In all the Andreas maps, the floodplains retain good-sized forests, and areas to the east of the Loess Hills are largely treeless.

Although the Andreas maps seem to give a comprehensive picture of the forested areas in 1875, they do not identify presettlement forest cover. A comparison of those maps with land survey records reveals that by 1875, the Loess Hills woodlands may have been reduced in size. In

---

withstanding environmental fluctuations and assaults far better than simple communities. Prairies have survived here for approximately 9,000 years, but croplands, lawns, and gardens would disappear within a few years without human intervention.

each of Iowa's seven Loess Hills counties, the number of forested acres is significantly higher in the earlier land survey records than in the Andreas maps. The decrease in timber coverage by 1875 ranges from 42 percent, in Mills County (50,790 timbered acres in the land survey to 29,584 in 1875), to 90 percent, in Plymouth County (3,640 to 365) (Thomson and Hertel, 1981). Of course, the decreases may reflect cutting of timber within county borders but outside the Loess Hills. However, timber cutting in some Loess Hills regions was sufficient to create a fear of firewood shortage. Governmental agencies such as the Iowa Geological Survey (White, 1870) and the Pottawattamie County Board of Supervisors (1875) encouraged tree planting in the Hills for fuel, shelter, and the like.

B. F. Bush (1895) provided a thorough description of Missouri's Loess Hills plant communities at the end of the nineteenth century, approximately 50 years after settlers arrived. Prairie-covered mounds extended from the Iowa border to a few miles south of St. Joseph, about 35 miles farther than today's most southerly prairies at the McCormack Natural Area. The steepest, most exposed bluff-face prairies were especially dry. On their north and east sides, the mounds were covered by short, thick shrubs. Trees grew at the base of the slopes, sometimes reaching well up the sides of east-facing slopes. East of the mound faces, a north-to-south belt of timber about one mile wide covered the rolling hills. High, rolling prairie extended east from the timber belt.

Louis Pammel (1915) reports that by the early 1900s much of the commercially valuable timber in the Hills had been cut and that virgin stands of oak, elm, hickory, ash, walnut, and other species had been replaced by second growth. Woodlands of that era included native and planted timber. Plantings, particularly extensive in Harrison County, often introduced exotic species such as catalpa, soft maple, pine, and spruce to an area. Pammel describes native timber as located primarily in ravines, with more extensive groves in the southern Hills.

Within 40 years, bur oak, American elm, and associated species were invading areas up to several thousand square acres in Harrison, Monona, and Woodbury counties (Loomis and McComb, 1944). Those young forests, which covered the less intensively farmed land on all but the steepest, most westerly line of bluffs, must have been similar to the young forests invading grasslands throughout the Hills today.

Where native communities remain, human land use practices have exerted pressures that have altered their distribution and abundance. The abundance of some plants and animals also has changed, because of the introduction of exotics or removal of sensitive native species. The health and vigor of some native species has increased because of human use, while that of other species has decreased.

The cessation of wildfire has produced all of those changes. Fire was an integral part of the natural environment for thousands of years before settlement. Woodlands were thinned and their species composition was shaped by fire. Fire in prairies killed shrubs and trees, helping fire-tolerant grassland species maintain the upper hand. Modern-day woodland expansion has meant a shrinking of prairies on all but the driest sites, the steep west and south-facing bluffs and ridge tops. Remaining prairies have been degraded by invading shrub and tree seedlings. Tall-grass prairies, typical of native grasslands originally surrounding the Loess Hills, have been nearly lost to invading woodlands. An entire new mosaic of communities now covers the Hills, with woodlands and croplands occupying sites previously dominated by prairies. Woodland expansion continues to the present day and threatens to obliterate Loess Hills prairies.

Another human-related pressure on native ecosystems has been the replacement of bison with pastured cattle. Bison may have preferred surrounding, lusher prairies to the steep-sloped, relatively sparse Loess Hills grasslands. But if bison did frequent the Hills, the animals' nonselective grazing and their habit of constantly moving on would have prevented permanent damage to the prairies.

In contrast, cattle confined to pastures tend to congregate in spots and to graze selectively on the species that are most inviting. Legumes and the more sensitive prairie grasses decrease in abundance. Plants able to invade cattle paths and other disturbed areas and plants not attractive to cattle (such as hoary vervain and the panic and grama grasses) increase. With time, the vigor of the prairie decreases along with plant height, plant density, and the prairie's ability to withstand invading species and erosion. Sensitive plants decline or disappear. Exotic species whose seeds are spread in cattle feces, by wind, and by birds find such degraded prairies prime areas for reproduction. Trees also invade massively when the pressures of cattle tramping are reduced. Those changes occur on all sites including steep bluff faces, where grazing cattle can easily kill a significant portion of the already sparse vegetation, cut trails deep into the bluff face, and leave steep bare ground susceptible to washing and slumping. Thus cattle-grazing has affected the hills' shape, the types of communities present, and their plant species' composition and vigor (fig. 24). (Specific changes in prairie plant composition due to grazing are described in chapter 5.)

Figure 24. Cattle have dramatically altered the Loess Hills by modifying the species composition and vigor of the prairies and the shape of the landscape. Bottom. Overgrazing has induced the slumping and terracing of loess. Top: Cattle also have cut paths into hillsides. Don Poggensee.

Variations in the abundance and distribution of a number of native animals also have been traced to human land use patterns. Native animals that are not specific in their requirements, adjusting to new habitats and the presence of humans with ease, have increased since settlement. Examples include the raccoon, coyote, house wren, American crow, deer mouse, and big brown bat. Native plants that do well on disturbed ground—snow-on-the-mountain, curly-top gumweed, western prairie clover, ragweed, and great-flowered beardtongue among others—also have increased in abundance.

Animals whose requirements are met by agricultural lands have increased in the Hills. In the past, the richest native grasslands probably were found on lowlands and gentle slopes, which today have been converted to agricultural land. Small birds of large open grasslands, such as the grasshopper sparrow, dickcissel, and western meadowlark, have been able to adjust to agricultural usage and now are most common in the Hills on agricultural fields rather than in the small, steep native prairies that remain. The meadow vole is abundant in hay fields, and the northern grasshopper mouse prefers cultivated fields to other community types. The southern bog lemming, a rare species, is found in low, moist, heavy stands of the introduced Kentucky bluegrass, in addition to communities of native plants. The thirteen-lined ground squirrel, which prefers short grasslands, has increased in heavily grazed grasslands.

Woodland and woodland-edge species such as the eastern cottontail, raccoon, white-tailed deer, and gray fox have benefited from woodland invasion into prairies. Woodland reptiles (the eastern hognose, ringneck, red milk, and other snakes) have increased in number, along with the increase of woodland plants and habitats. Bird species such as the chuckwill's-widow and summer tanager are pushing their range limits to the north as forests expand northward. Thus forest plants and animals are now occupying sites historically occupied by prairie species.

The destruction of moist valley marshlands and grasslands has in a small way been mollified by construction of upland farm ponds and other water impoundments, which were previously absent in the well-drained Hills. The ponds have become homes to bullfrogs, muskrats, and certain waterfowl that were previously rare or nonexistent within the Hills. Other animals such as the Great Plains toad and plains leopard frog, previously breeders in ponds on the Missouri River's floodplain, have found new breeding grounds in human-created roadside ditches. Even modifications such as construction of basin terraces (water catchment ridges at the base of slopes) have provided moist spots for proliferation of floodplain species such as cottonwoods. However, the newly created wetlands do not contain nearly the diversity and richness of the earlier valley marshlands and wet grasslands.

Unfortunately, many other Loess Hills natives have disappeared completely. Most large herbivores and carnivores were eliminated from the region within historic time. The black bear, mountain lion, elk, pronghorn, and bison all were eliminated through hunting pressure and habitat modi-

Figure 25. *The prairie rattlesnake remains in Iowa only in the northern Loess Hills. Randall D. Williams.*

fication, abetted by especially harsh winter weather. Venomous snakes were willfully destroyed there as elsewhere. A small number of prairie rattlesnakes have survived in only one spot in Iowa, the northern Loess Hills (fig. 25). Large birds such as the greater prairie chicken, long-billed curlew, and short-eared owl were probably present before settlement. This says nothing of the insects, plants, and other higher animals that undoubtedly were residents but disappeared from the region before their presence was recorded.

Many species have declined in the area without disappearing. Reptiles and amphibians (the fox snake and prairie king snake, for example) have decreased in response to loss of critical habitat. Habitat loss and exposure to pesticides have injured cricket frog populations. The ornate box turtle, Great Plains skink, and plains pocket mouse, all threatened or endangered in Iowa, have dropped to dangerously low numbers as the small prairie openings they inhabit have been invaded by woodlands. Several prairie butterflies also have been threatened with loss of crucial habitat as native grasslands throughout the Hills have fragmented and shrunk, at some point becoming too small to maintain viable breeding populations. A growing number of prairie plants are declining as their habitat is lost through human use and woodland invasion.

The effects of human intervention on this unique landscape continue to be felt in many ways—through direct destruction of plants and animals, destruction of required habitat and the gradual shrinking and fragmentation of habitat, loss of archaeological sites, environmental deterioration, and the effects of human-introduced species. Human land-use pressures are felt especially strongly by prairie species, several of which have become rare or endangered in the Hills. Ironically, they also are the species that make Loess Hills communities so unusual and interesting.

Human-produced pressures continue to create problems in the Hills. A damaged building perched on a collapsed slope or a field dissolving into an ever-expanding gully are obvious reminders of our species' negative interactions with the fragile landscape. Also obvious are continued efforts to deal with land-use problems—the routine dredging of a sediment-clogged ditch, the reconstruction of a washed-out bridge or roadway. The loss of native species and communities occurs more slowly and secretly but is equally devastating. Disappearance of native communities means the growth of communities that are less able to withstand the Loess Hills' demanding environment and survive regional environmental fluctuations. It also means the loss of a rich and irreplaceable natural resource, not duplicated elsewhere, which attracts interest from throughout the continent because of its mixture of western and midwestern species and its unusual topography. Once lost, those natural assets can never be replaced.

Maintaining the health of those special prairie communities and of remaining natural areas and geological formations is a task to challenge any naturalist, a task whose success is extremely important. (Attempts to combat some of the human-induced ecosystem alterations described in this section are discussed in chapter 6.)

☙ FOUR ❧

PHYSICAL CHARACTERISTICS
OF TODAY'S LOESS HILLS

An understanding of the physical characteristics of the Loess Hills is important for several reasons. For example, it lays the groundwork for comprehending patterns of human land use. The steepest, most precipitous bluffs, especially those desertlike bluffs next to the Missouri River valley, are the least accessible to humans. They are thus the least used and the least disturbed areas of the Hills. As slope lessens and accessibility to cattle and farm machinery increases, intensity of land use likewise increases. Thus, although steeper slopes remain in permanent pasture, the broad, flatter ridgetops and larger valleys have been cultivated as cropland. Intensity of human land use in general increases from west to east. Conversely, most remaining undisturbed native communities cling to a narrow band along the westernmost hills.

Physical features also shape the distribution of natural communities in the Loess Hills. The angular, steep hills, with their exposure to varying intensities of sun and wind, weave intricate patterns of ridges and valleys, creating multiple nooks and crannies and equal numbers of plant and animal habitats. Soils that are dry, erosive, and poorly developed on uplands give way to thicker, moister, richer materials coating valley floors. The climate, with its accentuated variations in temperature, precipitation, and wind, at times gently fosters life and at other times seems bent to destroy, especially on those uplands most exposed to the elements. Those myriad perturbations create the specialized habitats so important to the various plants and animals of the Loess Hills.

Details of the formation of certain physical features—the process through which first wind, then water molded the Loess Hills—have been discussed in the previous two chapters. This chapter concentrates on features that dominate the landscape today.

CHARACTERISTICS OF LOESS

The loess of which the Loess Hills are composed is mostly quartz silt—small-grained particles that are somewhat larger than clay but not as big as grains of sand, with quartz being the most abundant mineral. The accumulations of loose, lightweight, unconsolidated silt are remarkably homogeneous, commonly lacking gravel, rock, and the horizontal stratifications so typical of most rock and soil layers (fig. 26). Even the color of the loess below the upper soil layer is often a uniform yellowish brown, although color can range from gray to brown, and some deposits are strongly mottled.

Although the loess deposits consist of uniform-sized grains, a microscopic examination of loess from the western and eastern Loess Hills would show differences in particle size. Coarse silt, difficult for the wind to hold aloft, dropped first and is most concentrated in and near the westernmost bluffs. The concentration of lighter, smaller clay and fine silt particles increases with distance from the floodplain.

Being composed of loosely compacted particles, deep loess deposits remain highly permeable. Precipitation moves through loess rapidly, rather than slowly filtering through the substratum and gradually being released into streams. On steep slopes, rain runs off rather than into the soil. Where exposed to sun and wind, the well-drained loess maintains a state of aridity or semiaridity suitable for the unusual assemblage of drought-resistant plants and animals that thrive there. The highly porous material is incapable of holding standing water with any consistency, a trait explaining in part the lack of natural wetlands in the Hills.

Because precipitation is not held for any time within the loess, the quantity of water in local streams can change quickly. Rivers in the region fill rapidly during storms. They have been notorious for their flooding, overflowing their banks more frequently than any others in Iowa. In contrast, during dry summers, local streams dry up and the flow of larger streams decreases dramatically.

Dry undisturbed loess deposits are very cohesive, a trait that explains their ability to stand in walls with a 50-degree to 75-degree slope. Near-vertical faces form naturally as gullies eat into the loess deposits. Pre-

Figure 26. The Loess Hills consist of remarkably homogeneous, fine-grained quartz silt. Photo by the author.

cipitous bluffs of impressive stature line the Missouri River valley. That vertical stability and strength has been used to advantage by highway and railroad engineers, who routinely design steep cuts through loess deposits for roadbeds and railroad tracks. A truly vertical cut of as much as 16 feet can stand independently in the Hills, with cuts as much as 24 feet being stable when the slope angle is decreased a bit.

Unfortunately, the cohesive strength of loess deposits disappears when the loess is disturbed or becomes wet (fig. 27). Saturated loess is unable to support even its own weight, and during unusually wet periods masses of loess collapse. The seemingly solid loess blocks "dissolve like sugar," as some local residents say. Water also lubricates natural vertical partings that form near exposed loess faces, encouraging landslides as loess sloughs off of steep slopes. Natural slope failures are abundant after heavy rains. Fresh scars of such landslides can nearly always be seen along the loess bluffline. Collapse has become more frequent because of human land uses that have increased moisture within the loess and have also required that loess support the additional weight of structures or fill. Collapse and landslide are now perceived as serious environmental hazards and management problems.

Figure 27. *The cohesive strength of undisturbed, dry loess allows it to stand in stable, near-vertical walls. Unfortunately, its strength quickly disappears when water content increases. Don Poggensee.*

Erosion of loess by running water is another natural feature that has been intensified through human use. The Loess Hills are inherently susceptible to severe erosion because the loosely compacted loess lies in long steep slopes, and the inevitable periods of heavy rain produce high runoff. Disturbance and destruction of the protective cover of native prairie plants have increased the material's natural proclivity to erode (fig. 28).

Rates of erosion in the Hills and resulting sediment loads of local streams are among the highest in the nation. Stream sediments are boosted especially high by the slumping of gully walls into streams. The sediments block ditches and threaten aquatic wildlife. Erosion is easily seen during rainstorms, when ditch waters are murky and sheets of sediments wash down steep hillsides that no longer are protected by healthy prairie vegetation. Runoff from unprotected fields of row crops is thought to be 2 to 3 times what it was when prairies covered the soil, with peak runoff rates 10 to 50 times the presettlement rate. Erosion removes in the range of 30 to 40 tons per acre per year in the Hills, a threefold to fourfold increase over Iowa's average of 9 to 10 tons.

Upland slopes have been reshaped by sheet erosion, which washes the

Figure 28. *The Loess Hills are naturally susceptible to erosion. Note the development of gullies throughout the photo, the slumping of loess on steeper slopes, and the tendency to develop steep-sided scars across the landscape as erosion occurs. These tendencies are increased by overgrazing and removal of prairie vegetation. Don Kurz, Missouri Department of Conservation.*

top layer of soil downslope. Erosion of uplands has removed tremendous quantities of loess, redepositing it in layers on valley slopes and bottoms and at times filling gullies. Because the material is no longer in its original wind-deposited position, it technically ceases to be loess and instead is called alluvium (material deposited by running water) or colluvium (material moved from hillsides to the bases of slopes by gravity or local wash).

Erosion produces vertical-walled gullies that can reach huge proportions, sometimes cutting more than 80 feet into the loess with a width of up to 100 feet. The gullies form an extensive and dense drainage network with intricate patterns of dissection. The dramatic results of gully erosion are evident both in valleys and on uplands, where ravines slice down steep hillsides. Gullies enlarge rapidly, eroding upward into the hills when blocks of loess break free and slump into the creeks, which carry the material downstream. New gullies also may be initiated upstream at a creek's headwaters.

The dramatic expansion of the gully system in modern times is best understood within a historic perspective. Although erosion has been a persistent feature of the Hills, rates of erosion have not been constant. Instead, periods of gully formation have been staggered, alternating with periods when gullies were filled and valley floors leveled with deposits from gully walls and adjacent slopes. Geologists have dated episodes of prehistoric gully cutting and described them in terms of their duration and the size of the gully network they produced. Thus the present-day expansion of gullies, which began in the Hills between 1860 and 1900, can be seen as one of many gully-cutting episodes that have repeatedly reshaped the landscape throughout the Holocene and even before. Although human activities undoubtedly have accelerated and exaggerated today's massive gully expansion, the episode probably was initiated naturally by a climate and runoff regime, as were episodes in the past.

Lateral erosion was significant in shaping the Hills in past centuries. The Missouri River and its tributaries then wandered in their valleys, sometimes flowing at the base of the hills and washing away peninsulas of loess that jutted out into the valley floor. In 1804, Lewis and Clark described entire islands, huge chunks of soil and trees, washing downriver. What remained were the gigantic bluffs that today characterize the Hills' eastern edge. Lateral erosion against the bluffs has not occurred since humans channelized the Missouri River. The mighty river now cuts downward into its bed, rather than affecting land to either side.

SHAPES OF THE LOESS

Water has carved the loose accumulations of windblown dust continually since they were first laid down. Natural reshaping of the hills continues today, albeit at an accelerated rate because of the impact of human processes. Deep loess responds predictably to the forces of water, in accordance with the physical properties and erosional patterns described in the preceding section. Here the resulting characteristic Loess Hills shapes and topography will be examined.

The most picturesque description of this distinctive topography may have been that by Bohumil Shimek, who in 1910 wrote of "the billowy expanse of the inland loess ridges which appear like a giant swell of a stormy sea which has been suddenly fixed." Like storm waves, steep slopes of loess rise to long, narrow ridge crests, which poise angularly above gully-bottomed valleys. The ridgetops invite hikers. Gently sloping, prairie-covered crests seem to stretch ever onward, branching into an in-

Figure 29. *Steep-sided undulating ridges, often topped by inviting hiking trails, seem to lead on forever. Don Poggensee.*

terconnected network that sometimes leads for miles through the hills (fig. 29). A narrow crestline walking trail often is present, offering visitors expansive views to either side wherever vision is not blocked by trees. The crestline itself is fairly level, although small swells produce an irregular skyline when seen from below. Those undulations have been termed "peaks and saddles," although occasionally the peaks may appear more as saddle horns where steep-sided knobs of loess jet upward.

Slopes on either side of the long ridges are steep and undulating. Numerous side ridges, or side spurs, extend outward from the branching ridgeline and are likewise steeply pitched and undulating. Seen from the ground, the terrain is rough and corrugated. The shapes are most obvious when grasslands dominate. The expanding forests may mask the view of those features, although the undulating steep slopes quickly become obvious to the cross-country hiker. From the air the hills present an angular and intricate topography, impressively sharp-featured, one of ridges and troughs continuously flowing into one another (fig. 30).

Vertical-walled gullies cut into valley floors. Gullies deepen and widen and continually expand upstream and upslope, sometimes stretching to a length of several miles. They are joined by ravines that cut into sideslopes to form well-developed drainage systems. Characteristic dendritic (branching like a tree) drainage patterns, which are exceptionally intricate and dense, are distinctive from the air. On the ground, the network of deep, vertical-sided gullies, ranging from 3 to 100 feet wide and dropping downward 80 feet or more, seriously hinders cross-country travel.

Lateral erosion has carved the gigantic bluffs along the Missouri River valley, which are technically named truncated spurs (see fig. 2). Bluff faces continue to be carved as vertical slabs of loess break free and slump downward, sometimes covering roads and railroad tracks at their base. The height of the prominent bluffs is greatest in the north, reaching more than 300 feet above the valley floor in Plymouth, Woodbury, and Monona counties, Iowa, and decreasing to 220 feet above the valley bottom in Holt County, Missouri. The bluff tops offer spectacular views of the valley below and the surrounding hills.

Those are the patterns peculiar to water-carved deep loess. One additional feature, that of catsteps, is limited to the steepest loess slopes near the Missouri River valley (fig. 31). A series of long, narrow benches cuts uniformly across upper hillsides, like a flight of stairs or a set of innumerable terraces. Each catstep is typically less than a foot wide, but as a series catsteps often extend for hundreds of feet across a slope.

Several explanations have been offered for the formation of the small-stepped terraces, which have been observed on steep grassy slopes in many parts of the world. For example, Charles Darwin in 1882 suggested

Figure 30. *Aerial views of the Loess Hills reveal a distinctive, angular, corrugated landscape. The network of narrow, branching ridge crests is flanked by steep slopes and numerous side spurs with intricate drainage patterns. Geological Survey Bureau, Iowa Department of Natural Resources.*

Figure 31. *Catsteps: naturally formed, long, narrow terraces cutting across upper hillsides. Don Poggensee.*

that in some places they resulted from the action of earthworms. He thought that the small terraces were formed of disintegrated worm castings (earth brought to the soil's surface by worms) and later accentuated by grazing animals. The catsteps of the Loess Hills, though, are likely to be a geological phenomenon, created by the repeated slipping and downslope movement of shelves of loess. They are seen as a natural result of loess's inherent tendency toward failure on steep slopes and of loess's tendency to shear off in vertical planes, resulting here in numerous small soil slumps rather than one massive collapse. Although some scientists cling to the idea that the Hills' catsteps were created by grazing animals (bison or cattle) traveling repeatedly across slope faces, that explanation is not probable for catsteps on steep upper loess slopes. However, cattle may be responsible for the enlargement or formation of horizontal terraces on lower slopes, in particular for the large terraces frequently seen near the bases of heavily grazed bluffs.

Although characteristics of loess dominate the Loess Hills landforms, underlying deposits (bedrock and glacial till) continue to have some influence on the shape of the hills. The scalloped edges of the bluffline along the Missouri River valley result in part from the sporadic presence of older underlying deposits near the land's surface. In previous centuries, those underlying materials resisted the Missouri River's erosive powers. Where especially resistant Pennsylvanian bedrock lies at the base of the hills, to the south of Harrison and Monona counties, Iowa, the entire Missouri River floodplain narrows abruptly.

A sudden change in the slope of a hill, from very steep to less severe, in many cases reflects the presence of underlying glacial till or water-deposited sand and gravel. The underlying deposits prevent the loess from assuming its characteristic near-vertical pose. They create a gentle foot slope, typically mantled by reworked loess from the steeper hillsides above.

Variations in topography do occur from north to south and from east to west. The precipitous bluffline rising abruptly from the flat Missouri River valley floor forms a sharp and unmistakable western boundary to the Loess Hills. The roughest, most corrugated, and most sharply dissected terrain lies directly adjacent to that bluffline. As the loess stretches eastward, its thickness decreases and the characteristic Loess Hills features become more subdued.

The far northern hills, especially those in Plymouth County, are more open and rolling than areas to the south, possibly because the underlying bedrock has greater control over broad drainage patterns in the north than elsewhere. Ridge crests toward the north are long, unbroken, and relatively broad. Views there are less restricted by expanding woodlands than in the southern hills. Toward the south, ridge crests become shorter and narrower and more divergent, side spurs become more numerous, and dissection patterns in general become more intricate and angular.

Throughout its length, the long, narrow band of hills is interrupted by broad river valleys that connect to the Missouri River valley. Tributaries of the Missouri River—the Floyd, Little Sioux, Willow, Boyer, Nishnabotna, and Tarkio, among others—all cut through the Loess Hills from the northeast to the southwest. When the waters of those rivers ran more freely, before they were restricted by humans to today's ditches, the rivers carved into ancient floodplains to form elevated, flat landforms called terraces. Today the terraces are a striking and distinctive feature of the river valleys. Some tributaries left alluvial fans, roughly triangular deposits of sediments at the mouths of small valleys. At the foot of the Loess Hills, the Missouri River also left terraces, which today are loess-covered and especially prominent in the Sioux City and Council Bluffs areas.

The bluffs bordering the west side of the Missouri River valley in Nebraska differ significantly from those in Iowa and Missouri. Nebraska's bluffs vary in height from small banks to cliffs exceeding 200 feet, with those at Fontenelle Forest Nature Center (just south of Omaha) being among the largest. Although not a part of the Loess Hills, the bluffs west of the Missouri River are formed in part by significant accumulations of loess. Bedrock, however, is far more dominant in Nebraska's bluffs. The irregular bedrock surface in places reaches far above the valley floor, coming close to the bluff top. Bedrock is exposed in massive bluffs at both Ponca State Park and Indian Cave State Park. In general, Nebraska's loess is rarely deep or extensive enough to assume the steep, highly dissected, angular topography typical of the Loess Hills. In a few places (e.g., Indian Cave State Park, parts of Thurston County, and southern Dakota County), a rugged loess landscape does extend a mile or two west of the bluff faces, but for the most part the terrain becomes subdued at the top of the bluffs.

Another major difference in Nebraska's bluffs is the substitution of the Loess Hills' typical near-vertical slope for a gentler slope at the base of the bluffs. The change in slope steepness reflects the dominance of underlying geological formations other than loess.

HIDDEN WITHIN THE LOESS

Although loess is remarkably uniform from the top to the bottom of a large bluff face, variations and inclusions are sometimes apparent in natural vertical exposures and in human-made cuts along roads. Especially common are loess kindchen, natural products of weathering of the loess (fig. 32). Water dissolves grains of calcium carbonate (the major component of limestone, but also found as particulates within loess) and moves the dissolved carbonate downward. The carbonate then segregates to form whitish, irregular, rocklike bodies (concretions), which may reach grapefruit size. Sometimes rounded, they also can be elongate or branching, resembling a human figure. In Germany, where nodules are found in thick loess along the Rhine River, they are called *kindchen*, the German term for "small children." The term has been imported to the Loess Hills.

Pipestems, less commonly seen products of weathering, are reddish brown, tubular concretions of iron vertically oriented in the loess. The hollow cylinders formed along old plant-root channels in the loess.

More recent reminders of plant occupation are living roots themselves (fig. 33). Because of the inclination of loess to shear away in massive vertical slabs, the Loess Hills is one of the few places where the pattern of a tree's entire root system can be readily observed. Other types of substrata do a better job of concealing their forest's footings.

Occasionally, deep layers of loess differ in color from the yellowish brown upper layers. Low, gray zones with dark brown iron stains indicate that a layer of loess was saturated by water in the distant past. Fluctuations in the water table promoted segregation of iron to form the brown mottles and the pipestems.

Thin, dark, horizontal bands within the loess represent ancient layers of topsoil that formed during periods of slow loess deposition, when plants growing on the hills had time to modify the uppermost loess layers, darkening them by adding organic matter. Soil formation halted when loess deposition once again speeded up, and the fresh loess buried and preserved the ancient soils. Sand and gravel river deposits and wind-borne sand also occasionally interfinger with the loess.

Signs of previous life are often found within the loess. The region's rich fossil collection has been described in chapter 2. Snail fossils are by far the most abundant. Fossils of larger animals, the most impressive being the diverse collection of gigantic prehistoric mammals, are frequently found

Figure 32. *Loess kindchen, naturally formed irregular concretions of calcium carbonate, are commonly seen in roadcuts through the Hills. Photo by the author.*

Figure 33. *Root systems of trees are commonly revealed in vertical cuts through the loess. Photo by the author.*

buried in valley and river deposits. Prehistoric remains of Indian cultures—
artifacts, hearths, ash lenses, bones of prey, and the like—also are predictably located within the layers of valley sediments and alluvial fans. Village
and burial sites have been excavated on Loess Hills uplands.

Much older deposits can be seen sporadically, at the base of some roadcuts and loess bluffs, along some streambeds, and in quarries cut into the
bluffs. Bedrock, formed of sediments deposited hundreds of millions of
years ago in and along the coast of shallow seas, is the most obvious. Occasionally, ancient glacial tills lie between the fine-textured loess and solid
bedrock. Finer-grained layers within or on top of glacial and alluvial sand
and gravel deposits may be very old soils indicating an ancient land surface. Patches of whitish volcanic ash, blown there from now-extinct volcanoes in today's Yellowstone National Park, also may be seen occasionally. All of those older deposits underlying the loess have been described
in chapter 2.

SOILS

Soil is the loose material covering the earth's surface that has been changed
by surface processes, such as weathering, and within which plants grow. In
some places, the soil layer is easily identified as the fine-textured material
lying on top of rock. In the Loess Hills, where loess may extend more than
200 feet downward, "soil" refers only to that top layer modified by vegetation and weathering. Loess Hills soil is distinctly different in color and texture from the little-modified loess below and from fresh loess exposed in
slumps or gully walls.

The Loess Hills and areas with deep loess immediately to the east have
produced soils that are unique to their region, reflecting the particular in-
teraction of climate, vegetation, and loess that has occurred there. Those
soils extend as far east as Shelby, Crawford, and Ida counties, Iowa. In
accordance with tradition, soil scientists have grouped Loess Hills soils
with similar characteristics into soil series, each with its own name and set
of distinctive, defining traits. Soil series of Loess Hills uplands differ dramatically from those of the valleys.

The Loess Hills uplands are dominated by three soil series that together
form the Monona-Ida-Hamburg soil association. Generally speaking, Monona soils cover gently sloping ridge tops and slightly to steeply sloping
hills. Hamburg soils are found on extremely steep catstep slopes, and Ida
soils occur on narrow divides and on slopes of intermediate steepness.

The upland soils are silt loams that are various shades of dark brown. They tend to be dry. Precipitation either rapidly runs off the steep slopes or moves through the well-drained material shortly after heavy rains. Except for fairly level ridgetop soils, the erosion hazard is classified as severe or very severe. The soils are as susceptible to erosion as soils anywhere in the Midwest, and more so than many. Indeed, except on hills with less than 9 percent slope, erosion has already been severe. Often only a few inches of surface soil remain. On most cultivated sideslopes, the surface layer of soil is completely gone. Erosion sometimes even eats into materials below the topsoil. When not depleted or removed through erosion, the surface layer of Monona soils can be 8 to 14 inches thick and that of Ida soils 6 to 10 inches thick. Hamburg topsoils are always very thin.

Because of rapid erosion of surface soil layers, upland soils are minimally developed. Ida and Hamburg soils are entirely lacking a subsoil, or B-horizon—that layer where iron and clay typically accumulate, which is immediately below the blackest, richest topsoil and is lower in organic matter and biological activity than the uppermost soil layer. Instead of the standard three-tiered soil profile, those soils have a thin A-horizon directly on top of the yellowish brown loess parent material from which the soil formed.

The loess substratum typically contains calcium carbonate concretions (the loess kindchen). The calcium has been partially washed from the substratum of Monona soils on more gently sloping hills.

Valley soils are much better developed than those of uplands. Since valleys are flat or slightly sloping, water is less likely to remove their surface soils. The sheet erosion potential is slight; therefore, the surface soil (A-horizon), a fertile black or dark brown silt loam or silty clay loam, can be thick. For one of the major Loess Hills valley soils (the Napier series), surface soils may be 20 to 30 inches deep.

Most valley soils have a well-developed B-horizon. The exception is the McPaul series, which consists of freshly deposited river sediments up to 36 inches thick that have not yet developed any sort of soil profile. The new sediments cover older, darker, better-developed soils.

Valley soils are moderately to well drained, although they generally are more poorly drained and moister than their upland counterparts. Bottomland soils are especially wet.

Valley soils are derived from reworked loess that has slid or been washed into place. Napier soils, found at the base of slopes (on "footslopes") and along upland drainage ways and narrow streams, have formed from colluvial parent material; that is, from sediments that have moved downslope through the action of gravity and soil wash. Soils of bottomlands (the McPaul, Colo, and Kennebec series) derive from alluvium, sediments deposited in floodplains by running water. All of those soils continue to be affected by the movement of sediments downslope and downstream, which can alter and cover topsoil.

One last major soil series covers high, fairly steep footslopes that lie midway between upland slopes and valleys. Castana soils bear characteristics of soils in both locales. Like upland soils, the dark brown Castana silt loams are well drained and lack a B-horizon. However, although their potential for erosion is rated as high, Castana soils have been far less stripped by erosion than have soils on the hillsides above them. Therefore, like the valleys, the footslopes retain a deep topsoil, 20 to 24 inches thick, derived from colluvial parent material.

CLIMATE

The climate of the Loess Hills is shaped by the region's distance from large bodies of water. Being far from the temperature-moderating influences of large lakes or oceans, the Loess Hills region has a midcontinental climate, with extreme temperature variations from season to season and year to year. Winters are fairly long and cold, with average temperatures in the teens or twenties in Sioux City and average lows usually between 5° and 15° F. The temperatures warm by approximately 10 degrees at the southern terminus of the Hills, in Oregon, Missouri, to the point that winter cold spells there are seldom prolonged. (Selected climatic data are listed in table 2.) Summers are long and quite warm, with average temperatures in the seventies and average highs in the eighties. July is the hottest month. January is the coolest. Record highs exceed 100° F and record lows drop to 20° or more below zero. The average annual temperature is about 50° F.

Sunshine is abundant in the Loess Hills. In fact, the region boasts more sunny days without a trace of precipitation than any other region in Iowa, and extreme northwestern Missouri is the driest region of that state. Precipitation often falls as thunderstorms that may bring heavy rainfall over a short time, accentuating erosion. Between two-thirds and three-fourths of the year's precipitation falls during the growing season. Annual precipitation averages range from 25.6 inches in the northern Loess Hills to 34.3 inches in the south. Droughts occur periodically and are best tolerated by native grasslands.

TABLE 2. Loess Hills Climatic Data

	Northern Hills (Sioux City, Iowa)	Central Hills (Glenwood, Iowa)	Southern Hills (Oregon, Missouri)
Temperature (°F)			
Average annual	48.4	51.1	52.8
Average January	16.1	20.8	24.5
Average July	75.6	76.7	77.2
Record high (July)	107 (1955)	108 (1974)	108 (1974)
Record low (January)	−26 (1970)	−28 (1974)	−20 (1974)
Precipitation (inches)			
Average annual precipitation	25.6	32.3	34.3
Average annual snowfall	31.8	28.5	18.8

Note: Data included in this table and in the text have been taken from the most recent local climatological summaries. The three sites represent weather stations closest to the northern and southern termini of the Loess Hills and the station closest to the midpoint between those two. Sioux City is a first-class weather station; data are summarized for the period 1957–1986. Glenwood and Oregon are smaller weather stations, with data collection limited to temperature and precipitation. Glenwood data are summarized for 1951–1980, Oregon data for 1951–1974. Oregon data were compared with those collected at the larger station at nearby St. Joseph and found to be nearly identical, with the exception that St. Joseph had a slightly higher mean annual and monthly snowfall.

Winter is the dry season, with snowfall being fairly light. Annual averages range from 31.8 inches in the northern Hills to 18.8 inches in the south. Actual water content of that snow is limited to a few inches annually. Between 3.5 and 7.9 inches of snow, on average, fall each month from November through March in the Sioux City area, although extreme snowfalls of up to 29 inches are possible. The southern Hills may have snowfalls as high as 23 inches, but monthly averages range from only 1.2 to 5.1 inches in Oregon, Missouri. Precipitation also may fall as sleet or hail.

Prevailing winds in the Sioux City area, near the northern terminus of the Loess Hills, are from the south or southeast during the warm season (May through October) and from the northwest during cool weather (November through April). Mean speeds are lowest in midsummer, around 9 miles per hour, increasing gradually in fall and winter to reach spring maxima exceeding 13 miles per hour. Although wind data for elsewhere in the Hills are unavailable, they would probably be similar. In St. Joseph, just below the Loess Hills' southern terminus, average wind speeds are close to those in Sioux City. However, the prevailing direction is south year-round except in March and April, the windiest months, when the prevailing direction is northwest. Changes in wind direction are frequent throughout the year. Occasionally, strong and persistent winds, with gusts of 60 to 75 miles per hour, are generated during severe thunderstorms. Air movement is significant in promoting water loss of plants. The hot, dry winds of summer place extreme stresses on plant life.

Those climatic specifics are produced by the air masses that sweep across the continent from distant regions. The winter's cold, dry air arrives as continental polar air masses from northern and western Canada or as somewhat warmer maritime polar air masses. The maritime masses move across the northern Pacific Ocean and into the Midwest from the northwest, dropping their moisture on mountain ranges west of the Great Plains. Occasionally, strong high-pressure cells from the Canadian Arctic produce bitterly cold winter weather. In contrast, summer months are dominated by a strong flow of warm-to-hot moist air primarily from the Gulf of Mexico. Milder periods (including Indian summer) reflect a mixture of maritime polar air masses and continental polar air masses, with their cooler, drier air. Intense heat and severe drought are also possible.

Compared with surrounding areas, the Loess Hills occupy a middle point in temperature and precipitation regimes. Temperatures tend to decrease to the north and increase to the south but remain similar in areas to the east and west, while precipitation tends to decrease to the west and increase to the east. The deciduous forests of more-eastern states are considerably more humid, with lower evaporation rates than those of Loess Hills communities, which in turn are typically more humid than the shorter, sparser grasslands farther west.

However, because isolines for temperature and precipitation cut diagonally across the Loess Hills, significant changes in both temperature and precipitation occur from north to south, as reflected in table 2. Extremes of cold and drought are moderated in the southern Hills, where winter, sum-

Figure 34. Intense sunlight and hot summer winds reduce moisture to desert levels on west- and south-facing bluffs overlooking the Missouri River valley. Drought-resistant prairies persist here. Photo by the author.

mer, and average annual temperatures are warmer. Thus the growing season, which is fairly long throughout the Hills, increases from approximately 160 days in Sioux City to approximately 190 days just south of the Hills, in St. Joseph. Annual average precipitation increases nine inches, or 35 percent, from north to south (although snowfall decreases in response to higher southern temperatures).

Those increases in temperature, precipitation, and growing season are significant for plant communities and may be major factors in explaining the more expansive woodlands in the southern Loess Hills. The larger remaining prairies in the northern Hills are better able to withstand the drier, more stressful climate that persists to the north. Climatic factors also explain the southern Hills' earlier onset of growth in the spring.

Equally important to Loess Hills plant communities are local variations in climate. Desertlike conditions on the steepest south-facing and west-facing bluffs were eloquently described in 1910 by the natural historian Bohumil Shimek. Those slopes are prairie rather than woodland because they "burn in the heat of the midday sun" and are "swept by the hot blasts of summer winds," he writes, and again, "when the summer has advanced, when the rains have ceased and the blistering winds and scorching sun have robbed the southwesterly prairie slopes of their moisture, the sheltered groves and the exposed prairie surfaces stand out in sharp contrast, visible for many miles."

Shimek hypothesized that prairies grew where the early afternoon sun, the day's hottest, and the prevailing winds were most intense. Those two factors, which increase temperature and evaporation rate and decrease relative humidity, had the strongest influence on south-facing and west-facing bluffs directly adjacent to the Missouri River floodplain, where the driest Loess Hills prairies grew in Shimek's time (fig. 34). On the upper portions of those slopes prairies persist today, often surrounded by woodlands that have invaded slopes that are a bit more humid and protected, a bit less harsh. The desertlike prairies, with their drought-resistant western plants, grow in sites climatically as dry as those of the Great Plains a hundred miles or more to the west.

⟪☙ FIVE ☙⟫

NATURAL COMMUNITIES OF
THE LOESS HILLS TODAY

Webster's dictionary defines "community" as "an interacting population of various kinds of individuals . . . in a common location." To many readers, that definition brings to mind collections of humans, people similar enough to find their common needs within one locale but different enough to fulfill the requirements of one another. But the term applies equally well to a grouping of animals and plants. "Community" is used here in that second sense.

Specifically, this chapter focuses on the natural communities of today's Loess Hills, those not directly created by humans. Of primary interest are associations of native animals and plants that arrived here long before Euro-American settlement. The organisms colonized the Loess Hills because their dusty, sun-beaten, windblown knobs provided just the right amounts of heat, water, and sunshine. Over the years, the organisms became interdependent, one animal species feeding upon another, using a certain type of plant for shelter, which in turn was nourished by droppings of yet another animal. Eventually, interconnected circles tied all the residents together into a web of mutual need-fulfillment, a complex natural ecosystem. The term "ecosystem" refers to both the organisms and the nonliving features, or environment, of a given area.

The chapter concentrates on the two dominant natural ecosystems of the Loess Hills today: prairies and woodlands. Prairies are diverse associations of grasses and broad-leaved flowering plants that have dominated large portions of the Midwest for much of the past 8,000 to 9,000 years.

The woodlands include those bands of shrublands that commonly separate forests from prairies. Discussion of human-created communities—croplands, cities, roadsides, farmsteads, planted pastures—is limited to comments interspersed where relevant. (The creation of those communities was described in the last part of chapter 3.)

A listing of community members is prerequisite to understanding a community. Therefore, birds, mammals, reptiles and amphibians, common prairie plants, common trees and shrubs, and rare species (along with features such as their range and primary habitat) have been listed throughout the chapter, in tables designed as checklists. The tables give a sampling of the common and obvious Loess Hills species but omit myriad small and inconspicuous organisms such as nonvascular plants, invertebrates, and soil organisms. Where data for Missouri are not available, tables are limited to listings of Iowa's organisms. Plants are referred to by common name in text and tables, but because common names often vary from place to place, Latin names are also included in the tables, and in the text for plants not listed in the tables. Plant nomenclature and distributional information follow *Flora of the Great Plains* (Great Plains Flora Association, 1986).

Patterns of Community Distribution

Wild species can survive only where the environment meets their inborn needs—where temperatures are neither too hot nor too cold, where appropriate food abounds, and where water, sunlight, and shelter are adequate. If any of a species' inherited requirements are not met, individuals will die and the species will disappear from the area. Thus patterns of species distribution can be correlated with environmental characteristics.

Predictable relationships of organisms and environments have allowed biologists to map major communities throughout the United States. Some areas meet the environmental requirements of more than one community type. That occurs in the Loess Hills with grasslands of the central United States and eastern deciduous forests. Before Euro-American settlement, native grasslands, which are fairly drought tolerant, stretched from the base of the Rocky Mountains eastward across the dry central plains. Deciduous forests, which require more moisture than grasslands, spanned the landscape from the prairies eastward to the Atlantic Seaboard, where precipitation was higher. That pattern was generally true for more than 9,000 years, although the exact location where forest and prairie met varied from north to south and also moved back and forth in response to climatic fluctuations. The interfingering of Loess Hills forests and prairies remains obvious today.

Because the edges of two major communities overlap in the Hills, the region contains many species at or near the edge of their distributional range, a number of which are rare. One special feature of the Hills is the presence of numerous Great Plains species, animals and plants with centers of distribution in the dry, hot, sparse grasslands much farther to the west. Enticed by the unusually hot, dry climate of the Hills, those species have extended their ranges eastward into Iowa and Missouri only here.

Within the Hills, some sites provide a satisfactory environment for prairies, while others are optimal for woodlands. Woodlands and prairies typically are separated by a band of shrubs. The communities' distribution reflects their differing needs for moisture (fig. 35). Moisture-demanding forests dominate in the southern Hills, covering all but the driest, most exposed ridgetops and bluffs. Forests spread northward along the moister sites, including ravines and lower slopes of any exposure, reaching onto upper slopes facing north and east, which are sheltered from intense sun and wind, in all but the most northerly Hills (see fig. 30). Forests also dominate the sheltered, inner, more easterly Hills not converted to agricultural use. In contrast, drought-tolerant prairies maintain dominance in the far northern Hills, extending southward on upper slopes (particularly those facing south and west, which are most exposed to the drying sun and wind) and on westernmost bluffs and the tops of ridges.

The southern dominance of forests corresponds with a climatic gradient favoring woody plant growth in the south. The southern Hills receive significantly more precipitation than the northern Hills and are less subject to severe drought. The growing season is shorter and average temperatures are lower in the north. Days with rainfall are more frequent and the average daily evaporation rate is lower in southern forests, while humidity and soil moisture are greater than in northern prairies—features that favor tree growth toward the south.

Although prairie and woodland communities may appear to be static and stable, their distributional patterns have always been dynamic. The climate of many sites within the Hills is thought to be capable of supporting either community type. Tension between the two communities has always existed, each one vying for the other's territory and expanding at the cost of the other when conditions permitted. Although forests probably always

Figure 35. *Deciduous forests of the eastern states and native prairies of the central states mix naturally in the Loess Hills. Woodlands climb uphill into drought-resistant prairies wherever moisture is sufficient for tree growth. In this photograph, woodlands snake uphill along ravines on the dry southwestern exposures in the distance, while in the foreground (a somewhat moister northeastern exposure) woody species are invading prairies nearly to the top of the hill. Thomas Rosburg.*

have occupied the moister sites—ravine bottoms and lower slopes facing north and east—the exact locations of prairies and the extent of forests in the past remain unknown. In the mid-1800s, when the region was being settled, prairies were undoubtedly far more extensive than now (see sidebar 4).

Changes in the distribution of woodlands and prairies have been especially dramatic in recent times. Shrubs and trees have rapidly entered grasslands, and woodlands have taken over prairies, through a process called invasion. Accelerated by several factors, including the elimination of prairie fires and an increasing supply of tree and shrub seeds, tree and shrub invasion of grasslands is now so massive that the unique Loess Hills prairies, along with their many rare plants and animals, may disappear (see fig. 65). One researcher, P. Heineman, from the University of Nebraska (who was working on bluff communities in Monona County), demonstrated that canopy cover of woody plants increased 66 percent from 1853 to 1981, with canopy cover of lower slopes increasing the most (85 percent). He estimated that woody plant invasion will obliterate bluff prairies by the year 2060 if a proper prairie management plan is not established. Forest invasion is most advanced or rapid in the southern Hills and has already nearly obliterated many of Missouri's Loess Hills prairies.

Tree invasion of prairies typically proceeds from the wooded base of a slope to the top, and north- and east-facing slopes are more conducive to tree growth because they are more sheltered from the wind and sun (fig. 36). The numerous ravines also are a bit lower and moister than adjacent hilltops and so form a route for upward and outward migration of shrubs and trees. Standing on a bluff top and turning in a circle, one can easily see the net result of those invasion patterns. When looking south at north-facing hillsides, one may see nothing but forests, for often invasion has occurred to the very tops of the ridges (fig. 37). Turning to look north at south-facing slopes, the observer sees prairies, at least on the upper hillsides; woodlands may creep partially up the hillsides, fingering their way a bit higher in the ravines (fig. 38).

Many individual hillsides show that same gradient from woodland to prairie. In the past, the typical streamside woodland was bordered by tall prairie grasses that gradually gave way to shorter and sparser plants as one climbed the ever-drier hill. Today trees invading from the base of the slope upward are likely to have obliterated taller grasses. Instead, somewhere on the slope, scattered shrubs with an understory of prairie grasses mark the woodlands' move into prairie, forming a band below which lie dense trees and above which extend grasslands.

Human land use is yet another factor influencing the distribution of today's natural communities. Native communities, especially prairies, have survived best where rugged topography has prevented conversion to agricultural use—prairies are largest and least disturbed on the steepest bluff faces directly adjacent to the Missouri River's floodplain and in the rugged, westernmost hills that are least accessible to the cow and plow. (Smaller, more gently rounded outer bluffs are intensely used for grazing or other agricultural purposes.) Indeed, native prairies in private ownership lie almost entirely within that narrow, westernmost strip. East of the front line of bluffs, as the hills become lower and more gently rounded, agricultural use increases. Natural communities disappear within a few miles of the western bluff faces, although farther to the east a steep knob of prairie-covered loess sometimes sticks awkwardly up from a cornfield.

Native communities occupy the broadest east-west belt where topogra-

Figure 36. *A band of shrubs similar to the one in the center commonly separates Loess Hills forests and prairies. The shrubs are soon invaded by trees and converted to woodlands. Thomas Rosburg.*

phy is roughest. Generally speaking, native communities extend farther to the east from the middle of Harrison County northward. In the southern Hills, native communities and indeed the Loess Hills landscape itself occupy a narrow strip that rapidly gives way to more rolling agricultural land.

Even within areas of rugged topography, all but the steepest slopes may have been plowed at one time. Today valley bottoms bordered by rugged slopes are likely to be cropland, and gentler lower slopes are planted pastures or heavily grazed prairies. Healthy native prairies are most likely to survive near hilltops or wherever a sharp increase in slope steepness prevents other use, such as on protruding loess knobs.

In Nebraska, a bluffline of irregular height is dominated today by woodlands wherever bluff steepness precludes agricultural use. Woodland dominance is logical there, given the eastern aspect of the bluffs; they are not as sunny, windy, or dry as Iowa's west-facing bluffline. Agricultural use claims the smaller bluffs, as well as land from the base of the bluffs eastward and from the top of the bluffs westward, except in the few sites where rugged terrain is not immediately replaced by gently rolling land. Thus in Nebraska

Figure 37. Looking south along better shaded, moister, north-facing hillsides, Loess Hills visitors typically see extensive forests. Notice that prairies still cover the convex hillsides toward the foreground—hillsides that are extremely dry because they are well drained and are exposed to strong western winds and intense sunshine. Photo by the author.

Figure 38. Looking north at south-facing hillsides, which have little shelter from the drying sun, one might assume that prairies still dominate the Loess Hills. Forests often can be seen only in lowlands and lining the tops of the north-facing slopes. Photo by the author.

native communities different in type from those of the Loess Hills have been reduced to a narrow and interrupted north-south thread.

Diversity and Distribution of Species

As a mixing ground for major biological communities, the Hills always have supported a large and interesting variety of species, creating an ecological richness that has long fascinated naturalists. The richness of the region was multiplied in the past by the Loess Hills' proximity to the fecund wetlands of the Missouri River floodplain. Today the wetlands have all but disappeared, although the floodplain still serves as a major migration corridor for waterfowl, which, by the hundreds of thousands, enrich the native bird life of the region as a whole.

The original diversity has survived in the Loess Hills in large part because the rugged hills have remained relatively remote and isolated, resisting conversion to cropland, lawn, pasture, and settlement. More than 700 species of vascular plants have been identified in the Hills. Remaining native prairies are large enough to maintain viable populations of rare butterflies that have declined or disappeared on smaller prairie remnants elsewhere. The wildness of the region also allows safe refuge for wintering hawks, rare species such as bobcat, secretive lizards and snakes, and numerous other types of animals, many of which are uncommon or absent elsewhere in Iowa and Missouri.

Because they constantly intermix, the diverse Loess Hills plant communities provide food and refuge for an abundance of animals (fig. 39). Everywhere prairies, woodlands, and shrublands intermingle—shrublands reaching into prairies along ravines, and woodlands interrupting prairies on ridgetops. That interfingering may eliminate sensitive species that require large, unbroken plant communities of a single type, but it also produces a greater-than-expected richness of animal species that do not require such large tracts because of what ecologists call the edge effect: the animals present are not only those typical of woodlands or shrublands or prairies but also those requiring a combination of those habitats.

The resulting richness of animal life is most easily observed among birds (listed in table 3). Although their diversity is probably impoverished in comparison with the presettlement bird fauna, more than 100 species are thought to still nest in the Hills. Add to them the waterfowl that migrate along the adjacent Missouri River floodplain and the raptors and songbirds that migrate along the Hills, and the result is a treasure for any bird-

Figure 39. Interfingering woodlands, shrublands, prairies (foreground), and agricultural lands (note the cultivated fields covering distant lowlands) provide homes for a rich diversity of animal species. Thomas Rosburg.

watcher. The Hills are thought to house Iowa's highest population densities of several bird species, including the turkey vulture, American kestrel, Bell's vireo, orchard oriole, chuck-will's-widow, and summer tanager.

Because of the intermixing of plant communities and because several animal species freely utilize more than one plant community, specific animal-plant associations often are impossible to define. That is especially true of birds, many of which flit freely from forest to prairie to shrubland. Birds common and conspicuous throughout the Hills and in all types of habitat include the brown-headed cowbird, northern cardinal, brown thrasher, house wren, mourning dove, American crow, blue jay, and red-headed woodpecker. Mammals in the same category include the eastern mole, big brown bat, coyote, red fox, white-tailed deer, and raccoon. The most common mammal in western Iowa, the deer mouse, inhabits a variety of unforested habitats in the Hills. Several reptiles are nearly equally adapted to woodlands and prairies, the western fox snake and western chorus frog being among the generalists. (Iowa's Loess Hills mammals and their typical habitats are listed in table 4; reptiles and amphibians of Iowa's Loess Hills together with their typical habitats are listed in table 5.)

TABLE 3. Birds of Iowa's Loess Hills

CICONIIFORMES (herons and allies)
☐ Green-backed heron, *Butorides striatus*
ANSERIFORMES (waterfowl)
☐ Wood duck, *Aix sponsa*
☐ Mallard, *Anas platyrhynchos*
☐ Blue-winged teal, *Anas discors*
FALCONIFORMES (birds of prey)
☐ Turkey vulture, *Cathartes aura*
☐ Cooper's hawk, *Accipiter cooperii*
☐ Sharp-shinned hawk, *Accipiter striatus*
☐ Broad-winged hawk, *Buteo platypterus*
☐ Red-tailed hawk, *Buteo jamaicensis*
☐ American kestrel, *Falco sparverius*
GALLIFORMES (chickenlike birds)
☐ **Ring-necked pheasant**, *Phasianus colchicus*
☐ Wild turkey, *Meleagris gallopavo*
☐ **Northern bobwhite**, *Colinus virginianus*
CHARADRIIFORMES (shorebirds, gulls, and auks)
☐ Killdeer, *Charadrius vociferus* (northern grasslands)
☐ Upland sandpiper, *Bartramia longicauda*
☐ American woodcock, *Scolopax minor*
COLUMBIFORMES (pigeons)
☐ Rock dove, *Columba livia*
☐ Mourning dove, *Zenaida macroura*
CUCULIFORMES (cuckoos and allies)
☐ Black-billed cuckoo, *Coccyzus erythropthalmus*
☐ **Yellow-billed cuckoo**, *Coccyzus americanus*
STRIGIFORMES (owls)
☐ Eastern screech owl, *Otus asio*
☐ Great horned owl, *Bubo virginianus*

☐ Barred owl, *Strix varia*
CAPRIMULGIFORMES (goatsuckers and allies)
☐ Common nighthawk, *Chordeiles minor*
☐ Chuck-will's-widow, *Caprimulgus carolinensis* (southern forests)
☐ **Whippoorwill**, *Caprimulgus vociferus*
APODIFORMES (swifts)
☐ Chimney swift, *Chaetura pleagica*
☐ Ruby-throated hummingbird, *Archilochus colubris*
CORACIIFORMES (kingfishers and allies)
☐ Belted kingfisher, *Ceryle alcyon*
PICIFORMES (woodpeckers and allies)
☐ **Red-headed woodpecker**, *Melanerpes erythrocephalus*
☐ **Red-bellied woodpecker**, *Melanerpes carolinus*
☐ **Downy woodpecker**, *Picoides pubescens*
☐ Hairy woodpecker, *Picoides villosus*
☐ **Northern flicker**, *Colaptes auratus*
PASSERIFORMES (perching birds)
☐ Eastern wood pewee, *Contopus virens*
☐ Acadian flycatcher, *Empidonax virescens* (southern forests)
☐ Willow flycatcher, *Empidonax traillii*
☐ Eastern phoebe, *Sayornis phoebe*
☐ **Great crested flycatcher**, *Myiarchus crinitus*
☐ Western kingbird, *Tyrannus verticalis*
☐ **Eastern kingbird**, *Tyrannus tyrannus*
☐ Horned lark, *Eremophila alpestris* (northern grasslands)

TABLE 3 (*continued*)

☐ Purple martin, *Progne subis*

☐ Tree swallow, *Tachycineta bicolor*

☐ **Northern rough-winged swallow**, *Stelgidopteryx serripennis*

☐ Bank swallow, *Riparia riparia*

☐ **Barn swallow**, *Hirundo rustica*

☐ **Blue jay**, *Cyanocitta cristata*

☐ **American crow**, *Corvus brachyrhynchos*

☐ **Black-capped chickadee**, *Parus atricapillus*

☐ Tufted titmouse, *Parus bicolor* (southern forests)

☐ **White-breasted nuthatch**, *Sitta carolinensis*

☐ Bewick's wren, *Thryomanes bewickii* (southern forests)

☐ **House wren**, *Troglodytes aedon*

☐ Blue-gray gnatcatcher, *Polioptila caerulea*

☐ Eastern bluebird, *Sialia sialis*

☐ Wood thrush, *Hylocichla mustelina*

☐ American robin, *Turdus migratorius*

☐ **Gray catbird**, *Dumetella carolinensis*

☐ Northern mockingbird, *Mimus polyglottos*

☐ **Brown thrasher**, *Toxostoma rufum*

☐ Cedar waxwing, *Bombycilla cedrorum*

☐ Loggerhead shrike, *Lanius ludovicianus*

☐ **European starling**, *Sturnus vulgaris*

☐ White-eyed vireo, *Vireo griseus*

☐ Bell's vireo, *Vireo bellii*

☐ Yellow-throated vireo, *Vireo flavifrons*

☐ Warbling vireo, *Vireo gilvus*

☐ Red-eyed vireo, *Vireo olivaceus* (southern forests)

☐ Blue-winged warbler, *Vermivora pinus* (southern forests)

☐ Yellow warbler, *Dendroica petechia*

☐ Black-and-white warbler, *Mniotilta varia*

☐ Ovenbird, *Seiurus aurocapillus*

☐ **Northern cardinal**, *Cardinalis cardinalis*

☐ **Rose-breasted grosbeak**, *Pheucticus ludovicianus*

☐ Blue grosbeak, *Guiraca caerulea* (northern grasslands)

☐ **Indigo bunting**, *Passerina cyanea*

☐ **Dickcissel**, *Spiza americana*

☐ Louisiana water thrush, *Seiurus motacilla* (southern hills)

☐ Kentucky warbler, *Oporornis formosus* (southern forests)

☐ **Common yellowthroat**, *Geothlypis trichas*

☐ Summer tanager, *Piranga rubra* (southern forests)

☐ Scarlet tanager, *Piranga olivacea*

☐ **Rufous-sided towhee**, *Pipilo erythrophthalmus*

☐ Chipping sparrow, *Spizella passerina*

☐ **Field sparrow**, *Spizella pusilla*

☐ Vesper sparrow, *Pooecetes gramineus*

☐ Lark sparrow, *Chondestes grammacus*

☐ **Grasshopper sparrow**, *Ammodramus savannarum*

☐ Song sparrow, *Melospiza melodia*

☐ Bobolink, *Dolichonyx oryzivorus*

☐ **Red-winged blackbird**, *Agelaius phoeniceus*

☐ Eastern meadowlark, *Sturnella magna* (southern grasslands)

TABLE 3 (*continued*)

- ☐ **Western meadowlark**, *Sturnella neglecta*
- ☐ **Common grackle**, *Quiscalus quiscula*
- ☐ **Brown-headed cowbird**, *Molothrus ater*

- ☐ **Orchard oriole**, *Icterus spurius*
- ☐ **Northern oriole**, *Icterus galbula*
- ☐ **American goldfinch**, *Carduelis tristis*
- ☐ **House sparrow**, *Passer domesticus*

Note: Common species are printed in bold. Distributional limits are indicated for species with a limited range or habitat. Waterfowl and other species of the adjacent Missouri River floodplain are not included. Species of Missouri's loess deposits are expected to be similar to those listed here; woodland species would predominate, and prairie species may be absent. Adapted from the appendix in Howe, Roosa, Schaufenbuel, et al., 1985.

TABLE 4. Mammals of Iowa's Loess Hills

MARSUPIALIA (marsupials)
- ☐ **Opossum**, *Didelphis virginiana* (woodland)

INSECTIVORA (insectivores)
- ☐ Masked shrew, *Sorex cinereus* (woodland or tall herbs near standing water)
- ☐ Hayden's shrew, *Sorex haydeni*
- ☐ **Northern short-tailed shrew**, *Blarina brevicauda* (grassland)
- ☐ **Elliot's short-tailed shrew**, *Blarina hylophaga*
- ☐ Least shrew, *Cryptotis parva* (prairie)
- ☐ **Eastern mole**, *Scalopus aquaticus* (grassland and woodland)

CHIROPTERA (bats)
- ☐ Keen's myotis, *Myotis keenii* (forest)
- ☐ **Big brown bat**, *Eptesicus fuscus* (widespread)
- ☐ **Red bat**, *Lasiurus borealis* (urban and rural wooded areas)
- ☐ Evening bat, *Nycticeius humeralis* (woodland)

LAGOMORPHA (rabbits and hares)

- ☐ **Eastern cottontail**, *Sylvilagus floridanus* (open woodland, woodland edge)
- ☐ White-tailed jackrabbit, *Lepus townsendii* (prairie, pasture)[1]

RODENTIA (rodents)
- ☐ Eastern chipmunk, *Tamias striatus* (woodland)
- ☐ **Woodchuck**, *Marmota monax* (woodland)
- ☐ **Franklin's ground squirrel**, *Spermophilus franklinii* (tall grassland)
- ☐ **Thirteen-lined ground squirrel**, *Spermophilus tridecemlineatus* (short grassland)
- ☐ Gray squirrel, *Sciurus carolinensis* (forest)
- ☐ **Fox squirrel**, *Sciurus niger* (woodland)
- ☐ **Plains pocket gopher**, *Geomys bursarius* (grassland)
- ☐ Plains pocket mouse, *Perognathus flavescens* (prairie)[1]
- ☐ Beaver, *Castor canadensis* (wetland)

TABLE 4 (*continued*)

☐ **Western harvest mouse**, *Reithrodontomys megalotis* (prairie/grassland)

☐ **White-footed mouse**, *Peromyscus leucopus* (forest/shrubland)

☐ **Deer mouse**, *Peromyscus maniculatus* (widespread)

☐ Northern grasshopper mouse, *Onychomys leucogaster* (grassland/cultivated fields)[1]

☐ Southern bog lemming, *Synaptomys cooperi* (moist grassland, southern Hills)

☐ **Prairie vole**, *Microtus ochrogaster* (dry grassland)

☐ **Meadow vole**, *Microtus pennsylvanicus* (grassland/hay fields)

☐ Woodland vole, *Microtus pinetorum* (forest)

☐ **Muskrat**, *Ondatra zibethicus* (wetland)

☐ **House mouse**, *Mus musculus* (farmsteads/cultivated fields; uncommon in prairie; exotic)

☐ **Norway rat**, *Rattus norvegicus* (farmsteads/cities; exotic)

☐ **Meadow jumping mouse**, *Zapus hudsonius* (grassland)

CARNIVORA (carnivores)

☐ **Coyote**, *Canis latrans* (widespread)

☐ **Red fox**, *Vulpes vulpes* (widespread)

☐ Gray fox, *Urocyon cinereoargenteus* (forest, southern Hills)

☐ **Raccoon**, *Procyon lotor* (widespread)

☐ Long-tailed weasel, *Mustela frenata* (widespread)

☐ **Mink**, *Mustela vison* (widespread)

☐ **North American badger**, *Taxidea taxus* (grassland)

☐ **Striped skunk**, *Mephitis mephitis* (widespread)

☐ Bobcat, *Lynx rufus* (shrubland)

ARTIODACTYLA (even-toed ungulates)

☐ **White-tailed deer**, *Odocoileus virginianus* (widespread)

Additional species expected to be present:

☐ Little brown myotis, *Myotis lucifugus*

☐ Indiana myotis, *Myotis sodalis*

☐ Silver-haired bat, *Lasionycteris noctivagans*

☐ Eastern pipistrelle, *Pipistrellus subflavus*

☐ Hoary bat, *Lasiurus cinereus*

☐ Richardson's ground squirrel, *Spermophilus richardsonii*

☐ Southern flying squirrel, *Glaucomys volans*

☐ Least weasel, *Mustela nivalis*

☐ Spotted skunk, *Spilogale putorius*

☐ Mule deer, *Odocoileus hemionus*

---

[1] Western species typical of Great Plains grasslands.

Note: Common species are printed in bold. Others are found either in localized populations or in low densities only. Habitat preference is indicated in parentheses. Species of Missouri's loess deposits are expected to be similar, although woodland species would predominate and prairie species may be absent. Adapted from Lampe and Bowles, 1985.

TABLE 5. Reptiles and Amphibians of Iowa's Loess Hills

AMPHIBIANS

ANURA (frogs and toads)

☐ American toad, *Bufo americanus americanus* (woodland)

☐ Woodhouse's toad, *Bufo woodhousii woodhousii* (prairie)[1]

☐ Great Plains toad, *Bufo cognatus* (prairie)[1]

☐ Plains spadefoot, *Scaphiopus bombifrons* (prairie)[1]

☐ Bullfrog, *Rana catesbeiana* (generalist)

☐ Northern leopard frog, *Rana pipiens* (generalist)

☐ Plains leopard frog, *Rana blairi* (prairie)[1]

☐ Blanchard's cricket frog, *Acris crepitans blanchardi* (generalist)

☐ Western chorus frog, *Pseudacris triseriata triseriata* (generalist)

☐ Gray tree frog, *Hyla versicolor* (woodland)

CAUDATA (salamanders)

☐ Small-mouthed salamander, *Ambystoma texanum* (woodland)

☐ Eastern tiger salamander, *Ambystoma tigrinum tigrinum* (generalist)

REPTILES

TESTUDINATA (turtles)

☐ Common snapping turtle, *Chelydra serpentina serpentina* (generalist)

☐ Western painted turtle, *Chrysemys picta bellii* (generalist)

☐ Ornate box turtle, *Terrapene ornata ornata* (prairie)[1]

SQUAMATA, LACERTILIA (lizards and skinks)

☐ Prairie, or six-lined, racerunner, *Cnemidophorus sexlineatus viridis* (prairie)[1]

☐ Great Plains, or Sonoran, skink, *Eumeces obsoletus* (prairie)[1]

☐ Northern prairie skink, *Eumeces septentrionalis septentrionalis* (prairie)

SQUAMATA, SERPENTES (snakes)

☐ Graham's water snake, *Regina grahamii* (generalist)

☐ Northern water snake, *Nerodia sipedon sipedon* (generalist)

☐ Red-sided garter snake, *Thamnophis sirtalis parietalis* (prairie)

☐ Western plains garter snake, *Thamnophis radix haydenii* (prairie)

☐ Northern lined snake, *Tropidoclonion lineatum lineatum* (prairie)

☐ Texas brown snake, *Storeria dekayi texana* (woodland)

☐ Northern red-bellied snake, *Storeria occipitomaculata occipitomaculata* (woodland)

☐ Eastern hognose snake, *Heterodon platyrhinos* (woodland)

☐ Western worm snake, *Carphophis amoenus vermis* (woodland)

☐ Prairie ringneck snake, *Diadophis punctatus arnyi* (woodland)

☐ Eastern yellow-bellied racer, *Coluber constrictor flaviventris* (prairie)

☐ Bullsnake, *Pituophis melanoleucus sayi* (prairie)

☐ Western fox snake, *Elaphe vulpina vulpina* (generalist)

☐ Black rat snake, *Elaphe obsoleta obsoleta* (woodland)

☐ Prairie kingsnake, *Lampropeltis calligaster calligaster* (generalist/prairie)

☐ Red milk snake, *Lampropeltis triangulum syspila* (woodland)

TABLE 5 (*continued*)

☐ Speckled kingsnake, *Lampropeltis getulus holbrooki* (woodland)

☐ Prairie rattlesnake, *Crotalus viridis viridis* (prairie)[1]

---

[1]Western species typical of Great Plains grasslands.

Note: Habitat preference indicated in parentheses. The term "generalist" indicates no specific habitat preference. Species of Missouri's Loess Hills are expected to be similar, although woodland species would predominate and prairie species may be absent. Adapted from Christiansen and Mabry, 1985.

Human use of the Hills has created new associations of exotic (introduced) plants and animals and has altered distributional patterns of some native species. Indeed, human-made communities occupy much of the Hills today, and exotic species now mix with most of the native communities. Some of the mixtures have been intentional—cattle, for example, have been put to graze on native prairie since the Hills were first settled. Kentucky bluegrass and brome (*Bromus* spp.) were introduced for lawns and pasture, alfalfa and other crops were grown, and apple trees were planted for food and beauty.

Not all additions to Loess Hills communities were planned. The house mouse and Norway rat accompanied settlers as uninvited guests and now are numerous around farmsteads and cities. Native species have responded to the changes in land use by humans. Species unable to adjust have been pushed toward extinction, and those finding suitable habitat in altered communities have proliferated. The eastern red cedar, for example, has benefited greatly from human land use. An evergreen that was probably rare in presettlement times, it now proliferates on grasslands (fig. 40).

One noticeable example of native species' adaptations to new environments is the response of wetland species to the creation of farm ponds and artificial impoundments. Wetlands never were abundant in the porous loess soils. Construction of bodies of standing water such as farm ponds has resulted in a marked increase in the number of bullfrogs and muskrats within the Loess Hills. Birds such as the green-backed heron, wood duck, mallard, and blue-winged teal now can be seen on artificial waterways.

Thus the Loess Hills communities of today differ from presettlement native communities in type and in composition and abundance of species. Those alterations are a few of the many factors that determine the characteristics of Loess Hills prairies and woodlands.

Figure 40. The eastern red cedar, probably rare in presettlement times, is now abundant on overgrazed grasslands and can be a major nuisance. Don Poggensee.

PRAIRIES

Many of the Loess Hills' special qualities lie within upland prairies. Clinging to the westernmost line of hills where porous soil, intense sunlight, and strong winds combine to create a desertlike environment, the native grasslands contain an unusual association of drought-resistant animals and plants typical of the Great Plains. Those species form midheight grasslands that are a radical departure from the lusher, denser tall-grass prairies typical of the remainder of either Iowa or Missouri. Today many Loess Hills prairie species are rare or endangered.

Prairies are the oldest native communities of the Hills, where they presumably have thrived for approximately 9,000 years. Before settlement, the prairies probably dominated a majority of the Hills. Today they are much diminished, having suffered from both forest invasion and human use for more than a century. However, the Loess Hills contain a good proportion of Iowa's remaining prairies, including the state's largest. Elsewhere in Iowa the prairie's thick soil was plowed to form today's rich cropland, and only an infinitesimal portion remains intact. Because of their many special qualities and because they are imminently threatened by forest invasion and human use, Loess Hills prairies have attracted far more attention from researchers and preservationists than the more extensive forests. As a result, the prairies are the best understood of the Loess Hills natural communities.

Prairie plants exhibit four major traits that allow observers to distinguish Loess Hills prairies from grasslands of exotic species, such as planted pastures or weedy roadsides.

1. Season of growth and color: Prairies contain many warm-season grasses; they green up in late spring. (Exotic species commonly green up much earlier.) As a result, many prairie grasses produce seed in late summer or autumn, later than exotic grasses. Prairie grasses turn a warm, rich russet color in fall. The color is retained through winter. (Exotic grasses may stay bright green through late fall and then turn a washed-out tan.)

2. Growth form: Many prairie grasses grow in distinct bunches or clumps, giving prairies an undulating surface. (Most exotic species form sod, producing a smoother appearance.)

3. Location: Prairies have survived in the most rugged bluffs and on the steepest slopes. (Planted pastures or other agricultural uses have claimed more gently sloping hills and valleys.) Within the rugged bluffs, prairies cover the driest, most exposed slopes: ridgetops, upper hillsides, south- and west-facing slopes, and the westernmost bluff faces. (Woodlands have invaded moister sites.) Prairies are more extensive in the northern Hills and are better maintained in managed preserves.

4. Species and diversity: Prairies contain a diversity of flowering plants, some of which can be recognized as typical prairie species by using a guidebook. Long after the flowers have bloomed, dried pods or seed heads of typical species (such as yucca and coneflower) distinguish prairies. (Exotic grasslands are often less diverse and more uniform, sometimes consisting of a single planted crop species or a few weed species. Exotic grasslands lack characteristic prairie species.)

Grasses. Loess Hills upland prairies are dominated by midheight grasses, reaching two to three feet high, that grow in distinct clumps or bunches and are separated by patches of bare soil (fig. 41). Little bluestem is by far the most abundant, sometimes composing as much as 90 percent of the total plant cover. Side-oats grama, easily recognized because all the seed spikelets extend from one side of the slender flower stalk, is a common codomi-

Figure 41. *Dominant prairie grasses: side-oats grama (left; ½ ×), hairy grama (center; ⅖ ×), and little bluestem (right; ½ ×). Bellamy Parks Jansen.*

nant that increases relative to the bluestem during periods of drought. The seed heads of the two grasses seem to compose the entire late summer and fall prairie. Other prairie grasses, such as June grass and needle grass, often occur in patches. (Grass species and common broad-leaved flowering plants, or forbs, of prairies are listed in table 6.)

Beneath the midheight bunchgrasses, sod-forming short grasses—most commonly hairy grama—produce a mat only inches high (fig. 41). Mats of blue grama are also present, and buffalograss occurs in Missouri's Hills. All three short grasses are on Missouri's Watch List of special-concern species; buffalograss is endangered in Iowa.

Loess Hills prairies are not completely devoid of tall grasses such as big bluestem and Indiangrass, which dominate the moister prairies to the east in Iowa and Missouri and the native grasslands of eastern Nebraska. They commonly reach heights of five to eight feet in favorable environments, although they may be much smaller in the Loess Hills. Thick clumps of tall grasses mix with shorter prairie species on inland and lowland prairies wherever moisture is sufficient: at the bases of slopes, in ravines, along moist roadsides, on east-facing slopes that are sheltered from the wind, on slopes of any exposure that are inland from the hottest, driest bluff faces. The line between midheight grasses and taller species is pronounced in the Loess Hills Wildlife Area, where seed heads of tall grasses form a distinct band between the crests of east-facing slopes and the woodlands below them; shorter grasslands are evident on the west-facing slopes.

In favorable sites, big bluestem and Indiangrass may intermingle with patches of other tall grasses (switchgrass and Canada wild rye) and with a few of the hardier forbs associated with tall-grass prairie, to form an impoverished tall-grass prairie. Many familiar moisture-loving forbs common in tall-grass prairies elsewhere are absent in the Hills. Tall-grass prairies were undoubtedly more extensive in presettlement times; the bulk have been lost to cropland and to invading woodlands, both of which seek out the sheltered, moist sites that would have been covered by tall-grass species.

The few loess bluff prairies remaining in Nebraska resemble tall-grass prairies rather than the drier Loess Hills prairies. Nebraska's bluff prairies remain as tiny slivers, primarily in Indian Cave State Park, with small patches also in Ponca State Park and southern Thurston County. Tall-grass prairies also grow immediately to the west of Nebraska's wooded bluffs, in the handful of sites where they have not been replaced by other human uses. A few prairie species can still be found as understory in the

TABLE 6. Typical Grasses and Forbs of Loess Hills Prairies

AGAVACEAE (agave family)
☐ Yucca, *Yucca glauca*[1]
ASCLEPIADACEAE (milkweed family)
☐ Green milkweed, *Asclepias viridiflora*
ASTERACEAE (sunflower family)
☐ Western ragweed, *Ambrosia psilostachya*
☐ White aster, *Aster ericoides*
☐ Aromatic aster, *Aster oblongifolius*
☐ Silky aster, *Aster sericeus*
☐ Flodman's thistle, *Cirsium flodmanii*[1]
☐ Purple coneflower, *Echinacea angustifolia*[1]
☐ Daisy fleabane, *Erigeron strigosus*
☐ Cutleaf ironplant, *Haplopappus spinulosus*[1]
☐ Stiff sunflower, *Helianthus rigidus*
☐ Western false boneset, *Kuhnia eupatorioides*
☐ Dotted gayfeather, or blazing star, *Liatris punctata*
☐ Skeleton weed, *Lygodesmia juncea*[1]
☐ Wavyleaf false dandelion, *Microseris cuspidata*
☐ Prairie coneflower, *Ratibida columnifera*
☐ Prairie ragwort, *Senecio plattensis*
☐ Prairie goldenrod, *Solidago missouriensis*
☐ Gray goldenrod, *Solidago nemoralis*
☐ Rigid goldenrod, *Solidago rigida*
BORAGINACEAE (borage family)
☐ Gromwell, puccoon, *Lithospermum incisum*
CYPERACEAE (sedge family)
☐ Sedge, *Carex heliophila*

FABACEAE (bean family)
☐ Leadplant, *Amorpha canescens*
☐ Ground plum, *Astragalus crassicarpus*
☐ Lotus milk vetch, *Astragalus lotiflorus*[1]
☐ Missouri milk vetch, *Astragalus missouriensis*[1,2]
☐ Nine-anther prairie clover, *Dalea enneandra*[1]
☐ Purple locoweed, *Oxytropis lambertii*[1]
☐ Western prairie clover, *Petalostemon occidentale*[1]
☐ Purple prairie clover, *Petalostemon purpureus*
☐ Silverleaf scurf pea, *Psoralea argophylla*
☐ Prairie turnip, or breadroot scurf pea, *Psoralea esculenta*
☐ American vetch, *Vicia americana* var. *minor*[1]
IRIDACEAE (iris family)
☐ White-eyed grass, *Sisyrinchium campestre*
LOASACEAE (stickleaf family)
☐ Ten-petal blazing star, or sand lily, *Mentzelia decapetala*[1,2]
MALVACEAE (mallow family)
☐ Cowboy's delight, or scarlet globemallow, *Sphaeralcea coccinea*[1,2]
ONAGRACEAE (evening primrose family)
☐ Plains yellow primrose, *Calylophus serrulatus*
☐ Scarlet gaura, *Gaura coccinea*[1]
POACEAE (grass family)
☐ Big bluestem, *Andropogon gerardii*[3]

TABLE 6 (*continued*)

☐ Little bluestem, *Andropogon scoparius*
☐ Red three-awn, *Aristida longiseta*[1]
☐ Side-oats grama, *Bouteloua curtipendula*
☐ Blue grama, *Bouteloua gracilis*
☐ Hairy grama, *Bouteloua hirsuta*
☐ Prairie sandreed, *Calamovilfa longifolia*
☐ Scribner dicanthelium, *Dicanthelium oligosanthes*
☐ Wilcox dicanthelium, *Dicanthelium wilcoxianum*[2]
☐ Canada wild rye, *Elymus canadensis*[3]
☐ June grass, *Koeleria pyramidata*
☐ Plains muhly, *Muhlenbergia cuspidata*
☐ Switchgrass, *Panicum virgatum*[3]
☐ Indiangrass, *Sorghastrum nutans*[3]
☐ Rough dropseed, *Sporobolus asper*
☐ Sand dropseed, *Sporobolus cryptandrus*

☐ Porcupine grass, *Stipa spartea*
☐ Green needle grass, *Stipa viridula*
POLYGALACEAE (milkwort family)
☐ Stiffstem flax, *Linum rigidum*[1]
RANUNCULACEAE (buttercup family)
☐ Pasqueflower, *Anemone patens*[2]
☐ Prairie larkspur, *Delphinium virescens*
ROSACEAE (rose family)
☐ Prairie wild rose, *Rosa arkansana*
SCROPHULARIACEAE (figwort family)
☐ Gerardia, *Agalinis aspera*
☐ Downy paintbrush, *Castilleja sessiliflora*
☐ White beardtongue, *Penstemon albidus*[1,2]
☐ Great-flowered beardtongue, or shell-leaf penstemon, *Penstemon grandiflorus*

---

[1]Western species typical of Great Plains grasslands, which for the most part do not extend eastward from the Hills. Some reach their eastern limits of distribution in the Loess Hills or more generally in western Iowa.

[2]Found only in the northern Loess Hills.

[3]Tall-grass species, found in the Loess Hills only in sheltered, relatively moist prairies.

Note: Adapted from Novacek, Roosa, and Pusateri, 1985.

---

forests that now claim much of the bluffline, evidence that prairie or savanna may have covered portions of the bluffs in presettlement times. Today forests claim nearly all of the more rugged bluffs, with agricultural use claiming sites where the bluffs are shorter and more gently sloping.

Forbs. A rich abundance of drought-tolerant forbs dot the Loess Hills prairies. First out are pasqueflowers, common in the northern Hills, fuzzy-leaved plants with flowers that mix among winter's dried grasses as early as March. By May, the deep-yellow flowers of gromwell (also called puccoon) mingle with purple-flowered prairie violets (*Viola pedatifida*), whose deeply divided leaves differ markedly from the heart-shaped leaves typical of other violets.

Blossoms of those smaller plants are followed by the three-foot-tall spikes of blossoming yucca, the hallmark of Loess Hills prairies (fig. 42). The large white, nodding, bell-shaped flowers light the driest of Hills prairies. When not in bloom, this member of the lily family is easily identified by its stiff, perennially green, spearlike leaves that also reach a length of three feet, and by its spikes of large dried seed pods. A western species that reaches its eastern limits of distribution in the Hills, the yucca brings with it other species from the West. Western fungi parasitize its leaves, and a small white moth pollinates the yucca flower as it lays eggs in the developing seed capsule, where the moth larvae will feed. Neither moth nor yucca could reproduce successfully alone. Yucca is classified as endangered in Missouri, where it clings to the remnants of Loess Hills prairies remaining in the state.

Midsummer prairies are marked by prairie coneflower, with its columnar flower center surrounded by drooping yellow petals, and by purple coneflower, a dome-centered flower surrounded by lavender petals. Those tall plants overshadow the pink-flowered skeleton weed, another of Missouri's endangered species, appropriately named because of its thin, nearly leafless branching stems (fig. 43). The stems commonly bear marble-sized bumps, galls formed after wasps lay their eggs within the plant tissues.

Leadplant, one of the most abundant of Loess Hills prairie plants, is also extremely conspicuous with its leaden gray, numerous oval leaflets colored by the dense coating of short hairs. The low shrub bears dense spikes of small purple flowers. Two additional common legumes, the western prairie clover and the purple prairie clover, bear smaller columnar spikes of tiny white and reddish flowers.

Late summer prairies see the appearance of the yellow blossoms of stiff sunflower, a common species up to five feet tall with long, leathery leaves. Numerous other composites now come into bloom—white- to purple-blossomed asters, yellow-plumed goldenrods, and brilliant violet-flowered dotted gayfeather to name a few. Those flowers and the drying of prairie grasses to golden and russet hues mark autumn's passage to winter.

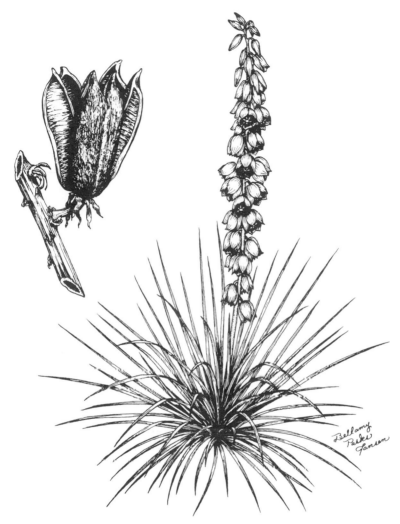

Figure 42. *Yucca, hallmark of Loess Hills prairies; blossoms and seed pod. Bellamy Parks Jansen.*

Many of the rare and endangered species in the Loess Hills are plants, most of which are prairie forbs or smaller shrubs, although there are some rare grasses as well and a few woodland plants. In fact, the dry prairies of northwestern Missouri have a greater concentration of restricted, rare, and endangered plants than any other community in that state, with the pos-

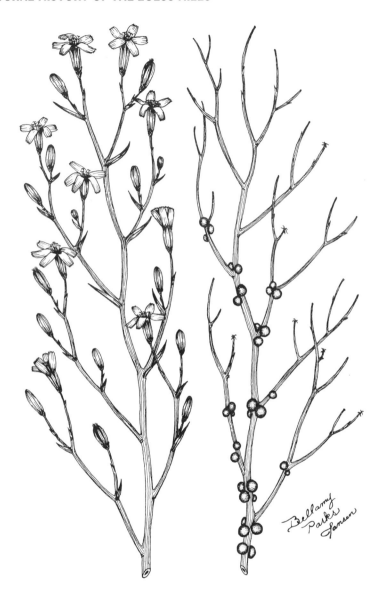

Figure 43. *Skeleton weed, in bloom and with insect galls. Bellamy Parks Jansen.*

sible exclusion of fens. More than half of rare Loess Hills plants are western Great Plains species, rare in Iowa and Missouri in part because they do not extend farther eastward in those states. For the most part, they are plants of the driest, westernmost Loess Hills.

Species common in Iowa's Loess Hills may be considered rare on Missouri's prairie remnants; species rare in Iowa may not extend south into Missouri's Loess Hills. Thus Missouri's and Iowa's listings of rare and endangered plants are very different. Of the 42 species listed, only buffalograss is common to both states.

Woody Plants and Woody Invasion. Loess Hills prairies are not naturally devoid of woody growth. The shrubs leadplant and New Jersey tea (*Ceanothus* spp.—growing to a few feet in height with balls of minute white flowers) are good indicators of native prairie. Today, however, the majority of woody plants are species that mark the prairie's destruction through woodland invasion.

The invasion process begins when a line of dense shrubs, usually smooth sumac or rough-leaved dogwood, grows outward in a band along the forest edge (fig. 44). The shade from the shrubs gradually kills the sun-loving prairie species, and shrubs provide perches for birds that import seeds of other woody species. Shade and a slightly cooler, moister climate are provided for tree seedlings, which grow within the shrublands and eventually overtop them. Shrubs in turn are forced out by the trees' shade, and an even cooler, shadier environment is created for successive tree species with higher moisture requirements. The forest has taken another step forward.

Many factors lend variety to the invasion product and process: seed availability, local climate, slope exposure, the character of the invaded community, and the presence of aggressive exotic plants. Bur oak and cedar can directly invade prairies. Sometimes an entire field is massively invaded by sumac or dogwood. All those species are common in today's prairies. Bur oak undoubtedly was present in presettlement prairies as well, in places remaining dwarfed by regular prairie fire and elsewhere maturing to form prairie savannas.

How did forests invade prairies in times past? Today's forests offer some possible answers. The trees in some present-day woodlands are dense and evenly sized, evidence that they all started growing at the same time. Such a flush of woody growth may have occurred when trees massively invaded a prairie; perhaps it was more common on disturbed prairie or on cropland, pasture, or logged forest that had been abandoned. Elsewhere, aged, broad-crowned bur oaks are surrounded by younger, denser trees and shrubs. Widespread bur oaks are especially prevalent near the tops of north-facing slopes. At one time in their lives, the trees may have grown as widely spaced individuals in grassland-dominated communities called sa-

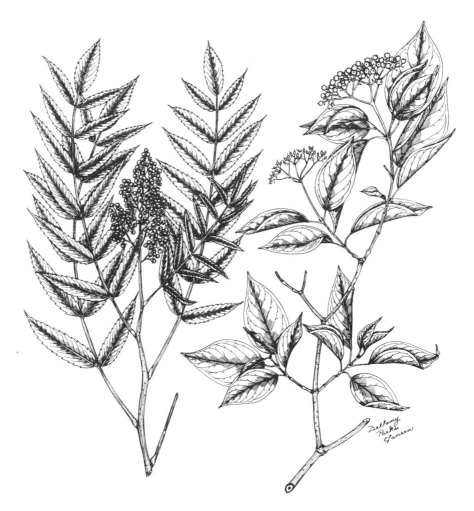

Figure 44. *Smooth sumac (left; ⅓ ×) and rough-leaved dogwood (right; ½ ×), woody invaders of Loess Hills prairies. Bellamy Parks Jansen.*

vannas. In such situations, the cessation of prairie fires would have allowed other woody plants to fill in the savanna and replace the prairie. (Earlier patterns of invasion are discussed further in sidebar 6.)

Are all Loess Hills prairies likely to disappear? Possibly not. The sites within this diverse region are not all equally susceptible to invasion. Some small prairie segments may be dry enough to resist forestation. Prairies on the highest bluff tops and steepest ridge crests facing west or south are prime candidates for survival. But without intensive human intervention, Loess Hills prairies on the whole have a grim future.

Animals. Searching for native animals in the Loess Hills prairies can be a frustrating experience, since neither a high diversity nor an abundance is casually encountered. The more expansive, less rugged inland prairies originally present undoubtedly had more obvious animal populations. Large ungulates (elk, bison, and pronghorn) were eliminated early in settlement, along with larger predators (gray wolf, black bear, mountain lion).

Remaining prairie habitats seem to be too small or too extreme (steep and inaccessible) for many animal species. That has been demonstrated with bird populations. Most Hills prairies of today simply lack the nesting sites and the broad, uninterrupted landscapes that ground nesters prefer, and so today's prairies contain fewer bird species than either the woodlands or the agricultural grasslands. Modern-day prairies were probably never rich in birdlife; conversely, prairie birdlife that remains in the Hills is noticeably poor in species adapted to moderate or moist prairie habitats, such as the bobolink, song sparrow, red-winged blackbird, and common yellowthroat, that are routine in other western Iowa prairies.

Animals that do remain are, for the most part, smaller species. Among grassland mammals, for example, common species include various mice and voles, smaller ground squirrels, the plains pocket gopher, the northern short-tailed shrew, and the badger. Larger common animals of the Loess Hills—coyote, white-tailed deer, and red fox—are widespread species, inhabiting woodlands or shrublands as well as open grasslands.

Although larger birds such as the greater prairie chicken, long-billed curlew, and short-eared owl probably dwelled here in previous centuries, smaller grassland birds have had more success adapting to postsettlement ecosystem changes. Common species include the field sparrow, grasshopper sparrow, western meadowlark, dickcissel, lark sparrow, eastern kingbird, brown-headed cowbird, and mourning dove. Many are birds of grasslands with scattered trees or shrubs, typifying the state of today's rapidly changing prairies. Barn swallows and northern rough-winged swallows are conspicuous aerial feeders. Because of the many woodlands and shrublands that are fingering their way into native grasslands, birds of the forest edge are commonly seen and heard in the grasslands, although they do not venture far from the woodland borders. Such birds include the rose-breasted grosbeak, indigo bunting, northern oriole, gray catbird, and many others.

Nearly half of all Loess Hills amphibians and reptiles are associated spe-

SIDEBAR 6. Woody Invasion: When Did It Commence and Why?

Plants have always been migrating into and within the Loess Hills in response to environmental factors, in particular climatic change. Presumably, for the last 9,000 years, the range of forests has expanded whenever the climate has grown wetter, because increased moisture favors woody growth. The prairies, with their drought-tolerant grasses, expand during dry periods; prairie dominance was aided by other natural factors such as periodic fire. Thus, the invasion of prairie by forest is not something new. Not that today's invasion is completely natural and therefore unworthy of our concern. Like many environmental problems, the invasion process has been greatly accelerated through human influence.

The beginnings of today's massive, rapid extension of woodland boundaries are incompletely understood. Modern-day invasion of prairies may have commenced with a trend toward a wetter climate that began before the Lewis and Clark expedition. Some observers believe that today's climate strongly favors woodlands and that the evidence is obvious in several preserves, where shrubs continue to invade despite attempts to control them through managed burns. Other observers argue that fire can be effective but sometimes is not because the trees and shrubs in many prairies are now too large to be killed by fire or because insufficient fuel keeps the fire intensity too low.

Dramatic and rapid changes in land use brought about by early settlers may have triggered or accelerated invasion, resulting in an immediate proliferation of woody growth. Substitution of cattle enclosed in fenced pastures for free-roving bison may have been one such change.

cifically with grasslands. Together with species inhabiting both woodlands and prairies, they give Hills grasslands a rich herpetofauna. Several of the prairie species (Great Plains toad, prairie racerunner, ornate box turtle, and others) are more widely distributed and abundant in western states (fig. 45). The most abundant amphibian, the plains spadefoot (a toad), is described later in the section on prairies (see fig. 51).

Several butterfly species are confined to prairies, the most noticeable being the regal fritillary. Males of the beautiful orange, white, and black species are easily seen flitting about ridgetops in midsummer. Their caterpillars are dependent on a few species of prairie violets for survival. Thus the butterflies cannot survive in agricultural land.

But probably most important were the settlers' attempts to halt prairie fires, which prehistorically had swept with legendary force and heat through the grasslands. Prairie and fire had evolved together, the fires being fed by the abundant fuel of dense dry grasses and the prairies being nourished by released minerals and the warm, dark soil surface of recently burned areas. Prairie plants survived because fires typically burned in spring or fall, when the prairies were dormant, and because their long roots stretched deep into protecting soil. The regular fires killed or top-killed any trees that were attempting to gain a foothold in the grasslands. Elimination of fire, together with other changes in land use, may have disrupted the integrity of prairies sufficiently to favor forest expansion. Plant communities and soil—once they were cut by the plow, trodden and heavily grazed by herds of cattle, compressed by wagon wheels and horse hooves, and eroded by water racing down scarred hillsides—were probably far less able to reject tiny shrub and tree seedlings than were their healthier, less disturbed predecessors.

Perhaps the trend toward expanded woodlands began even later. In 1910, the natural historian Bohumil Shimek testified that in Harrison and Monona counties, although existing groves of trees had grown denser since prairie fires had ceased 30 or 40 years before, there had been little or no expansion of woodlands since settlement.

Regardless of when invasion started, the extensive forested areas of the southern Hills imply either that woodlands have always been larger there than in the north or that prairie invasion started earlier or proceeded more rapidly there, where climate and seed abundance favored woody growth.

A number of prairie animals have been classified as rare or endangered in Iowa or Missouri (see tables 8 and 9), their populations shrinking as their required habitat disappears. Although many animals (for example, birds such as the dickcissel and grasshopper sparrow) are able to substitute agricultural land for native prairie, the plains pocket mouse, Great Plains skink, and others have been unable to do so. As growing woodlands and human use decrease the size of native prairies, those animals are constricted into smaller and smaller areas. At some point, different for each species, the area remaining is too small to assure food, shelter, and reproductive success, and the species disappears. Rare prairie butterflies— the ottoe, pawnee, and dusted skipper—are managing to survive, al-

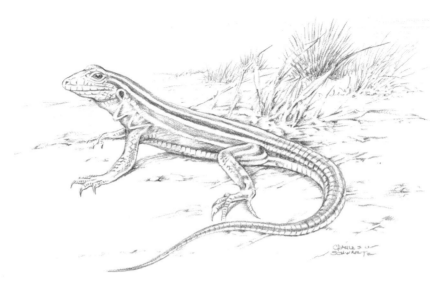

Figure 45. *The prairie racerunner: a typical lizard of dry, open Hills prairies, but more common in states to the west. Charles W. Schwartz.*

though they have disappeared on prairies elsewhere. However, nearly all declining reptiles and amphibians in the Hills are prairie species. Three—the prairie rattlesnake, Great Plains skink, and ornate box turtle—are extremely rare. They demonstrate today what may well be happening tomorrow to many more prairie species, if steps are not taken to assure the perpetuation of sufficiently large and abundant dry Loess Hills prairies.

The Western Element

The distinctive aspects of Loess Hills prairie vegetation were already recognized more than a century ago. Nineteenth-century naturalists commented on the intermingling of western and eastern prairie plants, which created a community quite unlike others in Iowa or Missouri. Because of the eastwardly displaced western plants, the Loess 'ills were of great botanical interest.

Eastwardly displaced animals and plants remain a major fascination for today's biologists, who describe the prairies as similar to the much drier Great Plains grasslands many miles to the west. Those western species are found within a state that historically has been the heart of the true prairie, the tallest, lushest, and most moisture-demanding of the midcontinental grasslands. Before settlement and the plowing of the prairie, approximately 85 percent of Iowa was such tall-grass prairies, proportionally more than any other state. They extended southward through the upper half and southwestern corner of Missouri and westward through the eastern third of Nebraska. As the prairies stretched toward the base of the Rockies, precipitation and height and lushness of the dominant grass species decreased. At 98 degrees west longitude or a bit farther to the west, 100 miles or so to the west of the Loess Hills, midheight grasses and mats of short grasses assumed dominance. They mixed with drought-tolerant forbs to form a mixed-grass prairie able to tolerate the drier climate.

The Loess Hills' western species, together with more-ubiquitous grasses and herbs that are sufficiently drought resistant, constitute the largest relatively contiguous mixed-grass prairie in Iowa and the only such prairie in Missouri, a narrow peninsular extension from the west into a region that typically supports tall-grass prairie. The community survives there because the environment is among the driest in Iowa and Missouri. The most drought-tolerant species are found on the steepest south- and west-facing bluffs most exposed to intense sunlight and southerly winds. (Their migration to the Loess Hills is described in sidebar 7.)

At least 40 Great Plains vascular plants extend eastward into the Hills. Table 6 identifies several such species: stiffstem flax, lotus milk vetch, scarlet gaura, yucca, and skeleton weed, among others. Species not common enough to be listed in the table include snow-on-the-mountain, tumblegrass, biscuit-root, sandhills bluestem (*Andropogon hallii*), curly-top gumweed, and buffalo berry. Almost half of the western plants (purple coneflower, purple locoweed, western prairie clover, ten-petal blazing star, cowboy's delight, and others), as well as several amphibians and reptiles and a few mammals, reach their eastern limits of distribution in the Hills. They cannot be found elsewhere in Iowa or Missouri. A number are rare. They are joined by western rust and other fungi that do not occur elsewhere in Iowa and by several soil lichens that are typical of western arid regions and grow throughout Iowa's western prairies. Several fungi enter the area as parasites of specific western plants.

Western animals also join the western plants. Most numerous are the amphibian and reptile species: the plains leopard frog, ornate box turtle (fig. 46), Woodhouse's toad, Great Plains toad, prairie racerunner, prairie rattlesnake, and Great Plains skink. Several are limited in Iowa or Missouri to the Hills. The plains pocket mouse, northern grasshopper mouse, and white-tailed jackrabbit also are more typical of western grasslands, and the

SIDEBAR 7. Migration from the West

The presence of so many western species prompts biologists to ask how they arrived in the Hills. The answer lies partially in observations of historic plant migrations. Scientists noted that during the seven-year Dust Bowl drought (1933 to 1940), mixed-grass prairie species moved eastward, replacing tall-grass species along a front of more than 1,000 miles. Their migration is thought to be illustrative of lengthier and more massive eastward migrations that must have occurred during dry periods throughout the Holocene, in particular during the very dry hypsithermal, which commenced in the Loess Hills about 9,000 years ago. Over the next several thousand years, grassland communities moved eastward many hundreds of miles. Areas as far east as present-day Ohio were transformed from moisture-loving deciduous forests to more drought-tolerant tall-grass prairies, and today's tall-grass prairie regions were invaded by even more drought-resistant communities from the West. When precipitation again increased, many species retreated, leaving scattered populations on locally dry sites as signs of their onetime more-expansive range.

Several species now found in the Loess Hills are thought to be such hypsithermal relicts, or possibly relicts from a more recent extended drought. A prime example is cowboy's delight, which is widespread on the Great Plains more than 100 miles west of the Missouri River but grows east of the river only in the Loess Hills in two widely separated locales. The ornate box turtle, plains pocket mouse, and prairie racerunner, among other species, are also thought to be left over from oncewidespread hypsithermal populations.

Examination of distribution maps of several Loess Hills plants reveals a second migrational phenomenon. The maps show plants that are widespread in the Great Plains extending eastward through Nebraska and into Iowa along a narrow strip bordering the Missouri River. Indeed, Iowa's mixed-grass prairie community as a whole is connected to the main body of mixed-grass prairie by a narrow band running along the Missouri River bluffs in South Dakota and Nebraska. The range of the

Loess Hills is one of the easternmost regular breeding habitats of the western kingbird. A few species such as the plains spadefoot have centers of distribution in the United States' Southwestern desert. (Western species of mammals, reptiles, and amphibians are noted in tables 4 and 5.)

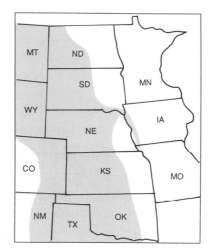

Distribution of *Yucca glauca*

western plants then extends southward along the Loess Hills, with some plants such as buffalo berry reaching only a short way into the Hills and others such as nine-anther prairie clover extending to the southern tip of the Hills. The largest number of Great Plains species (80 percent) is found in Plymouth County.

It appears that the Missouri River system has been a major migratory route for many of the Hills' Great Plains species. Plants presumably have migrated eastward along the dry upland bluffs or the sandy floodplains of the Missouri River, entering the Loess Hills in Plymouth County and then spreading southward. Water, birds, and other animals traveling along the river may have aided seed dispersal. Migration along the corridor may have occurred relatively recently and indeed may still be occurring. Botanists believe that some species, such as western prairie clover and ten-petal blazing star, may still be expanding southward in the Hills, demonstrating the natural expansion of plant species into habitats that meet their growth requirements. Unfortunately, species also become locally extinct in environments that no longer meet their needs. Careful management of remaining dry prairies will be necessary to prevent loss of the Loess Hills' special western species.

Variations among Prairies

These then are the typical Loess Hills prairies of today: an upland mixture of drought-tolerant, midheight and short grasses; speckled with a diver-

Figure 46. *The ornate box turtle, one of the many Loess Hills species dependent on dry prairies and more typical of western states. The rare populations of this species are thought to be relicts of larger populations from thousands of years ago, when the climate was drier. Charles W. Schwartz.*

sity of hardy, often western forbs; covering the west- and south-facing slopes of the westernmost Loess Hills and extending eastward into the Hills along ridgetops and upper dry slopes. Confined primarily to the harsh, dry, outermost bluffs, they rapidly give way to inland forests and to croplands as climate and rugged topography become more moderate. Occasionally tall grasses still intermingle when increased moisture is available, carrying Loess Hills prairies downslope and inland onto sites less drought-prone. But for the most part, today's prairies are shorter and sparser than the tall-grass prairies that originally encircled them. Those that remain fight for survival against invading woodlands and intensive agricultural use. Beyond those general traits, individual prairies can be described in terms of north-south variations, east-west variations, and variations related to particular disturbances.

North-South Variations. Typical upland prairies are best observed in central Loess Hills preserves such as the Loess Hills Wildlife Area. The wildlife area and surrounding tracts retain extensive prairies, many of which unfortunately show signs of transition to woodlands. Prairies in southern counties often are less than 100 yards wide and are limited to the tops of narrow ridges. Some of the steepest southern bluffs facing the Missouri River also maintain excellent prairies. Outstanding examples are the large vertical prairies on massive bluff faces at and immediately south of Waubonsie State Park, Iowa.

Missouri's Loess Hills prairies speckle the steepest outermost bluffs primarily in Atchison County (see fig. 77). The McCormack Loess Mounds Natural Area in central Holt County is the southernmost Loess Hills prairie of any size. Dry prairies that previously grew farther inland have been eliminated through grazing and quarrying of loess for highway construction. The remaining drought-tolerant prairies are dominated by midheight and short grasses, primarily little bluestem and side-oats grama, although hairy grama and blue grama also are common, and buffalograss may be present. Where moisture permits, on inland and lower slopes, taller grasses such as big bluestem and switchgrass may be present. Characteristic flowers include silky aster, prairie larkspur, silverleaf scurf pea, ground plum, and foxtail dalea (*Dalea alopecuroides*). Many species of those prairies, although common in Iowa, are rare in Missouri and are restricted to dry prairies in the northwest corner of the state.

Invasion is proceeding aggressively in Missouri's prairies. Even on the driest sites—the steepest, south- and west-facing knobs along the western bluffline—invading sumac are often obvious among the sparse prairie plants. Without active prairie maintenance efforts, most of those prairies are destined to disappear.

Prairies expand north of the central Hills, in Woodbury County and especially in Plymouth County, Iowa, where they may reach miles eastward into the Hills and cover all slope exposures (see fig. 75). Their character changes here. Although the steepest, most westerly bluffs and ridgetops maintain typical upland prairie associations, tall grasses increase dramatically on inland prairies such as the Sioux City Prairie. The inland prairies appear to be denser with less bare ground, sometimes speckled with moisture-loving forbs. Whether that change has resulted from the region's gentler slopes, the Cretaceous bedrock's closer proximity to the ground surface, past land-use practices, the survival of inland prairies in the northern Hills, or a combination of factors is not known.

The extensive far northern Hills prairies provide habitat for several open grassland bird species. There the upland sandpiper, a rare species in Iowa and Missouri, and horned lark have been observed. The killdeer, abundant in the Missouri River valley, has been sighted in the Hills in northern prairies and along roadsides. Grasshopper sparrows and dickcissels, found throughout the Hills in large planted fields of alfalfa and brome, inhabit the expansive northern prairies but are absent from smaller prairies elsewhere in the Hills. Thus these rich prairies contrast with those of the southern-most Hills, which lack birds that strictly inhabit grasslands. The expansive Plymouth County grasslands also provide habitat for Iowa's last few surviving prairie rattlesnakes.

Far northern grasslands contain the greatest number of prairie plant species, with diversity decreasing toward the south—a trend opposite that of woodlands, which are least diverse in the north. For undetermined reasons, some species (pasqueflower, tumblegrass, buffalo berry, and others) reach their southern limits of distribution in Monona County. (Northern prairie plants are indicated in table 6.) Other species such as yucca simply decrease in frequency toward the south.

East-West Variations. Variations within Loess Hills prairies occur from east to west as well. These variations have been well explained since the turn of the century, when naturalists observed that certain factors lowered humidity to desert levels on the west- and south-facing bluff fronts and on ridgetops close to the Missouri River valley. Specifically, the combination of heat from the sun (beating directly on the slopes at the hottest time of the day), strong winds (coming primarily from the south and southwest), and steep-sloping, well-drained loess (which neither soaks up nor holds much water) drives the evaporation rate upward to levels intolerable to most species.

Those factors create an environment conducive to the mixed-grass upland prairies that contain plants and animals adapted to similarly hot and dry environments in the western Great Plains. Westward from the inland forests and croplands toward the ever drier outermost bluffs, the upland prairies become more sparse, more interrupted by dry ground, and more dominated by grass bunches and by Great Plains vegetation. On the steepest south- and west-facing bluffs, short and sparse vegetation dots nearly bare, sometimes eroding ground (fig. 47). Yucca and skeleton weed abound, joined by nine-anther prairie clover, scarlet gaura, lotus milk vetch, and other species adapted to arid environments.

On nearly vertical loess faces, grasses such as prairie sand reed, sand dropseed, and plains muhly become common. The extremely steep loess bluffs facing the Missouri River valley and adjacent south-facing slopes contain the prairies most easily seen when driving along the base of the

Figure 47. Moisture decreases as one moves westward in the Hills toward the extremely dry westernmost bluff faces. There vegetation is sparse and interrupted by bare or eroding soil. Western plants such as yucca proliferate. Don Poggensee.

bluffs. Well developed throughout the central Hills, large vertical prairies also are found near Sioux City in the northern Hills and toward the south near Waubonsie State Park. They become smaller in Missouri's Loess Hills, where the deep loess landscape is reduced to a north-south sliver.

Disturbance-Related Variations. Disturbance is another major factor that creates variations among Loess Hills prairies. Often entire prairies have been obliterated. Some have been converted to cropland, pastures of brome, or fields of alfalfa (*Medicago sativa*); some left to become patches of ragweed (*Ambrosia* spp.), sweet clover (*Melilotus* spp.), or other exotic weeds; and some are now covered by human structures. The conversion process has sometimes been reversed, native prairie species being allowed to reclaim abandoned pastures and croplands. Conversion of prairies to other uses has occurred most frequently east of the rugged outer bluffs, where climate and topography inhibit cultivation of crops, and on gently sloping sections within the rugged bluffs, such as lower slopes and valley floors.

Where they survive, prairies suffer local disturbances from natural causes and from human use. Disruption by animals, slumping of soil, creation of trails or roads through prairies, even excessive mowing of prairies for hay can weaken prairie plants and create bare spots ripe for quick-growing, hardy invaders. Often exotic species invade. The introduced pasture grasses brome and Kentucky bluegrass (*Poa pratensis*) frequently mix with prairie species now. Sweet clover can be a common prairie weed.

But shifts in native prairie species occur as well, the sensitive plants decreasing while other native "weeds" increase. Snow-on-the-mountain (*Euphorbia marginata*), with its distinctive white-edged leaves; curly-top gumweed (*Grindelia squarrosa*), a yellow sunflower with sticky flower bases and sticky leaves; western prairie clover, with its dense spikes of small white flowers and narrow, linear leaflets; and great-flowered beard-tongue, with its magnificent three-foot-tall spikes of two-inch-long, tubular pink flowers, are examples of natives that increase wherever soil has been bared (fig. 48). Frequently Great Plains species are best adapted to the driest disturbed sites. Cowboy's delight and ten-petal blazing star, for example, invade bare, eroding soil on the westernmost bluff faces.

The most profound and extensive disturbances of Loess Hills prairies have been induced by grazing cattle. Practically all Hills prairies have been affected, since grazing has been common in the Hills for more than 100 years. Even prairies on extremely steep bluff faces and in today's preserves have been grazed at one time. The result is a patchwork of prairie communities that have been altered to a greater or lesser degree by grazing practices, specifically by differences in the duration of grazing, density of cattle, and slope steepness. The few prairies that are ungrazed today are readily recognized by their taller, healthier appearance, the dominance of grasses rather than forbs, and their abundance of litter.

Light to moderate grazing may have few effects other than shifting the abundance of native prairie plants already present. Cattle readily eat little bluestem, big bluestem, and other tall grasses, showing off the diversity and beauty of remaining forbs. Some native species may actually increase—the native weeds mentioned previously and the very drought-tolerant side-oats grama. Bare ground is likely to increase as litter decreases, the latter change also having been produced by fire in previous centuries.

Too often, however, prairies are so heavily grazed that their integrity begins a gradual decline (fig. 49). With time, the prairie's basic nature and composition change dramatically. Such prairies may appear to be close-cropped, with abundant bare soil, which, on steeper slopes, slumps to

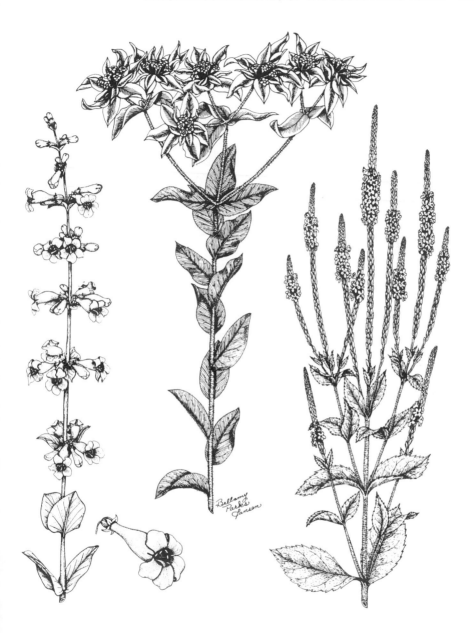

Figure 48. Great-flowered beardtongue (left), snow-on-the-mountain (center), and hoary vervain (right), native species that increase in disturbed areas. Bellamy Parks Jansen.

Figure 49. Heavy grazing changes the composition and nature of prairies. Weedy species increase, as do bare soil and hillside slumping. All of those changes can be seen here. Thomas Rosburg.

form large shelves or terraces. Those bare patches and cattle paths on uplands provide abundant space for invading weed species, whose seeds often are spread in cattle dung or bird droppings or by the wind. Prairie species selectively eaten by cattle decline or disappear. Most legumes fall into that category. Leadplant, ground plum, American vetch, the prairie clovers, silverleaf scurf pea, and prairie turnip (*Psoralea esculenta*) are examples. Toxic, spiny, or otherwise unpalatable species remain, along with exotic species that have invaded the weakened prairie sod and can tolerate chewing and trampling. Heavily grazed prairies may appear to be patches of common mullein (*Verbascum thapsus*), certain thistles (*Cirsium* spp.), sweet clovers, ragweeds, and other weeds, many of which are not native plants. Hoary vervain (*Verbena stricta*), a common member of native prairies but bitter enough to be avoided by cattle, can become dense in overgrazed prairies, where it seems to cover the land with its violet flower spikes (fig. 48).

Sensitive grasses disappear. Even side-oats grama declines in heavily grazed prairies. The introduced brome and Kentucky bluegrass increase, along with the most hardy of the native grasses, especially short grasses (blue grama and hairy grama) and panic grasses (*Panicum* spp.). If abandoned, the degraded grasslands often experience a flush of woody growth. Experience has shown that overgrazed grasslands do retain bluestem roots and seeds of prairie forbs, so if woody invasion is prevented and recovery is allowed, some of the prairie plants may return. Fire seems to stimulate the return of prairie grasses.

Animals have responded to the human-induced changes in grasslands. By definition, all Loess Hills grassland animals were once species of native prairies. Today some may find land altered by agriculture or roadside ditches an appealing substitute. Thus, Franklin's ground squirrel still inhabits the taller grasslands of abandoned pastures, ungrazed prairies, and roadsides, but the thirteen-lined ground squirrel, a short-grass species, has benefited from cattle grazing. It has increased its numbers in recent years. Although native prairie is most appealing to the plains pocket mouse and western harvest mouse, the meadow vole is abundant in hay fields, and the northern grasshopper mouse seems to prefer cultivated fields.

Birds of open grasslands also have shown an affinity for agricultural land. Fields of alfalfa and brome now seem to provide the open vistas, gentler slopes, and ground nesting sites furnished by the more expansive prairies of past centuries. The three most common birds of agricultural fields (the dickcissel, grasshopper sparrow, and western meadowlark) are all birds of open grasslands. In today's Loess Hills, the frequency of encountering those and other open-grassland birds is significantly higher in agricultural fields than in native prairies.

Adaptations of Prairie Species

The lack of standing water and the hot, dry climate of Loess Hills grasslands create an extremely harsh environment for animal species. Many escape the heat and dryness by burrowing, a habit that also protects them from predators. Burrows of the badger are commonly seen in Loess Hills prairies (fig. 50). Working the loose, friable soil with ease, the predator creates cavities later used by bumblebees, wasps, spiders, rabbits, spadefoot and Great Plains toads, tiger salamanders, and even hibernating prairie rattlesnakes. Even upland prairie snails hide themselves from the heat. Most are drought-tolerant types that live and breed underground.

Other animals have adapted other mechanisms for surviving in desert-

Figure 50. The badger, whose burrow provides a respite for numerous other species. Charles W. Schwartz.

like climes. The plains spadefoot toad, a southwestern species that is widespread in Iowa's Loess Hills, possesses opportunistic habits that help explain why it is the only Loess Hills prairie amphibian or reptile that may be increasing in abundance (fig. 51). As do other amphibians, the spadefoot requires an aquatic environment for its eggs and young. In the past, most Loess Hills amphibians bred during well-established breeding seasons on the predictably wet Missouri River floodplain; now, nearly all breed in farm ponds and puddles in roadside ditches. In contrast, the plains spadefoot is able to tolerate limited and unpredictable water supplies, remaining underground for much of its life. Heavy warm spring or early summer rains bring thousands of buried toads to the ground surface, where they congregate in small temporary pools. There they feed rapidly and lay eggs. If pools of water shrink, the tadpoles become cannibalistic, ensuring that at least a few of the future frogs will live. Within weeks the survivors burrow as deep as three feet back into the ground, where they will stay until the next breeding season.

Additional adaptations to the desertlike life are demonstrated by the plains pocket mouse, which is scattered through Iowa's and Missouri's Hills and is one of Iowa's endangered species (fig. 52). It is Iowa's only repre-

Figure 51. *The plains spadefoot has been found in the Loess Hills only recently. The amphibian shortens its aboveground life and breeding season to weeks to survive the desertlike climate. Charles W. Schwartz.*

Figure 52. *The plains pocket mouse, a relative of the kangaroo rat of Southwestern deserts, survives hot, dry environments by staying in covered burrows when the sun is shining and by living without drinking water. Charles W. Schwartz.*

sentative of a family of rodents that includes the kangaroo rat and other desert rodents of the southwestern United States. Like the better-known kangaroo rat, this small mouse has small front legs and well-developed hind legs. It stores its food, primarily seeds, in fur-lined cheek pouches (its pockets). It does not need to drink water since it can manufacture water from ingested solid food. The mouse escapes the day's heat in underground burrows, which are normally sealed, leaving home only at night or on overcast days.

Several prairie plants possess traits that prevent desiccation. Great-flowered beardtongue's waxy coating and cowboy's delight's hairy covering prevent excessive evaporation. Skeleton weed's near absence of leaves and yucca's thickening of leaves reduce moisture loss by reducing the surface-to-volume ratio. Silky aster's whitish hairs reflect the sun's heat. Yucca's long roots search out the deepest moisture. Yucca roots 40 feet long have been recorded. Loess seems to encourage long roots. Plants growing on loess on the whole are much more deeply rooted than plants of the same species growing on glacial till. Deep roots, low stature, small leaves, a thick outer covering, and abundant surface hairs are drought-resistant features typical of many species growing in dry Hills prairies and, for that matter, in deserts throughout the world.

Simpler plant forms found in the Hills also demonstrate adaptations to the harsh environment. For example, the rattlesnake fern (*Botrychium virginianum*), the only fern species of loess prairies, excluding the recently discovered prairie moonwort pictured in figure 60, attains a height of only one to two inches on prairie soils. In contrast, large, vigorous rattlesnake ferns commonly inhabit nearby Hills woodlands. The stunted size of prairie-grown plants may be a result of the arid climate, or it may be an adaptation to prevent excessive water loss.

In response to the prairie's extremely dry conditions and patches of exposed bare soil, soil lichens commonly form extensive crusts up to several square yards in diameter, crusts that are distinctive in Hills prairies. The lichens are well developed on steep, dry slopes of native prairies, maintaining a foothold in those erosion-prone sites because the small, compact plant bodies are interconnected by dense rootlike filaments. Plant bodies and reproductive structures may be covered with a gelatinous substance that allows them to withstand desiccation. Such lichens are found in arid regions throughout the world, where they have been shown to increase the soil's stability, moisture, and fertility. In addition, a limited number of mosses, 25 species in all, are capable of growing on the prairie soils.

Mosses commonly colonize dry, exposed sites. They check erosion of the fragile loess soils, upon which all Loess Hills prairie plants depend for nourishment.

WOODLANDS

Forests, woodlands, and shrublands dominate much of today's Loess Hills. Woody plants also dominate Nebraska's bluffline wherever it is too steep for agricultural use.

Most Loess Hills woodlands are relatively young, bearing little resemblance to presettlement communities and containing at most a smattering of presettlement trees. The forests' youth has been fostered by widespread nineteenth-century logging practices, the proliferation of woody species on land modified by agriculture, and the natural expansion of forests into prairies. Forest invasion of prairies, described in the previous section, is probably the dominating and certainly the most obvious ecological process occurring in the Loess Hills.

Woodlands are most prevalent and extensive on moister sites throughout the Hills—ravines, sheltered slopes, and inland sites not converted to agriculture. Those woodlands and their counterparts in eastern Nebraska form the most westerly outposts of the Eastern Deciduous Forest. In the Hills, where the environment just meets forest plants' growth requirements, the number of species is lower and the size of individuals may be smaller than in similar forests farther to the east.

Forests are most extensive and mature in the southern Hills, where a combination of factors produces a relatively humid climate especially conducive to tree growth. Proceeding northward in the Hills, several species reach their environmental limits, and the diversity of species decreases. (Table 7 lists the main woody species found in the Hills along with their ranges.) Of the 39 species listed for Missouri's Loess Hills, only 22 extend into Iowa's northern Hills. Loess Hills woodlands house a rich diversity of animals typical of deciduous forests and forest edges to the south and east. About a third of Iowa's Loess Hills mammals, amphibians, and reptiles (11 of the 36 amphibians and reptiles and 15 of the 44 mammals) have woodland affinities. Many of the remaining two-thirds are able to inhabit woodlands in addition to other ecosystems. An abundance of birds also makes itself conspicuous throughout Hills woodlands and shrublands. Woodland animals increase in diversity and abundance as one proceeds southward, in response to the increase in diversity and extent of woodland vegetation.

TABLE 7. Major Trees and Larger Shrubs of Loess Hills Woodlands

ACERACEAE (maple family)
☐ Box elder, *Acer negundo* 1[a]
☐ Black maple, *Acer nigrum* 4
☐ Silver maple, *Acer saccharinum* 1
ANACARDIACEAE (cashew family)
☐ Smooth sumac, *Rhus glabra* 1[a,b]
ANNONACEAE (custard apple family)
☐ Pawpaw, *Asimina triloba* 3
BETULACEAE (birch family)
☐ Hazelnut, *Corylus americana* 2[a]
☐ Ironwood, *Ostrya virginiana* 1[a]
CORNACEAE (dogwood family)
☐ Rough-leaved dogwood, *Cornus drummondii* 1[a]
CUPRESSACEAE (cypress family)
☐ Eastern red cedar, *Juniperus virginiana* 1[b]
FABACEAE (legume family)
☐ Redbud, *Cercis canadensis* 2
☐ Kentucky coffee tree, *Gymnocladus dioica* 1
FAGACEAE (oak family)
☐ White oak, *Quercus alba* 4
☐ Red oak, *Quercus borealis* 1
☐ Shingle oak, *Quercus imbricaria* 3
☐ Bur oak, *Quercus macrocarpa* 1[b]

☐ Chinquapin oak, *Quercus muhlenbergii* 3
☐ Dwarf chinquapin oak, *Quercus prinoides* 4
☐ Post oak, *Quercus stellata* 4
☐ Black oak, *Quercus velutina* 2
GROSSULARIACEAE (currant family)
☐ Missouri gooseberry, *Ribes missouriense* 1[a]
JUGLANDACEAE (walnut family)
☐ Bitternut hickory, *Carya cordiformis* 1
☐ Shagbark hickory, *Carya ovata* 2
☐ Mockernut hickory, *Carya tomentosa* 3
☐ Black walnut, *Juglans nigra* 1
MORACEAE (mulberry family)
☐ Mulberry, *Morus rubra* 2
OLEACEAE (olive family)
☐ White ash, *Fraxinus americana* 2
☐ Green ash, *Fraxinus pennsylvanica* 1
PHYTOLACCAECEAE (pokeweed family)
☐ Pokeweed, *Phytolacca americana* 3[a]
PLATANACEAE (sycamore family)
☐ Sycamore, *Platanus occidentalis* 3
ROSACEAE (rose family)

Even snails follow the pattern. The diversity of forest snails—and, in fact, the diversity of the snail population as a whole—increases as one progresses southward along the Hills, even though the snail fauna, as a whole, is much poorer than that of forests in eastern Iowa.

Plants. Hillside forests are predominantly species of oak (fig. 53). Hickories, basswood, elms, ashes, Kentucky coffee tree, and, in the far southern Hills, pawpaw and chinquapin oak are also present. Species composition changes on moist soils along well-developed watercourses. Floodplain forests consist of willow, cottonwood, box elder, ash, elm, and other species.

If one tree species were to be singled out, it would be the bur oak. Although eight oak species can be found in the Loess Hills, only bur oak

TABLE 7 (*continued*)

☐ Saskatoon serviceberry, *Amelanchier arborea* 3
☐ Summerhaw, *Crataegus mollis* 1[a]
☐ Wild plum, *Prunus americana* 1[a]
☐ Chokecherry, *Prunus virginiana* 1[a]
SALICACEAE (willow family)
☐ Cottonwood, *Populus deltoides* 1[a]
STAPHYLEACEAE (bladdernut family)

☐ American bladdernut, *Staphylea trifolia* 1
TILIACEAE (linden family)
☐ Basswood, or linden, *Tilia americana* 1
ULMACEAE (elm family)
☐ Hackberry, *Celtis occidentalis* 1
☐ American elm, *Ulmus americana* 1
☐ Slippery elm, *Ulmus rubra* 1

---

[a] Species commonly found at the edge of woodlands (some also occur within woodlands).

[b] Species commonly found in prairies (as well as in woodlands or along the woodland edge).

Note: The number following the species name indicates the northern range limit in the Loess Hills. The maximum diversity of woody plants is found in the southernmost Hills. A species may reach its northern limit slightly south of the boundary indicated; pawpaw, for example, does not extend north of Fremont County, Iowa.

1: Species naturally grows throughout the Hills or north to the border of Woodbury and Plymouth counties.

2: Species does not naturally grow north of Monona County, Iowa.

3: Species does not naturally grow north of Pottawattamie County, Iowa.

4: Species does not naturally grow north of the Missouri border.

Adapted from Novacek, Roosa, and Pusateri, 1985.

---

grows throughout the Hills. Red oak, also abundant and widespread, does not grow north of Woodbury County. Bur oak dominates many woodlands, in particular those of upper slopes. Where forests approach ridge crests on north- and east-facing slopes, large, old bur oaks often stand out along the uppermost edges. The trees frequently are open grown: their crowns have become broad and rounded because they matured in open parklands or savannas where sunlight was abundant (fig. 54). Elsewhere, the straight trunks and much narrower crowns of bur oaks reveal that they matured in a dense woodland, where branches did not have space or sunlight to extend laterally. Although bur oak often mixes with other species, sometimes nearly pure stands of it cover hills. In northern areas, such

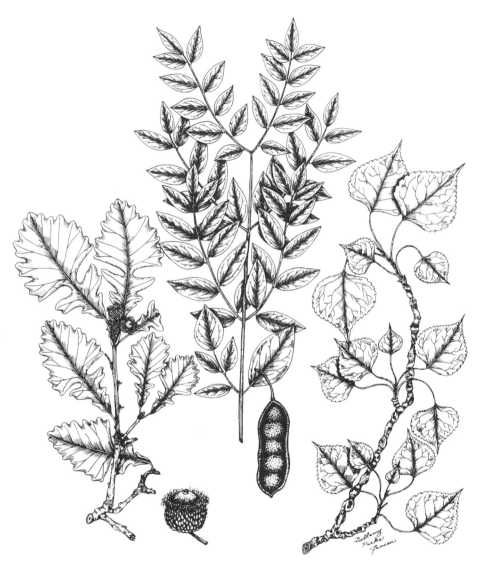

Figure 53. *The bur oak (left; ⅕ ×), Kentucky coffee tree (center; ¼ ×), and cottonwood (right; ⅓ ×), common trees of Loess Hills woodlands. Bellamy Parks Jansen.*

as Preparation Canyon State Park and Whiting Woods, stands may be strangely stunted and gnarled, a condition also described for bur oak growing in northern Nebraska.

Bur oak was the only tree species able to invade presettlement tall-grass prairies. Other tree species were killed by the heat of prairie fires, but bur

Figure 54. Open-grown bur oaks with broad and rounded crowns, reminders of the savannas of presettlement times, still speckle some Loess Hills prairies. Donald R. Farrar.

oaks survived if they were old enough to have a characteristically thick, corky, protective bark. If bur oaks were repeatedly burned back while young, they became grubs (small trees that continued to sprout from an aged rootstock). The grubs blossomed into trees when the frequency of fires diminished. Because of their ability to survive fire and because of their drought tolerance, bur oaks could invade prairies and survive as scattered individuals in savannas, which must have occurred in presettlement Loess Hills.

Basswood frequently dominates forests of lower slopes, along with red oak and other oak species, hickories, black walnut, elms, ashes, and Kentucky coffee tree. Along the base of the westernmost bluffs and along larger waterways, floodplain species, in particular cottonwood, can be seen climbing lower slopes and joining the hillside woodlands.

The upper edge of the forest is characteristically lined with shrubs and small trees, marking the woodland invasion of prairies. A typical pattern is a dense border of rough-leaved dogwood, in turn bordered by smooth sumac, which also dots the adjacent prairie. Western snowberry and coralberry (*Symphoricarpos orbiculatus*) may be intermixed.

Ironwood, a principal understory tree, is found throughout the Hills and often is quite numerous. Redbud trees make central and southern Hills woodlands especially colorful in spring. The herb layer of mature forests resembles a simplified, less diverse version of the more easterly oak-hickory forests. Jack-in-the-pulpit (*Arisaema triphyllum*), bloodroot (*Sanguinaria canadensis*), Solomon's seal (*Polygonatum biflorum*), violets (*Viola* spp.), columbine (*Aquilegia canadensis*), Dutchman's breeches (*Dicentra cucullaria*), and mayapple (*Podophyllum peltatum*) all grow in some older forests. Elsewhere, especially in younger forests, the understory may be more sparse, much less diverse, or absent, or may consist of a proliferation of a single species such as Virginia creeper (*Parthenocissus quinquefolia*).

Eastern red cedar has experienced varying human acceptance. Sometimes planted as a decorative evergreen or to grace Mormon cemeteries, at other times cedars were cut because of their role in maintaining cedar-apple rust, a fungal disease that decreases the vigor and yield of apple trees. Today cedar's aggressive invasion of pastures and prairies creates a serious nuisance in some areas. Cedars can form dense woodlands, or they can be scattered through grasslands or mix with other woody species.

Ferns, fungi, mosses, and liverworts of Loess Hills woodlands are basically a species-poor version of the assemblage found in more eastern, moister deciduous forests. Moss and liverwort diversity is held in check by the arid climate, lack of suitable soils, and absence of exposed bedrock with moist niches. Most mosses and liverworts that occur here are found on soil, trees, and decaying logs in the more protected, moister forests. Ferns, which in general are intolerant of drought, are represented by only

Figure 55. *The rose-breasted grosbeak, commonly heard singing in Loess Hills forests in early summer. Charles W. Schwartz.*

eight species in Iowa's Hills. Six of the ferns are restricted to the moistest woodlands. A seventh, rattlesnake fern, grows in woodlands and prairies. Fungal diversity is reduced by the limited rainfall and by today's woodlands' relatively low diversity of plants, which feed the parasitic fungi.

Animals. Common animals likely to be seen by visitors include the fox squirrel, eastern cottontail, opossum, woodchuck, white-footed deer mouse (the most common forest rodent), American toad, and species of both forests and other types of ecosystems such as the white-tailed deer, weasel, raccoon, red fox, and coyote.

Birds are perhaps the most conspicuous woodland animals. Rose-breasted grosbeaks (fig. 55), house wrens, and blue jays are ubiquitous, making their presence known in season by constant song. They and other woodland species are typical of oak forests throughout western Iowa. Forest-edge species (mourning dove, northern cardinal, red-headed woodpecker, rufous-sided towhee, indigo bunting, and others) and interior forest species (black-capped chickadee, eastern wood pewee, red-bellied woodpecker, and others) are common throughout the Hills, although several forest species (e.g., tufted titmouse, ovenbird, wood thrush, red-eyed vireo) are typical only of the more extensive forest tracts south of Monona County, Iowa. The eastern kingbird is one of the most conspicuous birds of sparsely wooded areas. Loess Hills forests, woodlands, and shrubby ra-

Figure 56. The gray fox, one of several animals that is benefiting from the expansion of Loess Hills woodlands. Charles W. Schwartz.

vines claim a richer diversity of birds than either grasslands or agricultural fields. That diversity is greatest in the southern Hills, although many species of forest birds are present throughout the Hills.

Some of the most interesting animals of Iowa's Loess Hills are woodland inhabitants: the rare Keen's myotis and the woodland vole, chuck-will's-widow and summer tanager (southerly birds uncommon in Iowa), the beautiful zebra swallowtail (an uncommon butterfly that feeds on pawpaw leaves), and several other rare woodland or woodland-edge butterflies (Henry's elfin, the hickory hairstreak, and the Olympia marblewing, among others). Well-studied Waubonsie State Park is known to be the home of all of those woodland species, a site where southern birds such as Bewick's wren and the Louisiana water thrush have been seen, and a refuge for the Great Plains skink (endangered in Iowa), which inhabits small, rugged prairie openings in the woods. The forest-dominated park is characterized as one of Iowa's most important habitats for rare butterflies and most interesting birding spots. (Rare woodland animals and their distributions are discussed in more detail in the last part of this chapter.) Although several woodland animals such as the woodland vole, evening bat, red milk snake, and spicebush swallowtail are uncommon or on Iowa's list of rare species, the vast majority are common. Few of Missouri's rare species have woodland affinities.

Several species, including uncommon ones such as the gray fox (fig. 56) and common species such as the white-tailed deer and eastern cottontail, are known to be benefiting from the upslope and northward expansion of woodlands. Reptiles such as eastern hognose, ringneck, red milk, black rat, and DeKay's snakes are increasing. In fact, all reptiles that are increasing in the Hills are woodland species. Birds such as the chuck-will's-widow and summer tanager are thought to be pushing their range limits northward. However, those birds, along with certain other animals such as the woodland vole, gray squirrel, gray fox, small-mouthed salamander, and zebra swallowtail, are presently limited to the southernmost Hills. Although some Hills animals are near the limits of their ranges, with centers of distribution in forests to the south and east, most woodland species tend to be widespread throughout the Midwest.

Variations among Woodlands

Loess Hills woodlands can be described generally, but outlining woodland communities precisely is difficult in part because of the lack of information and in part because of the woodlands' lack of uniformity. Variations in the woodlands are caused by human use of the land and by naturally occurring north-south gradients, such as changes in climate and in woody species. (Attempts to define woodland communities are described in sidebar 8.)

Although the exact extent and location of presettlement woodlands are not known, prairies are thought to have been far more prevalent then than now. Certainly some of today's forests are the product of a massive and relatively recent upslope sweep of forests into prairies. But to view all of today's forests as the result of prairie invasion is far too simplistic. We know that woodlands have become more extensive since the 1800s. We also know that since settlers have arrived in the area, they have been altering the locations and characteristics of forests by cutting trees, planting trees, removing some woody species and introducing others, changing the intensity and timing of fires or eliminating fire completely, grazing cattle, and participating in other agricultural practices. Even woodlands that appear to be old and undisturbed have felt the influence of the human hand at some

SIDEBAR 8. Community Associations of Loess Hills Woodlands

Ecologists describe plant communities in one of two ways: either as a set of individual species, each of which has its own distributional pattern, or as a grouping of species that predictably cluster together to form distinct associations. Because Loess Hills woodlands have not been studied in depth, this chapter has had to use the first approach, describing approximate distributions of major species to the best of our knowledge. Future research may well define the distinct associations of Loess Hills woodland plants and reveal what step-by-step changes in composition (successional patterns) each association will naturally pass through as the community matures. For example, if we were considering deciduous woodlands that today flourish in eastern Iowa, we could reliably predict that associations of oak and hickory species would eventually become dominated by basswood and maple.

Although relatively young and unstudied, Loess Hills woodlands might be partially understood through examination of their closest neighbors, the forests that border the Missouri River valley on the Nebraska side. Those forests were thoroughly studied in the first half of this century by J. M. Aikman (1926, Aikman and Gilly 1948), who identified three upland forest communities: a red oak–basswood community with intermixed ironwood, bur oak, Kentucky coffee tree, and bitternut hickory in the moistest sites, forming extensive forests in southeastern Nebraska and groves in sheltered sites in northeastern Nebraska; a black oak–shagbark hickory association found only in slightly drier sites in southeastern Nebraska, where it forms a band between the first and third communities; and a bur oak–bitternut hickory association with numerous other tree and shrub species on the dry slopes and tops of hills, the driest and most severe sites. Given sufficient time and probably a climate moister than today's, the latter two communities theoretically would become stable (climax) red oak–basswood forests. At the tops of slopes, Nebraska's forests are bordered by shrubland dominated by hazelnut, smooth sumac, coralberry, and western snowberry. At the

time. Intact woodlands representing those of presettlement times may be the rarest of Loess Hills natural communities or may be nonexistent. Instead, today's timbered areas consist of a patchy mosaic, which includes the following types.

1. Pre- or post-settlement savannas that have been invaded by trees and shrubs.

slope bottoms, upland forests are replaced by floodplain forests. Willows dominate young floodplain forests, but cottonwood and box elder gradually invade. They in turn are replaced by ash, elm, and walnut as the community matures.

As the northern Loess Hills become increasingly dominated by forests, it will be interesting to observe whether they manifest any of the several north-south vegetational changes observed in Nebraska. There, as in the Loess Hills, the climate becomes increasingly drier and more restrictive to tree growth toward the north. In addition to decreasing the number of species, the harsher northern climate restricts the abundance and size of woodland organisms. The average height of bur oak, for example, decreases from 70 feet in southeastern Nebraska to 20 feet in northeastern Nebraska. On the most severe sites, bur oaks are like shrubs, with fewer, smaller branches forming irregularly shaped, closely spaced trees. Upriver, Nebraska's woodlands become more and more restricted to protected sites, the moisture-loving species disappear completely, and the width of the forested band narrows. Conversely, shrublands increase in dominance.

A superficial examination of Loess Hills woodlands reveals some similarities between Iowa's and Nebraska's woodlands. Basswood abounds on lower slopes, for example, and bur oak dominates upper slopes. But future research undoubtedly will disclose many distinctive traits of Hills woodland associations and their successional patterns. The dearth of woody species and the dropping out of species of oak, hickory, and maple in the northern Hills will prevent replication of successional patterns occurring farther to the east. Loess Hills woodlands will continue to change, as the species present and the associations they form are influenced by environmental traits and land-use patterns.

Perhaps most important, the fate of Hills woodlands will depend on a climate that continues to favor tree reproduction rather than prairie expansion. But beyond such generalizations, until they are better studied, Loess Hills woodlands will remain poorly described associations with an unknown ecological future.

---

2. Groups of mature trees growing where intensive grazing has eliminated tree reproduction. A flush of woody growth will occur once grazing has ceased.

3. Forests that have been selectively cut. Multiple shoots sprouting from a central cut stump of basswood or bur oak indicate past logging or another such disturbance.

4. Planted timber, including catalpa (*Catalpa speciosa*), Kentucky coffee tree, cottonwood, silver maple, box elder, green ash, black walnut, and pine (*Pinus*) and spruce (*Picea*) species.

5. Second-growth forests, appearing after the original forests had been cut.

6. Woodlands of varying ages that have remained fairly undisturbed since they invaded prairies.

7. Woodlands of varying ages that have remained fairly undisturbed since they invaded abandoned cropland or pasture.

8. Invading woodlands that have been grazed to varying degrees.

Further definition of the woodland mosaic must await future research.

RARE SPECIES AND SPECIAL FEATURES

Several distinguishing features of Loess Hills natural communities have already been described. Relatively large and remote prairies, where Great Plains species thrive and where environments resemble Southwestern deserts more than midwestern plains, differentiate the Hills from surrounding natural areas. Add to them the Hills' wide biological diversity and distinctive deep-loess geological formations, features that have helped identify the Loess Hills as a premier natural area. The chapter, to this point, has only alluded to another special characteristic: the presence of numerous rare species in the Hills. Frequently animals and plants, and even communities as a whole, are rare because they reach the edges of their range of distribution in the Hills. This section examines first the rare species and their special distributional patterns and then discusses the importance of the Loess Hills as a migrational corridor for animals and plants.

Distributional Patterns and Rare Species

As explained at the beginning of this chapter, the Loess Hills theoretically lie in the heart of the tall-grass prairie. That is, looking at the regional climate and surrounding vegetation as a whole, the Loess Hills should be covered by tall-grass prairies. In fact, Hills native communities are quite different. They include plants and animals more typical of areas far to the east and or to the west, being dominated by some of the westernmost remnants of Eastern Deciduous Forest and by an unusual eastern extension of Great Plains mixed-height grasslands. Some western species are common in the Hills—yucca in Iowa, for example, and the plains spadefoot toad, both of which are hallmarks of regions hundreds of miles to the west. Most of the western elements can be observed in Iowa and Missouri only in the Loess Hills.

Native communities, at their outermost edges, often consist of species at the edge of their range of distribution. That is obvious among Loess Hills trees and shrubs, most of which extend their range northward into the Hills from southern and eastern forests. Many woody species—seven oak species, three hickory species, white ash, mulberry, and many others—reach their northern limits of distribution somewhere in the Hills. Conversely, several western prairie plants reach their eastern or southern limits of distribution in the Hills.

The presence of organisms at their limits of distribution is, in itself, a special feature of the Hills. Here biologists can study rates of migration as ranges expand or contract. And theoretically, individuals at the outposts of their range possess the greatest freedom to diversify genetically. In addition, animals or plants from different regions that are similar enough to interbreed may do so in the few places where the edges of their range overlap. In the Hills, that happens with the eastern and western subspecies of the red-tailed hawk, the area's most common raptor.

Species close to their environmental limits—those at the edge of their range—often do not find living conditions as favorable as they would toward the center of their range. Thus species frequently decrease in abundance toward the edge of their range. They then are classified as rare or, if they are in danger of disappearing completely, as endangered. Formal definitions of such terms vary from state to state. (Terms used in Iowa and Missouri are defined in sidebar 9.)

Iowa's Hills have been called the state's most significant region for unusual plants and rare animals, a retreat for the rarest mammals of the state. The dry prairies of northwestern Missouri, including Missouri's Loess Hills and surrounding loess regions, harbor one of the greatest concentrations of restricted, rare, and endangered plants of any terrestrial natural community in the state. In spite of dramatic alterations through human use, the Hills' rugged landscape maintains significantly large and intact wild lands to provide refuge for species that have decreased or disappeared elsewhere.

Because environmental conditions and thus the abundance of various species differ from state to state, one state's list of rare species is never identical to its neighbor's list. A total of 45 Loess Hills species are classified

SIDEBAR 9. Terminology for Categorizing Rare Species

General definitions of various terms for rare species are given below, followed by the official definitions used to classify rare species in the states of Iowa and Missouri.

Terminology and ranking systems for rare species vary from state to state because each state, as well as the federal government, prepares its own listing of rare species, which applies only to animals and plants within its own geographic boundaries. Because the terms apply to a species' abundance within a limited region rather than to its abundance on the earth as a whole, each state's listing of rare species is different. Thus a species might be rare in one state and common in a neighboring state.

"endangered"—threatened with extinction
Iowa: in danger of extinction throughout all or a significant part of its range.
Missouri: prospects for survival in the state are in immediate jeopardy.

"threatened"—about to become endangered
Iowa: likely to become an endangered species within the foreseeable future throughout all or part of its range.
Missouri does not use this category.

"rare"—uncommon, about to become threatened
Iowa: may become jeopardized in the future but is currently surviving; found in a limited number of sites.
Missouri: present in the state in small numbers; if the environment worsens, its continued presence in the state may become endangered.

"species of special concern"—thought to be uncommon; status is being monitored
Iowa: problems of status or distribution are suspected but not documented; no special protection is afforded a species under this rule.
Missouri: placed on the Watch List for any of a variety of reasons; the Department of Conservation seeks additional information on such species.

Note: Definitions have been taken from *Checklist of Rare and Endangered Species of Missouri, August 1985* (Missouri Department of Conservation), and from the Iowa Administrative Code (571), Chapter 77: Endangered and Threatened Plant and Animal Species List.

as rare in Iowa (table 8). Of those, 21 are on the state's threatened or endangered list. Nineteen of Missouri's 37 rare Loess Hills species are in danger of extinction in Missouri (table 9). In particular, the Hills house a
goodly number of rare prairie plants, mammals, and reptiles.

Only five of Iowa's and Missouri's rare species are held in common: the
Great Plains skink, upland sandpiper, Cooper's hawk, plains pocket gopher,
and buffalograss. That divergence is due in large part to north-south variations in the Loess Hills. Iowa's northern Hills, with their larger prairies and
greater diversity of prairie plants, provide habitat for the greatest number
of Great Plains species. Many are rare even in the northern Hills and do
not extend at all into Missouri's far southern Hills. Tumblegrass, buffalo
berry, and ten-petal blazing star are examples of such species. Great Plains
species that do extend south into Missouri may be rare there because Missouri's remaining dry prairies are so small. Several prairie species regularly
found in Iowa (such as yucca, skeleton weed, great-flowered beardtongue,
and the white-tailed jackrabbit) are classified as endangered on Missouri's
dry prairie remnants. The decrease in abundance and diversity of prairie
species from north to south is evident even within Missouri. The Hills prairies of Atchison County are more diverse and have a greater number of
rare species than do prairies to the south in Holt County.

An opposite gradient holds true for Loess Hills woodlands. Missouri,
with its greater abundance of diverse forests, classifies only a few of its
Loess Hills woodland species as rare. Species common in Missouri may be
rare in Iowa's Loess Hills, where woodlands are more restricted, drier, and
less diverse. Iowa's Hills contain more than a dozen rare woodland species.

Several of the region's rare species are western species, typical of the
Great Plains, which reach the eastern limits of their range in the Hills. That
is true of two of the Loess Hills' least common animals, Iowa's prairie
rattlesnake and Great Plains skink, both of which are widespread in more-
western states. The last few prairie rattlers east of the Missouri River survive in the extensive prairies of Plymouth County, Iowa. In contrast, low
numbers of the secretive Great Plains skink inhabit minuscule prairie openings at the edge of bur oak woodlands in the far southern Hills. Both animals are on the verge of extinction in the Loess Hills, the first because of
willful destruction by humans and loss of habitat, the second through
woody invasion of the last few prairie openings where the skink is still
found. The northern grasshopper mouse, a threatened species in Iowa,
reaches its southeastern limits in northwestern Iowa and the most northern

TABLE 8. Rare Plants and Animals of Iowa's Loess Hills

BUTTERFLIES
- ☐ Dusted skipper, *Atrytonopsis hianna* (prairies; special concern)
- ☐ Olympia marblewing, *Euchloe olympia* (woodlands, prairie openings; threatened)
- ☐ Zebra swallowtail, *Eurytides marcellus* (woodlands; rare)
- ☐ Ottoe skipper, *Hesperia ottoe* (prairies; rare)
- ☐ Pawnee skipper, *Hesperia pawnee* (prairies; rare)
- ☐ Henry's elfin, *Incisala henrici* (woodlands, prairie openings; rare)
- ☐ Olive hairstreak, *Mitoura gryneus* (cedar stands; rare)
- ☐ Spicebush swallowtail, *Pterourus troilus* (woodlands; rare)
- ☐ Hickory hairstreak, *Satyrium caryaevorum* (woodlands; rare)

REPTILES AND AMPHIBIANS
- ☐ Small-mouthed salamander, *Ambystoma texanum* (woodlands; rare)
- ☐ Western worm snake, *Carphophis amoenus vermis* (woodlands; rare)
- ☐ Prairie, or six-lined, racerunner, *Cnemidophorus sexlineatus viridis* (prairies; rare) [1]
- ☐ Prairie rattlesnake, *Crotalus viridis viridis* (prairies; endangered) [1]
- ☐ Great Plains skink, *Eumeces obsoletus* (prairies; endangered) [1]
- ☐ Speckled kingsnake, *Lampropeltis getulus holbrooki* (woodlands; endangered)
- ☐ Red milk snake, *Lampropeltis triangulum syspila* (woodlands; rare)
- ☐ Ornate box turtle, *Terrapene ornata ornata* (prairies; threatened) [1]

BIRDS
- ☐ Cooper's hawk, *Accipiter cooperii* (open woodlands; endangered; not confirmed as breeder in Hills)
- ☐ Upland sandpiper, *Bartramia longicauda* (prairies; rare)

MAMMALS
- ☐ Bobcat, *Lynx rufus* (shrublands; endangered)
- ☐ Woodland vole, *Microtus pinetorum* (forests; threatened)
- ☐ Keen's myotis, *Myotis keenii septentrionalis* (forests; rare)
- ☐ Evening bat, *Nycticeius humeralis* (woodlands; rare)
- ☐ Northern grasshopper mouse, *Onychomys leucogaster* (grasslands, cultivated fields; threatened) [1]
- ☐ Plains pocket mouse, *Perognathus flavescens* (prairies; endangered) [1]
- ☐ Southern bog lemming, *Synaptomys cooperi* (moist grasslands; special concern)

PLANTS
- ☐ Red three-awn, *Aristida longiseta* (prairies; rare) [1]
- ☐ Engelmann's milkweed, *Asclepias engelmanniana* (prairies; endangered) [1]
- ☐ Missouri milk vetch, *Astragalus missouriensis* (prairies; rare) [1]
- ☐ Prairie moonwort, *Botrychium campestre* (prairie edges; rare)
- ☐ Buffalograss, *Buchloe dactyloides* (prairies; endangered, last confirmed report Thorne, 1956) [1]
- ☐ Rocky mountain sedge, *Carex saximontana* (woodlands; endangered) [1]
- ☐ Wavy-leaved thistle, *Cirsium undu-*

TABLE 8 (*continued*)

latum (prairies, disturbed sites; endangered)

☐ Coralroot orchid, *Corallorhiza odontorhiza* (woodlands; rare)

☐ Prairie tea, *Croton monanthogynus* (prairies, open woodlands, roadsides; rare)

☐ Biscuit-root, or fennel lomatium, *Lomatium foeniculaceum* (prairies; endangered)[1]

☐ Ten-petal blazing star, or sand lily, *Mentzelia decapetala* (prairies, disturbed sites; threatened)[1]

☐ Rice grass, *Oryzopsis racemosa* (woodlands; rare)

☐ Slender penstemon, *Penstemon gracilis* (prairies, threatened)[1]

☐ Spreading yellow cress, *Rorippa sinuata* (wet sites; rare)

☐ Tumblegrass, *Schedonnardus paniculatus* (disturbed grasslands; threatened)[1]

☐ Sensitive briar, *Schrankia nuttallii* (prairies, open woodlands, roadsides; rare)

☐ Buffalo berry, *Shepherdia argentea* (prairies; threatened)[1]

☐ Cowboy's delight, or scarlet globemallow, *Sphaeralcea coccinea* (prairies; threatened)[1]

☐ Spear grass, *Stipa comata* (prairies; endangered)

---

[1] Western species typical of Great Plains grasslands, which for the most part do not extend eastward from the Hills.

Note: See sidebar 9 for definitions of rare species terms used in table. Table limited to resident or breeding species. Adapted from the 1987 Loess Hills rare species list provided by the Bureau of Preserves and Ecological Services, Iowa Department of Natural Resources, Des Moines, and from the Iowa Administrative Code (571), Chapter 77: Endangered and Threatened Plant and Animal Species List; with the use of Novacek, Roosa, and Pusateri, 1985. *Flora of the Great Plains* (Great Plains Flora Association, 1986) and *Atlas of the Flora of the Great Plains* (Barkley, 1977) used as references.

Hills. The plains hognose snake, a western species that is rare in Missouri and absent from Iowa's Loess Hills, is restricted in Missouri to the northwestern corner of the state.

Ten-petal blazing star is one of Iowa's many rare plants on the eastern edge of its range in the Loess Hills (fig. 57). As with most threatened species, casual observers are not likely to see this plant, but once viewed, its distinctive traits are easily remembered. Growing on steep and eroded west-facing bluffs, the three- to five-foot-tall stems bear cream-colored flowers sometimes more than four inches wide, the centers of which are

TABLE 9. Rare Plants and Animals of Missouri's Loess Hills

REPTILES AND AMPHIBIANS
- [ ] Western fox snake, *Elaphe vulpina vulpina* (wet prairies or marshes; endangered)
- [ ] Great Plains skink, *Eumeces obsoletus* (prairies; rare)[1]
- [ ] Plains hognose snake, *Heterodon nasicus nasicus* (prairies; rare)[1]

BIRDS
- [ ] Cooper's hawk, *Accipiter cooperii* (open woodlands; endangered, not confirmed as breeder in Hills)
- [ ] Sharp-shinned hawk, *Accipiter striatus* (open woodlands; endangered, not confirmed as breeder in Hills)
- [ ] Upland sandpiper, *Bartramia longicauda* (prairies, pastures, hay fields; rare)
- [ ] Marsh hawk, or northern harrier, *Circus cyaneus* (prairies, marshes; endangered)
- [ ] Common barn owl, *Tyto alba* (farmyards, fields, marshes; endangered)

MAMMALS
- [ ] White-tailed jackrabbit, *Lepus townsendii* (prairies, pasture; endangered)[1]
- [ ] Long-tailed weasel, *Mustela frenata* (widespread; rare)
- [ ] Least weasel, *Mustela nivalis* (prairies and other grasslands; rare)
- [ ] Plains pocket mouse, *Perognathus flavescens* (prairies; status undetermined)[1]
- [ ] Franklin's ground squirrel, *Spermophilus franklinii* (tall grasslands; status undetermined)
- [ ] Meadow jumping mouse, *Zapus hudsonius* (grasslands; status undetermined)

PLANTS
- [ ] Thimbleweed, *Anemone cylindrica* (prairies; rare)
- [ ] Silky wormwood, *Artemisia dracunculus, A. glauca* (woodland edge, dry open places; Watch List)
- [ ] Rayless aster, *Aster brachyactis* (disturbed areas, prairies; endangered)[1]
- [ ] Lotus milk vetch, *Astragalus lotiflorus* (prairies; endangered)[1]
- [ ] Blue grama, *Bouteloua gracilis* (prairies; Watch List)
- [ ] Hairy grama, *Bouteloua hirsuta* (prairies; Watch List)
- [ ] Buffalograss, *Buchloe dactyloides* (prairies; Watch List)[1]
- [ ] Wood's sedge, *Carex tetanica* (prairies; endangered)
- [ ] Downy paintbrush, *Castilleja sessiliflora* (prairies; endangered)
- [ ] Rocky Mountain bee plant, *Cleome serrulata* (prairies, waste areas; Watch List)[1]
- [ ] Nine-anther prairie clover, *Dalea enneandra* (prairies; endangered)[1]
- [ ] Scarlet gaura, *Gaura coccinea* var. *coccinea* (prairies; Watch List)[1]
- [ ] Western wild lettuce, *Lactuca ludoviciana* (prairies; endangered)[1]
- [ ] Blue lettuce, *Lactuca pulchella* (prairies, roadsides; endangered)[1]
- [ ] Dotted gayfeather, or blazing star, *Liatris punctata* var. *nebraskana* (prairies; Watch List)
- [ ] Skeleton weed, *Lygodesmia juncea* (prairies; endangered)[1]

TABLE 9 (*continued*)

☐ Purple locoweed, *Oxytropis lambertii* (prairies; endangered)[1]

☐ Great-flowered beardtongue, or shell-leaf penstemon, *Penstemon grandiflorus* (prairies; endangered)

☐ Silver-leaf scurf pea, *Psoralea argophylla* (prairies; Watch List)

☐ Alkali sacaton, *Sporobolus airoides* (prairies; endangered)[1]

☐ Western snowberry, or wolfberry, *Symphoricarpos occidentalis* (prairies, woodland edge; endangered)[1]

☐ Rock elm, *Ulmus thomasi* (woodlands; Watch List)

☐ Yucca, *Yucca glauca* (prairies; endangered)[1]

---

[1] Western species typical of Great Plains grasslands, which for the most part do not extend eastward from the Hills.

Note: See sidebar 9 for definitions of rare species terms used in table. Table limited to resident or breeding species. Adapted from Wilson, 1984, and Johnson, 1987 (animals), with plants compiled from *Checklist of Rare and Endangered Species of Missouri, August 1985* (Missouri Department of Conservation) with the use of Novacek, Roosa, and Pusateri, 1985. *Flora of the Great Plains* (Great Plains Flora Association, 1986) and *Atlas of the Flora of the Great Plains* (Barkley, 1977) used as references. With the assistance of Virginia K. Wallace (botanist), Dennis Figg (wildlife ecologist), and James D. Wilson (ornithologist), Missouri Department of Conservation, Jefferson City, Missouri; Doug Ladd (director of stewardship), the Nature Conservancy, St. Louis, Missouri.

---

filled with many dozens of stamens. While maturing, the flowers open during night and close during the day, giving the species another of its common names, "moonflower." Even more noteworthy are the rough, thistle-like leaves, which along with mature fruits are covered by multicellular hairs. The species, confined to a few sites in the northern Hills, fills an ecological niche similar to that of cactus in deserts. Other of Iowa's rare plants that reach so far eastward only in the Loess Hills include the threatened cowboy's delight, endangered Engelmann's milkweed, and endangered biscuit-root. (At least 17 Great Plains plants reach their eastern limits of distribution in Loess Hills prairies, but not all of them are rare.)

Three-fourths of Iowa's rare plants, 14 out of the 19 rare plants listed, are prairie plants; the figure is even greater for Missouri's rare species (21 out of the 23 listed). Most of those prairie plants are western species—tumblegrass, buffalo berry, buffalograss, and lotus milk vetch being a few ex-

Figure 57. *Ten-petal blazing star, a distinctive western species, is on the edge of its range and very rare in the Loess Hills. Bellamy Parks Jansen.*

amples. More than half of Loess Hills rare plants (11 of Iowa's and 13 of Missouri's) have centers of distribution in the Great Plains or farther to the west, where they may be quite common. They have developed mechanisms for surviving in the Hills' hot, dry, upland prairies, which are in danger of disappearing, especially in the southern Hills. A high percentage of rare reptiles and amphibians in both states also have western affinities.

Not all rare prairie plants are limited to the Hills in Iowa and Missouri. Red three-awn and spear grass, for example, are found in other western Iowa prairies, and prairie tea, wavy-leaved thistle, and sensitive briar are more widespread east of the Hills.

Loess Hills woodlands also claim a few of the rare plants—coralroot orchid, ricegrass, and Rocky Mountain sedge in Iowa, and rock elm in Missouri. None of Iowa's woody plants are considered to be rare, with the possible exception of pawpaw, which grows in Iowa only in Fremont County.

Although many rare or special animals are eastwardly displaced prairie species, some in Iowa's Hills follow other distributional patterns. The woodland vole, a species common in the southeastern United States but threatened in Iowa, extends northward in a few sites into Iowa's moist deciduous woodlands; two populations have been located in the Hills' southern forests. The rare evening bat reaches its northwestern limits in Stone State Park's woodlands. Small numbers of Iowa's rarest nonvenomous snake, the endangered speckled kingsnake, live on the periphery of larger populations in southern woodlands, along with the uncommon western worm snake and small-mouthed salamander. That pattern is copied by birds in Iowa that are uncommon but not officially classified as rare, such as the chuck-will's-widow and the summer tanager, and by the eastern chipmunk. A few isolated chipmunk populations in Iowa's Hills are near the western edge of the woodland species' range.

Modern-day distribution patterns demonstrate that in past years, some rare Loess Hills species were more widely distributed in dry habitats east of the Hills. Two such animals, the plains pocket mouse (described earlier in this chapter) and the ornate box turtle, today survive in the Loess Hills and in far eastern Iowa, on Big Sand Mound next to the Mississippi River. There and in a few other locations scattered across Iowa, dry environments and well-drained, friable soil provide the conditions that those species require.

The southern bog lemming is one of Iowa's few rare species that does well in ecosystems modified by humans, providing that they meet the lem-

Figure 58. *The southern bog lemming, one of the few rare species that inhabits certain exotic as well as native plant communities in the Loess Hills. Charles W. Schwartz.*

ming's need for heavy grass cover (fig. 58). In the Hills, it is found in low, moist, heavy stands of bluegrass, an introduced plant, although the mouse-like animal also inhabits moist woods, marshes, and prairie swales. Also found in surrounding states and Canada, the lemming joins several other Iowa rare species such as the bobcat, Keen's myotis, and red milk snake as animals that are uncommon but nowhere near their limits of distribution.

The relatively large number of Iowa's rare Loess Hills butterflies can be explained in part by researchers' concentration on that particular invertebrate. Perhaps more important is the inbred habitat specificity of the insects. Although larger animals typically rely on a variety of food sources, many butterflies lay their eggs on only one or a few plant species. Many of the small, drab butterflies called skippers, for example, are prairie obligates, species that cannot survive in other plant communities. If the prairie plants that the butterflies depend upon disappear, the butterflies also disappear. Most prairie obligates have declined considerably because of the loss of prairie habitat and are now rare across the United States. Few or no prairie obligates can be expected on tracts of less than 15 or 20 acres, and as much as 1,000 acres of prairie may be needed for long-term maintenance of such butterfly species. In Iowa, such large prairies exist only in the

Figure 59. *The ottoe skipper, one of several rare Loess Hills butterflies that can live only in prairies. Charles W. Schwartz.*

Loess Hills, and they are able to maintain substantial populations of two prairie obligates—the regal fritillary and ottoe skipper—as well as smaller populations of the rare pawnee skipper and dusted skipper. Hills populations of the ottoe skipper are among the largest remaining in the world (fig. 59).

The forests of Iowa's Hills also contain a rich assemblage of rare butterflies. Field biologists studying Waubonsie State Park have characterized it as one of the state's most important habitats for rare butterflies. Six uncommon or rare species (the zebra swallowtail—an obligate of the pawpaw tree, white-M hairstreak, hickory hairstreak, hoary edge, Olympia marblewing, and Henry's elfin) have been documented there. The latter three are known from only a few localities in Iowa. Most woodland butterflies, being users of woodland edges or openings, may have been species of the savannas that were found throughout presettlement Iowa. The spicebush swallowtail, another rare species of more northerly Hills woodlands, prefers shady forests to prairie openings.

No bird species are restricted to the Loess Hills, and only a few Hills bird residents are classified as rare, although in 1988 a nest of bald eagles was reported. Bald eagle nestings had not been previously recorded for the

Hills. Iowa's bird watchers appreciate that few places allow better opportunities to find the western kingbird, more abundant in western states, and
three species with more southerly ranges: the blue grosbeak, summer tanager, and chuck-will's-widow. All three are uncommon in Iowa's Hills but
rare or absent elsewhere in the state. The latter two are found only on the
Hills' southern woodlands, although they may be expanding their range
northward as the forests expand. Many of Iowa's Hills birds are included
in the National Audubon Society's 1982 Blue List of declining or special-
concern species: Bell's vireo, which is still common in the Hills' shrubby
ravines, dickcissel, grasshopper sparrow, upland sandpiper, ruby-throated
hummingbird, hairy woodpecker, western bluebird, eastern meadowlark,
and yellow warbler. The wild turkey, greater prairie chicken, and common
barn owl, once widespread in Iowa but then eliminated from the state,
have been reintroduced in the Hills. Only the wild turkey has successfully
established breeding populations.

Investigations in recent years have revealed some hidden treasures. In
1983, the supposedly extirpated ornate box turtle was rediscovered in
Iowa's Hills, 40 years after it had last been seen there. Two other rare species, the plains pocket mouse and southern bog lemming, also were rediscovered in the early eighties, more than a decade after they had last
been observed in Iowa's Hills. The plains spadefoot, a toad now known to
be widespread in Iowa's Hills, was first found in the state in 1967. It may
have recently migrated into Iowa or may be a long-term resident that was
missed in previous surveys.

Perhaps the biggest surprise was the 1982 discovery of the prairie moonwort, a rare species never before known to science (fig. 60). Persons attending a nature hike at the Loess Hills Prairie Seminar in Monona County,
Iowa, discovered the tiny fern, usually under two inches in height. Since
then, it has been found in several other Hills locations as well as in Nebraska, southwestern Minnesota, and possibly sites northward into Canada. The fern typically grows at the edge of woodlands, sheltered by a few
shrubs, where it survives the full rigor of the Hills' prairie climate by growing above ground for only a short period each year. Emerging in early
spring and shedding spores around late May, the fern's aboveground
leaves wither and disappear by mid-June. Only underground portions of
the species, rhizomes and gametophytes protected by overlying soil, remain to overwinter and give birth to more visible plants once again the
following spring.

Figure 60. *Prairie moonwort, a newly discovered fern that was first identified in the Loess Hills. Randall D. Williams.*

The Loess Hills as a Migrational Corridor

Today and for thousands of preceding years, the richness of the Hills has been augmented by the migration of plants and animals. Indeed the entire history of the Hills can be explained as an ebb and flow of species, entering or leaving the Hills in response to their environmental needs and the conditions offered by the Hills. Forest species gradually moved into the Hills from the south and east; the Loess Hills prairies were created when western species entered the Hills primarily from the north and west (see sidebar 7).

The Hills also demonstrate more obvious and rapid migrations, serving possibly as a significant migrational corridor for raptors. Such use is logical, since uplifting air currents along the loess bluffs provide the soaring conditions required by birds of prey. Species such as the red-tailed hawk, Cooper's hawk, sharp-shinned hawk, and rough-legged hawk have been observed moving along the bluffs in late fall. More research is needed to establish the importance of the flyway.

Informal observations suggest that the Hills, along with forests in northeastern Iowa, provide safe shelter for greater numbers of wintering raptors than are found elsewhere in Iowa. The fairly extensive, isolated ecosystems seem to provide abundant feeding grounds and resting sites for wintering great horned owls, red-tailed hawks, American kestrels, rough-legged hawks, and occasionally a golden eagle or prairie falcon.

Although evidence establishing the importance of the Loess Hills as a migrational corridor is still being collected, there is no doubt whatsoever that the Hills stretch out along one of North America's major flyways for migrating waterfowl (fig. 61). Migrations along the Missouri River, directly adjacent to the Hills, must have been a sight beyond belief before the river's wetlands and the waterfowl breeding grounds farther north were converted to agricultural land and dramatically reduced in size. But migration along that flyway still is spectacular and can best be appreciated where birds congregate to feed and rest: at Squaw Creek and DeSoto national wildlife refuges, and at Forney Lake and Riverton state wildlife areas in southwestern Iowa. Geese and ducks congregate by the hundreds of thousands during the peak of fall migration. Spring migration, in February and March, is a more leisurely affair, with bird populations spreading out over time. And, attracted by an abundant food source, the bald eagle, bird of our national emblem and now on the federal endangered-species list, fol-

Figure 61. *Snow geese migrating along the Missouri River valley. Randall D. Williams.*

lows waterfowl to those refuges. Squaw Creek is home to the nation's largest wintering populations of bald eagles east of the Rockies.

Plant communities and animals will continue their rhythmic and predictable movements up and down the Hills day after day, age after age. The Hills will never be static. Today, western prairie plants such as ten-petal blazing star and western prairie clover continue to migrate along the Hills. Forest plants push upslope and northward into prairies. In response, populations of woodland animals such as chuck-will's-widow, gray fox, and white-tailed deer increase and move northward, while populations of animals inhabiting small prairie openings (ornate box turtle, plains pocket mouse, Great Plains skink) shrink. Elsewhere animal populations migrate in search of a safe refuge, as their habitats are converted from natural areas to uses that will serve humans more directly. In future years, the species may change but the migrations will continue, as long as the Hills retain their wild and free character.

⋘ SIX ⋙

THE LOESS HILLS
OF THE FUTURE

Change is certainly not new to the Loess Hills. The landscape has been characterized by changes in the types of plant and animal communities present, their locations, and their exact species composition. But rapid change of the type that has occurred in the last 150 years has happened in the Hills only once. It can be traced to a single factor: the arrival of humans with modern technologies. With Euro-American settlement came a wave of local extinction and massive conversion of diverse native communities to simple associations introduced from eastern states. The natural processes of erosion, mass wasting, and gully cutting were accelerated. Those processes, along with construction of mines and roads and other topographic alterations, reshaped the Hills. The march of woodlands into prairies was set in motion. The shrunken prairies that remained were degraded through grazing and other agricultural uses. Sensitive native species declined, while adaptable natives increased along with species recently introduced to the region. Such changes occurred rapidly and produced dramatic alterations in the abundance, location, and nature of presettlement ecosystems. Both in the Hills and on adjacent floodplains, natural areas (especially communities dominated by sensitive native species) were reduced to a fraction of their original size. The remaining natural areas were controlled as much by human influences as by natural processes.

Those changes and the one species that induced them are here to stay. Thus, it is worth examining our relationship to the Loess Hills and questioning how our actions will alter the landscape in the future. What will a visitor 100 or 500 years hence find there? Will all sites be maximally utilized for food production, as is true for most of the Midwest now? Will large sections of the Hills be abandoned as too delicate for sustained agricultural use? Will they be allowed to revert to natural communities once again? If so what will those communities be—solid forest, or a mixture of prairie and woodland as in presettlement times? Or, perhaps, will erosion and mass wasting of the Hills increase to the point that the region is no longer worth describing and preserving?

The answers to those questions rest in part on what we humans do to preserve and manage the Loess Hills today. The Hills may never again be completely dominated by natural forces. Instead, human uses such as urbanization could continue to destroy native communities. Following a century-plus of intensive human use, only 3 percent to 5 percent of the original Loess Hills prairies remain. They are confined primarily to windswept ridgetops and steep slopes. Many have been degraded through agricultural use, overgrazing in particular, and through intensive recreational use, invading shrubs, and continued erosion.

Yet the Hills retain possibilities that are unseen in the rest of the Midwest, where prairies have been all but eliminated. The 3 percent to 5 percent of the Loess Hills covered by prairies greatly exceeds the fraction of a percent of prairie remaining elsewhere in Iowa. Prairie preserves of a thousand acres are conceivable in the far northern Hills, which contain one of Iowa's largest remaining roadless areas. Even larger natural areas, encompassing mixtures of prairie and woodland, could be established elsewhere in the Hills.

Furthermore, management for native species can be compatible with human use of the Hills (fig. 62). Maintenance of prairies and woodlands provides benefits for private landowners as well as public agencies. Sustained agricultural productivity can be achieved on well-managed prairie pastures. Prairies are increasingly seen as desirable recreational lands, with a special beauty and appeal not found in other plant communities. Woodlands can provide a cash crop while preventing soil erosion. Humans can live in and use the Hills productively without further destroying the land's natural features, especially if private landowners are encouraged and assisted in natural-area management.

Figure 62. *Possibilities for preservation of special features are great in the Loess Hills. Note this farm's backdrop of native prairie, showing that preservation need not conflict with human use. Proper management and preservation can be beneficial to private landowners and public agencies as well as to native species and natural areas. Don Poggensee.*

PRESERVATION OF NATURAL AREAS

To most people, preservation of natural areas is synonymous with public land acquisition, and indeed much of this section focuses on acquisition projects. But to equate the two in the Loess Hills is to do a disservice to the land and to residents interested in its long-term care, for two reasons. First, acquiring land is only one step toward assuring its preservation. Holding land without a management plan is, for most tracts, to relinquish the prairies to invading woodlands and the loess to continued substantial erosion. Second, the vast majority of land within the Hills is in private hands and will remain there. Preservation of the Hills must include plans for working with private landowners on techniques to blend human use with occupation by native species. Indeed, some private landowners have already shown concern for rare features found on their land. They have taken steps on their own to perpetuate those features.

On private tracts, as on public, the future of natural lands depends not on ownership but on how the lands are handled. Agricultural use of private land holdings and recreational use of public lands can continue without destroying natural features. The secret lies in wise management.

Publicly owned lands in the Hills are numerous, although they encompass a relatively small portion of the total land area. In 1986, an estimated 8,500 acres of the total 672,000 acres in Iowa's Loess Hills were in public ownership. In Iowa, public lands include three state parks (Stone State Park in the northern Hills, Preparation Canyon in the middle, and Waubonsie in Iowa's southern Hills), the Loess Hills Wildlife Area (currently the largest publicly owned tract in the Hills), and a few other state-owned areas, including the beginnings of a state forest. City parks within Sioux City and Council Bluffs and numerous smaller parks and preserves owned by Iowa's county conservation boards, only some of which contain native plant and animal associations, are also public lands. In Missouri, public lands include a corner of the federally owned Squaw Creek National Wildlife Refuge, two Department of Conservation tracts (one of which is jointly owned with the Nature Conservancy), and a state forest.

Most public acquisitions were made before the mid-seventies. Although many of the earlier purchases protect natural and rare features of significance, inclusion of such features was not a primary criterion in the land's selection. Since then, beginning with the building of today's Loess Hills Wildlife Area, selection criteria have changed. Purchases often have been made on the basis of exemplary geological and biological features.

That change in emphasis was given major impetus when the Nature Conservancy, an international nonprofit conservation organization dedicated to preserving rare species and natural ecosystems, proclaimed preservation of prime areas in the Loess Hills a national priority. Following a search for high-quality prairies with rare species, the Nature Conservancy purchased the 800-acre Five-Ridge Prairie in Plymouth County, Iowa (now owned by the Plymouth County Conservation Board), and the 157-acre Sioux City Prairie (fig. 63). The latter is dedicated to the memory of a revered local environmental educator, Carolyn Benne. The educational value of the Sioux City Prairie is heightened because of its location in the heart of Sioux City, adjacent to Briar Cliff College.

Formally recognizing an area's special features does not necessarily mean changing the land's ownership. In 1986, approximately 10,000 acres in Harrison and Monona counties, Iowa, were designated a National Natural Landmark. The designated land will remain in private ownership. Pri-

Figure 63. The Sioux City Prairie preserves a diversity of native species within a large metropolitan area. This prairie is a valuable recreational and educational asset to Sioux City residents and to students at the adjacent Briar Cliff College. Photo by the author.

vate land uses are not restricted, although conservation of natural features will be encouraged. The designation of the National Natural Landmark formally establishes the region as one of the nation's prominent natural areas and culminates a lengthy push for national recognition of the Loess Hills' unique features.

Two areas, Five-Ridge Prairie and Turin Loess Hills Preserve (the southern unit of the Loess Hills Wildlife Area), have been dedicated into the Iowa State Preserves System. To enter the system, an area must meet stringent qualifying criteria; its natural features must be selected as exemplary and worthy of the highest protection afforded by Iowa law, which all state preserves receive in perpetuity.

High-quality lands also can be registered with the Nature Conservancy. Registration does not mandate new land-use practices, but participating landowners have voluntarily agreed to protect important natural features and are given advice on how to do so. Well over a dozen publicly and privately owned sites in Iowa's Loess Hills, mostly prairies, have been registered with the state Nature Conservancy office.

One final land conservation effort promises to create the largest Loess Hills preserve in existence. The Loess Hills Pioneer State Forest in northern Harrison County and southern Monona County, now being purchased by the state of Iowa, will eventually exceed 17,000 acres in four separate management units. Some natural historians view the formation of a forest preserve as ironic, since invading forests are aggressively destroying Iowa's last major prairies. In answer to those concerns, Iowa officials state that management of the land will be focused on forests, but attempts also will be made to preserve prairies and other natural features of significance.

Future preservation of native communities through any of a number of means—purchase, preserve dedication, registry, easement, or simply management efforts of private landowners—is highly desirable. Sites of archaeological importance should also be preserved and respectfully managed. The amount of land designated for preservation should reflect the growing demand for human access to the Loess Hills and the requirements for propagation of special species and communities. Large, unbroken tracts and small tracts are both needed. Large tracts should be big enough to assure long-term breeding success of rare species. Certain prairie butterflies, for example, may need at least 1,000 prairie acres for long-term viability. Selection of small tracts should be based on the presence of rare plants, animals, and associations, especially those of prairies, since today's public lands already include the majority of the mature, diverse woodlands found in the Hills. Placement of future preserves also should allow migration of species up and down the Loess Hills. Preservation of dry prairies in Missouri, near their southern terminus, is especially critical since so few prairies remain there, and those that do remain contain a relatively large number of Missouri's rare species.

MANAGEMENT OF NATURAL FEATURES

Selection of natural areas for preservation will be for naught if the areas are not managed for perpetual survival of a balanced assemblage of native plant and animal residents. Ideally, a management plan addressing the necessary types and amount of human intervention would be produced for the region as a whole. The plan would propose actions to be taken on both public and private lands. The amount of erosion and stream siltation considered to be acceptable could be assessed. Practices that would aid in lowering erosion rates to those levels could then be encouraged. An estimate could be made of the amount of land needed to maintain in perpetuity the special communities unique to the Hills. That estimate, along with an inventory of areas containing rare and endangered species, would permit the selection of the best candidates for preservation as natural areas. Where use for other purposes was considered reasonable, ways to minimize degradation of natural communities while maintaining the land's productivity could be recommended. All of those plans could be meshed with increased opportunities for human access to public lands. Nondestructive recreational uses could be encouraged through educational and interpretive programs. Where preservation of natural features was the primary goal, permissible land uses could be designated. Qualities to be preserved could be outlined, along with a plan of action for maintaining the features. Although that is the intended goal on many public lands, a scientifically designed management plan focusing on perpetuity of prime natural features often is lacking.

Such a total Loess Hills land-use plan and policy would take time to develop, but components of the plan could be implemented immediately. The chief ingredient needed is the cooperation and assistance of agencies and individuals controlling Loess Hills lands, whether they are city, county, state, or federal land managers, conservation organizations, or private landowners. Persons in control of lands can consider taking steps to promote natural-area health, ranging from decreasing the density of grazing cattle to treating prairies to routine prescribed burns. Knowledgeable local residents and persons with training and experience, such as employees of Iowa's Department of Natural Resources, need to share their talents. Private landowners must have someone they can contact regularly, who will provide information and assistance as needed.

The following sections consider management of all lands within the Hills, regardless of ownership or use, and they address four proposed goals: (1) minimize further destruction of natural communities, (2) maximize the diversity of native species, (3) maintain the integrity of existing natural communities, and (4) control erosion, gully cutting, and slope instability to the greatest degree possible.

Minimize Further Destruction of Natural Communities. Only a small percentage of the original prairies remain in the Hills, and they generally are found on sites such as ridgetops and steep south- and west-facing slopes that are inaccessible and extremely erosion-prone. Further destruction of the prairies for purposes such as suburban spread, increased

Figure 64. Further destruction of natural communities must be weighed against the land's natural values. Here prairies were destroyed as loess was mined for construction of Interstate 29 in Missouri. Don Kurz, Missouri Department of Conservation

agricultural production, or procurement of loess for landfill must be weighed against the land's natural values (fig. 64).

The Hills' few diverse, mature woodlands also must be allowed special consideration. An assessment of any natural area for the presence of rare or endangered species or archaeological artifacts is highly desirable before the area is altered. Wanton destruction of native plant and animal life or of prehistoric human artifacts is inexcusable in any situation.

Unintentional destruction of natural areas through recreational use is another major problem. Dirt bikes play havoc with steep slopes and bluff faces, killing vegetation and accelerating erosion. Milder forms of recreational use can do the same on slopes and on ridgetops, which also are fragile and require long periods to recover from disturbance. Horseback riding can demolish those areas, as can all-terrain vehicles. Even heavy foot traffic can destroy vegetation and soil cover faster than nature can replace them.

Questions such as "What are the ramifications of intensive recreational use on sensitive communities?" and "How much should a natural community be allowed to degrade?" are not easily answered. Management plans need to consider the amount and type of use to be allowed. Certainly nondestructive activities should be permitted to the greatest degree possible. Because steep slopes and ridgetops are so sensitive to disturbance, their recreational use needs to be restricted to prevent excessive destruction. Major recreational uses such as camping, horseback riding, and vehicular use are least destructive in valleys and on gentle lower slopes. Complete closure of extremely fragile areas and of sites with endangered species struggling for survival may be justified.

Maximize the Diversity of Native Species. Identification of habitats with rare and endangered species, and preservation of those habitats to the best of our abilities, will go a long way toward preventing further species extinctions in the Hills. Maintenance of areas large enough to sustain healthy breeding populations is necessary. Populations of small, inconspicuous organisms must not be forgotten. They may be crucial to the survival of other species. Many prairie plants, for example, cannot reproduce without their insect pollinators.

The use of a diversity of management practices is known to be important for survival of certain rare prairie butterflies and may also be important for other invertebrates. Butterflies depend on a variety of plant species and environments for completion of their life cycle. Because butterflies may never travel more than 500 yards from their point of emergence, they require that diversity within a small area. Applying a variety of management practices to small patches of prairie is more likely to provide the required environmental diversity than is widespread application of any single management technique.

When species have been eliminated, their reintroduction can be considered. The wild turkey has been successfully reintroduced, and the large birds now strut through most Hills woodlands. Two attempts to reintroduce the greater prairie chicken have been unsuccessful. Perhaps other reintroduction schemes will return that hallmark of the prairie to the Loess Hills in future years. Wildlife biologists are considering stocking the sharp-tailed grouse in the northern Loess Hills, where topography seems to be suitable for the species.

Most northerly woodlands are species-poor. Being on the edge of the Eastern Deciduous Forest, the Loess Hills woodlands likely will always contain fewer species than forests to the east. Nevertheless, the diversity of plant species is expected to increase somewhat with time, as young woodlands mature and as plants typical of the association migrate northward into the Hills. To a limited extent, forest diversification in public areas (such as in the Loess Hills Wildlife Area) is being speeded up by efforts to plant a diversity of trees in existing species-poor woodlands. Various native oaks and hickory seedlings are being introduced primarily to increase the variety of nut foods for wildlife in future years.

Introduced plants and animals must not be allowed to displace the land's original inhabitants. Displacement of prairie plants can be prevented in part by maintaining the health of the plant cover, which minimizes the creation of large spots of bare soil and the decline in plant vigor that would allow exotic species to proliferate. Introduced species such as brome are more likely to be excluded by healthy prairie that is regularly burned and not fertilized by cattle droppings.

Leafy spurge (*Euphorbia podperae*), a fierce competitor introduced from Europe, presents special problems. The one- to two-foot-tall plant with small yellow flowerlike structures and milky juice spreads both by roots and by seeds and can invade and take over a healthy prairie. Its presence may justify sterilizing a site with herbicide to prevent its spread to surrounding areas. Eastern red cedar, another species that massively invades disturbed prairies, may require intensive physical removal efforts.

Maintain the Integrity of Existing Natural Communities. No single species can survive without a supportive environment. If the diverse assortment of native Loess Hills species is to continue, management must focus on preserving the integrity of natural communities as a whole. More specifically, the continued presence of western species that have migrated to the Hills over the millennia and of the many rare and endangered prairie species mandates that prairies as a whole remain healthy. And in the Hills, that implies intensive human management, for without interference the Loess Hills prairies will perish.

Because prairies are the oldest, the most threatened, and the most biologically unusual native communities, most of this section focuses on prairie preservation techniques. Woodland invasion is the major problem of every Loess Hills preserve (fig. 65). It is often rapid, especially when cattle are removed from lands that have been heavily grazed. Once a community of shrubs has become established in prairie, the process of conversion to forest is extremely difficult to reverse.

The survival of Loess Hills prairies depends on the reversal of factors

Figure 65. *Invasion of prairies by woody plants, such as this dense growth of sumac, is a problem throughout the Loess Hills. Don Poggensee.*

that trigger invasion: a moist climate, lack of prairie fire, and intense human disturbance. A prolonged dry spell might well reverse the present invasion patterns, but controlling climate is not within the realm of landscape managers. On the other hand, fire and intensity of land use can and are being controlled in some nature preserves to rebuild the health and integrity of native prairies. Prescribed burns are regularly scheduled for the Sioux City Prairie, Five-Ridge Prairie, sections of the Loess Hills Wildlife Area, and Gleason-Hubel Wildlife Area in Iowa (fig. 66). However, burned areas may rapidly refill with shrubs. When burns are carried out in the wrong season or too infrequently, fire even seems to promote the growth of invading sumac. The exposed tips of sumac may be killed, but many more sprout from underground stems called rhizomes. Additional management techniques—physically removing woody vegetation and selective use of herbicides on woody stumps—have been tried. All three techniques have been tested on the McCormack Loess Mounds Natural Area in Missouri, in an attempt to design mechanisms for saving the southernmost Loess Hills grasslands.

Unfortunately, the bulk of Loess Hills prairies are being transformed to

Figure 66. Prescribed burns, such as this one at Five-Ridge Prairie, are used to kill the trees and shrubs invading prairies while stimulating growth of native prairie plants. Kirk Payne.

woodlands without any human efforts to interfere. Research into the best methods of halting forest invasion is clearly needed, but Hills prairies cannot await research results. Fire and possibly cutting and toxins must be systematically applied soon or many prairies will be lost forever. Prairie maintenance techniques are appropriate on both public and private lands.

Land managers may argue that time and financial constraints limit such attempts to a small number of prime prairies, but that need not be so. Elsewhere in Iowa and in Minnesota, burn crews circulate among private and public prairies, taking with them the equipment and experience required to complete a large number of safe, well-planned burns in a short time. Crews may consist of paid seasonal help or of unpaid volunteers who join in because of their love of nature and the excitement generated by the rush, heat, and crackling of flames. Prairie burns offer a sense of participation in an ancient natural event, of revisiting prehistory. Many volunteers come away feeling that a spring day could not have been spent in a more satisfying and exciting way, and they vow to return annually.

Consideration of cattle grazing is also important to prairie preservation,

Figure 67. Grazing need not destroy prairie plants and may be beneficial to certain native animals. Note the similar nature of the ungrazed prairie in the foreground and the grazed prairie behind the fence. Thomas Rosburg.

since most prairies lie on private grazed land. Historically, many Loess Hills prairies have been seriously degraded by cattle grazing. The amount of degradation depends on the number of cattle and the size of the area, the duration of grazing, slope steepness, and restrictions (such as fencing) that limit cattle movement.

If managed with care, grazing need not destroy a prairie's health (fig. 67). In fact, haying or grazing a prairie, if not overdone, may help prevent shrub invasion and seems to be beneficial to certain prairie species. For example, mowing or light grazing may be alternatives to burning that are beneficial to rare prairie butterflies. Healthy prairies can be maintained if an area is not grazed too long or by too many cattle and if cattle are not given access to the steepest slopes most susceptible to damage. Thus, human use of the land need not be pitted against preservation of prairie communities. Well-managed private land in agricultural use can be compatible with prairie preservation efforts in the Loess Hills. However, care must be taken to assure that land management practices are not being used to justify economically rewarding but ecologically deleterious agricultural uses.

Although grazing can destroy a prairie, all prairies degraded by grazing are not necessarily destroyed forever. Because most prairie plants are deep-rooted perennials, and because the grasses reproduce from rootstocks even when seed heads are eaten or otherwise removed, some native prairie plants naturally return to vigor once grazing pressure is lessened. Most if not all Loess Hills prairies in today's preserves were grazed in the past. Burning a degraded prairie seems to strengthen the prairie plants and aid the recovery process. Also, a sufficient number of prairie plants survive in the Hills to produce seeds that will recolonize degraded prairies, if allowed, and even invade abandoned cropland—a process that probably has produced many of today's prairies since all but the steepest slopes have been plowed at one time.

Recovery or reconstruction of prairie communities in valleys or on gentle slopes would allow reestablishment of native grassland bird communities, since present-day prairies in all but the northernmost Loess Hills are too small and steep for those birds. Other animal associations might also respond positively to such prairie expansions.

Allowing natural recovery or reconstruction of prairies on private land adds exciting possibilities to the future of Loess Hills land management, as does the potential of tying management of land for agricultural production to practices that assure the perpetuation of the Hills' irreplaceable grasslands. Prairie restoration also is a potential alternative to tree planting and forest promotion in the state forest that is now being established in Iowa's Hills.

To date, little thought has been given to techniques for preserving Loess Hills forests, in part because the forests are surviving well on their own. Future management efforts would do well to identify and preserve the small percentage of Loess Hills forests that are mature, diverse, and contain rare or endangered species. Diversification of other forested areas should be encouraged.

Controlled burns may prove to be a helpful management tool for some Loess Hills woodlands. Studies of records of Missouri's presettlement forests have revealed that they were typically more open, with a richer ground cover than today's forests. Differences in the nature of presettlement forests can possibly be explained by the influence of fires routinely set by Indians. Research done in Missouri's oak woodlands elsewhere in the state suggests that prescribed burns can be helpful in increasing species richness per unit of area and in sustaining the diversity of mature forests.

Figure 68. The Loess Hills Pioneer State Forest, now being established in Iowa's central Hills, will provide opportunities to work with woodlands and develop forest management techniques while protecting prairies and geological features. Don Poggensee.

Establishment of the Loess Hills Pioneer State Forest will offer ample opportunities to experiment with forest management (fig. 68). Forested land and wood production are to be the central focus of that potentially large public unit in the central Hills. In addition to managing existing forests for wood production, the state will plant trees to upgrade existing woodlands, and a large percentage of land now in agricultural production will be planted to trees. It is hoped that those woodlands will provide local wood-using industries with a sustained yield of raw materials. Wood production in the forests will be combined with diverse, nonintensive, primarily forest-based recreation. Sound conservation practices and land management techniques will be demonstrated to the public. Examples of existing natural resources, including prairies, rare and endangered species, and geological features, will be protected.

The state forest's emphasis on conservation, demonstration projects, and bringing more Loess Hills land into public recreational use is laudable. However, managers planning the state forest's future would do well to reconsider the current emphasis on woodland expansion. Woodlands do offer an attractive alternative to row crops in the Loess Hills, promising to decrease erosion and increase habitat for some native species. But prairies are the truly special asset of the Hills. Creation of a state forest offers tremendous opportunities to restore and learn to manage large prairie tracts within the central Loess Hills. Public interest in the recreational assets, aesthetics, and natural history of prairies has increased dramatically in recent years. And in an area with so many rare and endangered grassland species, management to preserve prairie organisms must be equal in importance to the currently stated policy of management to enhance habitat for game species. Timber production would be a welcome addition to Loess Hills economies and residents, but overemphasis of that one facet will rob present and future residents of a special heritage.

Control Erosion, Gully Cutting, and Slope Instability to the Greatest Degree Possible. Water and gravity have always actively reshaped the Hills. The intensification of those natural processes through human land-use practices has created some practical problems in the Hills. Gully cutting removes thousands of acres of potential cropland from production each year. Gullies widened by erosion threaten bridges, pipelines, and roads (fig. 69). Replacing or relocating those structures is a recurrent and costly problem. Loess washing down slopes and collapsing into gullies releases enormous volumes of sediment into streams and drainage ditches, which must constantly be maintained.

Under the pressure of increased moisture or under the weight of structures and fill dirt, loess settles, and expensive new buildings are damaged or destroyed. Bluff faces also collapse, covering structures and roads at their base and, in populated areas, posing a safety hazard. A spectacular collapse occurred at War Eagle Park in Sioux City, in March 1988. At least 25 feet of the bluff top and many tons of earth slid downhill, burying railroad tracks and two lanes of Interstate 29 (fig. 70). The landslide threatened Chief War Eagle's grave and massive statue, which were perched on the bluff's top, and necessitated movement of the monument.

Slope failures such as that are often natural processes. However, the likelihood of slope failure is raised when humans increase the flow of water into loess or cut into the base of the bluffs. Safe and beneficial use of the Hills requires recognition of such natural processes. Inhabitants need to avoid situations that, because of traits inherent to loess, are dangerous or unstable. People also need to develop management practices that limit the effects of humans in reshaping the Hills.

Figure 69. Newly formed gullies, such as the one in this road, pose hazards to human use, threaten structures, remove land from agricultural use, and routinely require costly repairs. Kirk Payne.

Figure 70. *Collapse of bluff faces is a natural process that is often intensified by human use. Here a massive collapse at War Eagle Park in Sioux City covered railroad tracks and two lanes of Interstate 29.* Ed Porter, Sioux City Journal.

Guidelines have been developed for reducing increases in erosion, gully cutting, and slope instability caused by humans. Control of hillside erosion now relies primarily on no-till farming techniques (planting directly into the previous year's stubble) and on continued construction of basin terraces. Terraces at the base of grazed slopes slow water that is flowing downhill.

The water then soaks into the loess rather than draining downhill in a soil-eating torrent. Siltation structures at the base of drainages serve the same function. Along with the field terraces commonly constructed in rolling cropland east of the most rugged Hills, they have slowed erosion somewhat.

On public lands and to a lesser degree on private lands, reversion to permanent grasslands and seeding of waterways have been used. A dense cover of prairie grasses is ideal for holding soil in place. Other conservation tillage techniques and decreases in the intensity of grazing, which would allow grasses to increase in density and size, also would help. Some of those practices may be encouraged by the federal government's Conservation Reserve Program or by a current U.S. Department of Agriculture policy that ties eligibility for government farm subsidies to an erosion control strategy.

Direct control of gully growth would be a major effort, involving costly structures and vegetation conservation treatments. Given present land-use practices and economic constraints, solutions to the problem are not forthcoming. If the present gully-cutting episode is indeed a natural cyclical event, natural changes in climate and precipitation may decrease the intensity of such erosion. Today's human-intensified gully cutting would not, however, cease completely without changes in land management.

Reducing the effects of slope instability will require other techniques. The shearing off of loess along the westernmost bluffs is largely a natural process and will continue to freshen the dramatic bluff faces. Caution would preclude the building of highways, houses, and other structures at the base of bluffs. If care is taken to avoid cutting into loess at the foot of bluffs and to plan construction so that water is not injected into the loess, human use will not increase the frequency of such shearing.

To prevent collapse of loess on upland surfaces, extreme care must be taken in planning and executing construction. Test borings can determine water content and the need to drain subsurface loess. Loess should not be cut into too deeply. Surface runoff and water from downspouts and gutters must be diverted. Leaks in sewer and water lines must be prevented. Care must be taken to avoid overwatering of lawns. Flattened areas must be adequately drained. Failure to take such steps will result in continued loess collapse and damage to structures.

Erosion, gully cutting, and slope instability today pose practical problems to those living and working in the Hills. If today's land-use practices continue, those forces will threaten the continued productivity of the Hills and, ultimately, the very survival of the landscape. Development of techniques that effectively minimize those problems is imperative.

RESEARCH EFFORTS IN THE HILLS

Preservation and management efforts will be misdirected if they are not continually fed by new research information. Such information has been forthcoming since 1804, when Lewis and Clark first wrote their impressions of the region. Within 20 years, botanists were recording newly discovered plant species there. Explorers and visitors throughout the nineteenth century commented on the unusual landscape and its associations of native organisms. Artists such as George Catlin and Karl Bodmer sketched the Hills as their steamships carried them up the Missouri River.

Nineteenth-century surveys of the region's geological features were among the first such surveys published in Iowa. A flurry of research was published around the turn of the century when Iowa's classical natural historians Bohumil Shimek and Louis Pammel took an interest in analyzing the region's plant communities. They studied the correlation of the Hills' plant associations and climatic variables. They theorized about how the Hills had been formed and what vegetation and now-extinct creatures had inhabited the region long ago.

Despite that early research, the Loess Hills remained remarkably poorly understood through most of the twentieth century, in part because of their distance from Iowa's and Missouri's major research universities. The distance did not faze local residents of the Glenwood, Iowa, area, such as Paul Rowe and D. D. Davis, who became archaeological experts. They devoted much of their lives to studying the remains of previous Indian residents, collecting artifacts that today are available for public viewing in the Mills County Historical Museum. But compared with natural history studies as a whole, the Glenwood archaeological studies are an anomaly. Until recently work on natural communities was spotty, modern studies being limited to a sprinkling of plant, animal, and insect surveys. Before the mid-seventies, many Hills species remained unknown.

Since then, the situation has reversed. Natural historians, realizing that the Hills' unique features were being threatened, have made a concerted effort to accelerate scientific investigations and to inventory and protect specialized ecological habitats (fig. 71). Their work was given a thrust forward in 1980, when the Iowa State Preserves Board (a program of Iowa's

Figure 71. Further scientific research in the Loess Hills will provide the understanding for wise management decisions. Don Poggensee.

Department of Natural Resources) initiated a biological survey of the Loess Hills. The survey was aimed at preparing comprehensive documentation of the occurrence and distribution of Hills plants and animals. Over the next several years, researchers traveled to the Hills to investigate the region's biological diversity, geology, paleontology, and cultural history. Experts from the Smithsonian Institution and from natural history museums throughout North America met to survey the Hills for small, rare prairie butterflies called skippers. On four occasions, natural historians from throughout Iowa converged to study in depth the ecology of a single section of the Loess Hills. During the resurgence of interest, several species thought to have disappeared from the Hills were rediscovered, and a fern previously unknown to science was identified. Archaeologists and geologists, working together, discovered a wealth of Indian artifacts preserved in valley deposits throughout the Hills.

Research findings on the Loess Hills were presented at a scientific symposium held in 1984 and also have been published in scientific journals. The majority of publications are included in two issues of *The Proceedings of the Iowa Academy of Science*, volumes 92(5) and 93(3), where 17 papers provide natural historians with the first definitive compilation of scientific information on the region's features.

Continued research is imperative, both for further characterizing the special features and ecological dynamics of the Hills and for refining management practices. Wise management depends on firm knowledge, which in turn rests on research oriented toward answering questions such as "What additional species are present in the Hills?", "What processes determine their abundance and location?", and "How are various forms of land use affecting patterns and processes in natural communities?"

Wise management also requires knowledge sufficient to integrate the interests of different scientific disciplines, for what might be preservation to one concerned scientist may be destruction to the next. Archaeologists understand that dualism well when they talk of the gullies cutting through the Hills as agents that simultaneously expose and destroy prehistoric sites. Archaeologists also state that impoundments built to control soil erosion have destroyed prehistoric sites.

Loess Hills forests are poorly described and not well understood. Tracing their maturation will make a fascinating study. Such studies should be fostered by formation of Iowa's Loess Hills Pioneer State Forest. Maintaining that potentially large forest and managing it as a woodland, a wood-producing resource, and a repository of rare natural features will, in effect, be a major research project in itself.

The best populations of rare species and associations need to be identified so that they can be preserved. Rates of conversion from prairie to forest have yet to be defined, and even more important, effective techniques for halting and possibly reversing that process must be established. Current management attempts to prevent forest invasion of existing high-quality prairies are, in effect, research and demonstration projects. The same is true of current efforts to lessen the high rates of erosion and gully cutting. Such linkage of research and control efforts is mandated in areas such as the Loess Hills, where natural areas are degrading too rapidly to await the results of pure research. However, future research need not be limited to applied efforts. In an area as diverse, dynamic, and different as the Loess Hills, the number of questions to be answered is limited only by the imagination of researchers.

EDUCATION AND INTERPRETATION

If the public is to be interested in preserving natural features, people must understand the value of preservation. Also, the best-made plans of natural-

Figure 72. *The Loess Hills Prairie Seminar, held annually in the spring, provides excellent, enjoyable opportunities to learn more about the region's features. Here Shirley Schermer, archaeologist with Iowa's Office of the State Archaeologist, lectures on Indian artifacts. Photo by the author.*

area managers will accomplish nothing if counteracted by persons using the land. It is significant that the lay public's interest in the Loess Hills and the educational programs to teach about the Hills have risen along with preservation and management efforts.

Educational efforts have taken various forms: the construction of self-guided nature trails and auto tours, initiation of nature hikes led by Iowa's County Conservation Board naturalists and private citizens, a traveling art exhibit of photographs of the Hills, and the book you are now holding. A historical museum and two excellent nature centers (near Omaha) have been established. An increasing number of articles on the Hills are being published in periodicals. Educational displays have been constructed at various land preserves. A television documentary has been devoted to the Hills' natural features.

The proposed Loess Hills Pioneer State Forest may serve as a future educational resource in several ways. The preliminary management plan calls for construction of interpretive trails. The forest will promote consideration of woodlands and wood products as less erosion-prone alternatives to row crops. Demonstration plots displaying woodland thinning, various types of tree plantings, and maintenance of prairies will passively promote wise land management practices.

The most innovative educational development to date has been the Loess Hills Prairie Seminar (fig. 72). Annually since 1975, up to 300 participants, from infants to persons in their eighties, spend an early June weekend in the Loess Hills Wildlife Area. They attend talks and nature hikes on biology, ecology, archaeology, geology, and nature appreciation. Participants normally camp in the wildlife area, sharing meals from a chuck wagon. Learning is combined with a convivial and cheery spirit, so that attending the seminar has become a tradition for citizens throughout the state. Attendance is open to all, with no previous training required.

Projects and activities such as those attempt to point out the natural features and species that exemplify the Loess Hills, while promoting wise and healthy land-use practices. They develop an appreciation for the plants that migrated there from the western plains, the humans that occupied the Hills long ago, the depth and homogeneity of the fine-textured silt, the birds that migrate along the bluffs and adjacent floodplain; for the desert-like bluff faces and the tenacity of deep-rooted, wind-battered plants that cover them; for the undulating, angular tops of the Hills, the gullies that cut like knife blades into valley floors, and the rare butterflies that flit between the two; for the hundreds of natural features that set the Loess Hills apart as something special.

Being both extremely fragile and rugged, posing a barrier to human desires, the Loess Hills have suffered devastating attempts to transform them into "usable" form. In a brief 150 years, natural balances that have dominated the Hills for thousands of years have been thrown out of kilter. Nearly all of the surrounding prairies have been transformed to cropland. Yet the rugged, fragile nature of the Hills also has meant that here, unlike elsewhere in the region, there is something left to preserve. Many of the region's species have been pushed to the brink of extinction, yet they do still survive in the Hills. The shape of the Hills is being altered by accelerated erosion. Yet they remain, massive and free. Despite changes, the essential character of natural areas in many places remains intact. If preservation and management of the Loess Hills are not effective, a natural heritage of value far beyond the local area will be lost to all. If successful, a landscape and assemblage of species not duplicated elsewhere in the world will be passed on to future generations.

SEVEN

EPILOGUE: TAKING
A BROADER VIEW

Preserving the natural heritage of the Loess Hills is but one part of a larger discussion now occurring among natural scientists, about destruction of natural ecosystems and features worldwide. Why is that topic of such concern? In part, because the rapidly growing human population, with its ever more sophisticated technologies, is eliminating the earth's natural features at an accelerating rate. The natural world is being transformed into one dominated by human decisions rather than natural balances. At the same time, we are learning how dependent we are on natural features to provide our basic needs—on the earth to filter and clean our water, on the forests and oceans to produce our oxygen, on the soil to provide our food, on the atmosphere to filter out the sun's harmful rays and maintain livable temperatures.

One concern receiving special emphasis is the accelerating decline in the earth's species diversity—that is, the rapid decrease in the number of types of plants and animals occupying the earth. Some observers predict that as many as one-fifth of the earth's estimated 5 million to 10 million species will become extinct by early in the twenty-first century. Because genetic diversity (that is, the diversity of species) is associated with environmental stability, a loss of so many species could mean a dramatic increase in the number and severity of environmental crises. Ecologists state that a great decline in the number of species could produce environmental effects similar in magnitude to those of a nuclear holocaust. Such statements often produce feelings of hopelessness and powerlessness.

Seen as part of that broader picture, maintaining the health of the Loess Hills environment takes on a new importance. In this one relatively small region, species can be pushed back from the brink of local extinction, an act that will help to maintain the region's genetic diversity and, ultimately, its environmental stability (fig. 73). It is one area where concerned citizens can act positively to combat environmental threats. Private citizens can work with researchers, landowners, public land managers, and conservation organizations on educational, management, and preservation-related goals. And they can work together powerfully, with the assurance that their efforts will have much broader implications than one might first think.

If you would like to find out how you can help efforts to preserve natural areas and native species in the Loess Hills or elsewhere in Iowa, Missouri, or Nebraska, please contact any of the following organizations or agencies.

The Nature Conservancy

Iowa Chapter
431 East Locust St., Suite 200
Des Moines, Iowa 50309
phone (515) 244-5044

Missouri Chapter
2800 South Brentwood Blvd.
St. Louis, Missouri 63144
phone (314) 968-1105

Nebraska Chapter
1001 Farnam-on-the-Mall
Omaha, Nebraska 68102
phone (402) 342-0282
A nonprofit conservation organization dedicated to preserving natural diversity through locating, protecting, and managing rare natural communities and endangered species throughout North, Central, and South America.

County Conservation Boards, Iowa
Consult the listings in the next chapter for addresses and activities.

Figure 73. *The far northern Loess Hills, home to many rare species and large, diverse native prairies, are one Hills site where the earth's natural genetic diversity and environmental stability can be preserved. Michael P. Greiner.*

Iowa Department of Natural Resources
Wallace State Office Building
Des Moines, Iowa 50319-0034
phone (515) 281-5145
The state agency that is broadly concerned with preservation and management of Iowa's natural features and state-owned public lands, including state parks, state forests, and nature preserves.

Iowa Natural Heritage Foundation
1005 Insurance Exchange Building
505 Fifth Ave.
Des Moines, Iowa 50309
phone (515) 288-1846
A nonprofit organization that assists agencies and individuals in a broad range of projects leading to the conservation, protection, and long-term wise management of Iowa's natural features, including natural areas and native species.

State Ecologist
State Preserves Advisory Board
Iowa Department of Natural Resources
Wallace State Office Building
Des Moines, Iowa 50319-0034
phone (515) 281-8676
An independent advisory board that helps to identify and maintain the state's finest natural, archaeological, geological, historical, and scenic sites and dedicates those sites into the Iowa State Preserves System, which preserves them in perpetuity.

Missouri Department of Conservation
Natural History Section
Box 180
Jefferson City, Missouri 65102
phone (314) 751-4115
The state agency charged with conservation of the state's forest, fish, and wildlife resources. It manages wildlife areas, state forests, natural areas, and other public lands. The Natural History Section maintains the Natural History Data Base.

Missouri Department of Natural Resources
Division of State Parks and Historic Preservation
Box 176
Jefferson City, Missouri 65102
phone (314) 751-2479
The state agency that manages the state park system, including administration and management of wild areas and natural areas occurring on state park lands.

Missouri Prairie Foundation
Box 200
Columbia, Missouri 65201
A not-for-profit membership organization consisting of volunteers dedicated to the preservation of prairies through acquisition, management, and protection of native prairie in Missouri and through educational programs. It publishes the *Missouri Prairie Journal* quarterly, produces and

disseminates other educational aids, holds field trips, and occasionally sponsors Missouri prairie conferences.

Nebraska Game and Parks Commission
2200 North 33rd St.
Lincoln, Nebraska 68503
phone (402) 471-0641
The state agency charged with conservation and management of fish, wildlife, and outdoor recreation resources. It manages wildlife management areas, state recreation areas, and other state-owned lands.

Prairie/Plains Resource Institute
1307 L St.
Aurora, Nebraska 68818
phone (402) 694-3307 or (402) 694-5535
A nonprofit membership organization, dedicated to preservation, restoration, and educational activities regarding native grasslands and other natural habitats of Nebraska through publication of a periodic newsletter, distribution of other scientific publications, and land preservation projects.

PART TWO

TOURING THE LOESS HILLS

In the last 150 years, humans have transformed the rich lowlands bordering the Missouri River, but nature retains control of the rugged Loess Hills. Donald R. Farrar.

The southern Loess Hills display the same finely dissected topography as those farther north, but woodlands are more extensive and better developed toward the south. Don Kurz, Missouri Department of Conservation.

The far-northern Loess Hills retain some of the largest prairies and roadless areas remaining in Iowa. Rare and endangered species abound here. Michael P. Greiner.

Invading trees continue to transform flower-rich native prairies into woodlands. Notice the series of catsteps—a distinctive feature of the Loess Hills. Carl Kurtz.

Abundant leadplant and purple coneflower grace Loess Hills prairies.
Thomas Rosburg.

Looking south along the western bluffline, one might think that the Loess Hills were nearly completely forest-covered. Woodlands thrive on relatively moist north-facing hillsides, while prairies still dominate the very dry ridgetops and south-facing slopes. Carl Kurtz.

When seen from the air, the Loess Hills' intricate landscape of alternating ridges and troughs contrasts sharply with the flat, cultivated Missouri River valley. Geological Survey Bureau, Iowa Department of Natural Resources.

With the coming of winter, drying prairie grasses turn a rich reddish-gold.
Carl Kurtz.

EIGHT

INTRODUCTION

To fully understand the Loess Hills, you have to see them. By walking in the Hills, scanning their topography from high points and kneeling to study details of features and species, travelers can understand and enjoy this wild land with a depth impossible to attain from reading alone. But where are travelers to go, and how can they know how to interpret the features that they are examining?

This part of the book presents two aids for Loess Hills visitors. Together, they should serve the needs of everyone, from the person who wishes to follow a guided nature walk through a prairie to someone who wants to wander alone and simply needs to know where to go.

The first aid, public use areas and educational resources, lists federal, state, county, local, and private areas where public access is permitted. The listings are intended to be a comprehensive guide to public use areas within the Loess Hills. Each site is described in terms of its ownership and management, size, location, facilities and activities permitted, and natural assets. Sites also discussed in the second aid, the car tours, are marked as such. The sites are listed by county, with counties ordered from north to south.

The listings also include educational centers and programs throughout the region. The Loess Hills Prairie Seminar (see Monona County, Iowa, listing), held annually in the spring, is a delight to anyone interested in the region's natural history (fig. 74). Guided nature walks are commonly offered in the northern Hills. Selected noteworthy public use areas near the Loess Hills (primarily those on the adjacent Missouri River floodplain) are included, as are selected sites in Nebraska's easternmost line of bluffs

Figure 74. *Nature hike at the Loess Hills Prairie Seminar. Don Poggensee.*

that have some educational merit with regard to deep loess. Not listed are numerous additional roadside or riverside parks, river access areas, and the like located on the Missouri River floodplain that lack natural features relevant to the understanding of the Loess Hills. County conservation boards or Iowa's and Missouri's conservation departments can provide further information on omitted sites.

Following the listings is the second aid: three self-guided auto tours, which recommend a travel sequence and describe features seen along the way. The Northern Tour leads through a variety of contrasting landforms and communities in the northern Hills of Woodbury and Plymouth counties, Iowa. Starting at Sioux City's massive vertical prairies, the route proceeds to inland, rolling prairies and woodlands within the city limits and then northward to the largest remaining prairies in the Loess Hills, and perhaps the most spectacular view of any Loess Hills prairie. The more subdued landscape and the dominance of the prairies are unlike scenes seen elsewhere in the Hills.

The Central Tour leads along the western edge of the central portion of the Loess Hills, in Harrison and Monona counties, Iowa, following the road along the base of tall, rugged bluffs that rise dramatically from the Missouri River valley. Occasional detours extend eastward into the Hills. The tour proceeds through the heart of the Loess Hills, for those two counties contain the deepest loess, with all the characteristic landforms typical of deep loess. Woodlands may appear to dominate the route, since the road skirts lower hillsides where woodlands predominate. But prairies are abundant also, increasing in number and size toward the northern end of the tour. Of the three tours, this one gives perhaps the most representative taste of Loess Hills features, including fine examples of many ecological and geological qualities characteristic of the Hills. The tour certainly includes areas as beautiful and dramatic as those that can be found anywhere in Iowa.

Unlike the first two tours, which proceed through characteristic and exceptional features of deep loess, the Southern Tour covers four widely spaced major sites in southern Iowa and Missouri's Loess Hills and along Nebraska's bluffs, with intermediate stops at sites with less natural history significance. Each major site claims distinctive features well worth visiting, but none is representative of the Loess Hills as a whole. The tour is more for the woodland enthusiast than for the prairie lover. Although it includes the southernmost prairies in the Hills and some dramatically large and beautiful vertical prairies, forests dominate the southern Hills and Nebraska's bluffs. The dominance and diversity of woodlands makes the tour especially beautiful when leaves are in fall colors. Sites for the most part are more intensively developed, offering more human amenities and a greater diversity of experiences than sites farther north. This tour is ideal for someone who enjoys strolls down well-developed woodland trails, a self-guided nature tour or two, a Sunday visit to a museum, a nature class or a good browse through a shelf of natural history books, or a stop at one of the most productive wildlife refuges in the nation.

In addition to following the three tours, one also could travel the roads that run along the western base of the bluffs for most of the length of the Hills. The roads often form the line separating the Loess Hills from the Missouri River floodplain. Following them is the best way to see the most rugged Hills that are still dominated by native communities. Views can be exceptionally beautiful, especially when lit by vibrant colors of changing seasons—the springtime green of trees budding out, the reds and golds of autumn's trees. From those roads, occasional excursions can be taken eastward into the Hills, although the rugged sections of bluffs prevent east-west transit. The entire bluff-bottom sequence of roads could be pieced together from county or topographic maps since state maps do not show all the smaller roads, or one could simply follow whatever roads skirt the bluffline without referring to maps.

Before you begin, please consider the following points:

Care of natural areas: Please leave the landscape just as you found it for others to enjoy. *Do not disturb or destroy animals, plants, or any natural features.*

Roads: Gravel roads are passable in all weather, although they may become a bit slick when wet. *Dirt roads in loess are considered impassable when wet* and should be avoided when saturated and during heavy rain. The roads drain and dry rapidly.

Maps: Map 2 locates all sites listed in this section. Maps 3, 4, and 5, which outline routes for the car tours, may help you locate some public sites more specifically. However, good-quality state, county, or city maps, as well as a compass, will also be useful, especially if you are traveling remoter areas of the Loess Hills. Short segments of each auto tour are not included on state maps.

Maximizing your enjoyment: Get out of your car frequently, hike in the Hills, picnic or camp here. See the land and its communities from a moving vehicle, but then hear, smell, and touch the Hills as well.

Binoculars and field guides will be useful if you wish to identify species. Because little has been published specifically on the Loess Hills, general guides for birds, reptiles and amphibians, mammals, insects, and woodland plants should be consulted. T. Van Bruggen's *Wildflowers, Grasses, and Other Plants of the Northern Plains and Black Hills* is an excellent reference for novice prairie botanists, since the book contains color pictures of all included species. The Loess Hills issue of the *Iowa Conservationist* describes and illustrates some of the native plants and animal residents. Publication data for those and other sources are given at the end of part II.

NINE

PUBLIC USE AREAS AND
EDUCATIONAL RESOURCES

IOWA

Plymouth County

Five-Ridge Prairie (Northern Tour). 790 acres; purchased by the Nature Conservancy, now owned by Plymouth County Conservation Board; managed jointly by the board, the conservancy, and the Iowa Department of Natural Resources; dedicated into State Preserve System in 1986.

Location: from Stone State Park, follow Iowa Hwy. 12 north for 6 miles, take County K-18 north a bit more than 3 miles, follow sign to west, proceed 1 mile on dirt road. Must hike into preserve from parking area.

Facilities and permitted activities: hiking and cross-country ski trails; guided nature hikes; hunting permitted.

Natural assets: woodlands, ridgetop and hillside prairies; good birding; one of the largest remaining roadless areas in Loess Hills; managed as nature preserve, with intensive program to prevent forest invasion of prairie.

NEARBY ATTRACTIONS

Hillview Recreation Area. 210 acres; Plymouth County Conservation Board.

Location: 1.5 miles west of Hinton, on County C-60, just east of the Loess Hills.

Facilities and permitted activities: hiking, bridle, and cross-country ski

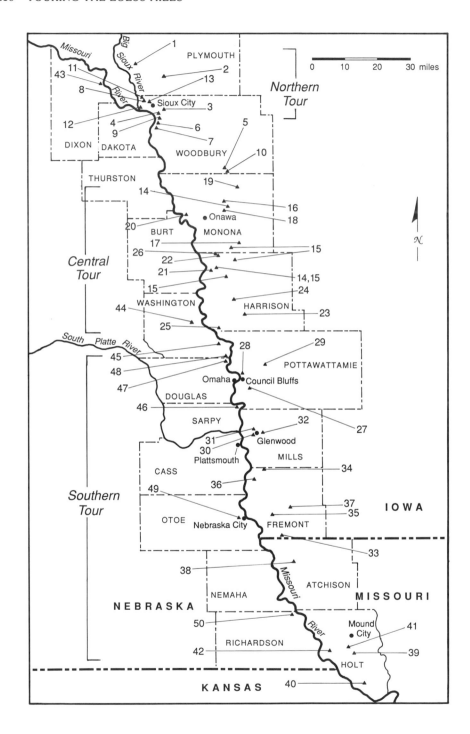

1. Five-Ridge Prairie
2. Hillview Recreation Area
3. Bacon Creek Park
4. Floyd Monument Park
5. Fowler Forest Preserve
6. Green Belt Park
7. Green Valley Golf Course and Park
8. Sioux City Prairie
9. South Ravine Park
10. Southwood Conservation Area
11. Stone State Park
12. War Eagle Park
13. Sioux City Public Museum
14. Loess Hills National Natural Landmark
15. Loess Hills Pioneer State Forest
16. Loess Hills Wildlife Area
17. Preparation Canyon State Park
18. Turin Loess Hills Nature Preserve
19. Whiting Woods
20. Lewis and Clark State Park
21. Gleason-Hubel Wildlife Area
22. Murray Hill Scenic Area
23. Niles Historical Village
24. Sawmill Hollow Wildlife Area
25. DeSoto National Wildlife Refuge
26. Sioux Dam Fishing Access
27. Fairmount Park
28. Lewis and Clark Monument
29. Smith Area
30. Mile Hill Recreation Area
31. Pony Creek Park
32. Mills County Historical Museum
33. O. S. Wing Area
34. Pinky's Glen
35. Waubonsie State Park
36. Forney Lake Wildlife Area
37. Riverton Wildlife Area
38. Brickyard Hill Loess
    Mound Prairie Natural Area
39. McCormack Loess Mounds
    Natural Area
40. Riverbreaks State Forest
41. Squaw Creek National Wildlife Refuge
42. Big Lake State Park
43. Ponca State Park
44. Cuming City Cemetery and Nature Preserve
45. Fort Atkinson State Historical Park
46. Fontenelle Forest Nature Center
47. Hummel Park
48. Neale Woods Nature Center
49. Arbor Lodge State Historical Park
    and Arboretum
50. Indian Cave State Park

Map 2. Public use areas and educational resources in the Loess Hills. Heidi Perry.

trails; lake fishing; picnic area; modern campground; hunting permitted; guided nature hikes.

Natural assets: gently rolling hills, woodland, retired agricultural land, some reconstructed prairie; good birding.

EDUCATIONAL RESOURCES

Plymouth County Conservation Board. Phone (712) 947-4270; write RFD 1, Hinton, Iowa 51024.

A full-time naturalist conducts regularly scheduled guided nature hikes at Five-Ridge Prairie and Hillview Recreation Area; hikes also conducted on request as time permits; indoor talks on the Loess Hills and on prairies are given upon request throughout the year to small groups, school classes, and organizations.

Woodbury County

Bacon Creek Park. 239 acres; Sioux City, Public Works Department. Location: far western Sioux City; 5015 Correctionville Rd.

Facilities and permitted activities: highly developed park with many facilities—hiking trails, picnic areas, shelters, playground equipment, fitness trail, rest rooms, boat concessions, fishing; no camping; primitive area for hiking and nature study.

Natural assets: large lake, lawn, retired agricultural land, woodland, nonnative grasslands, reconstructed prairie; gently rolling topography.

Floyd Monument Park. 120 acres; Sioux City, Public Works Department.

Location: southern Sioux City, access via U.S. 75 (also known as South Lewis Blvd.), which transects park; monument entrance just south of intersection with Glenn Ave.

Facilities and permitted activities: overlook, rest room; Sergeant Floyd Monument, a registered National Historic Landmark, grave of the only member of the Lewis and Clark expedition to die on the journey; golf course.

Natural assets: woodland, lawn, small bluff prairie; scenic view of adjacent Missouri River and urban developments.

Fowler Forest Preserve. 108 acres; Woodbury County Conservation Board.

Location: 0.5 mile west of Smithland on Iowa Hwy. 141; just north of Southwood Conservation Area.

Facilities and permitted activities: hiking trails, picnic area, shelter, playground equipment, rest rooms, fishing.

Natural assets: well-developed forest, reestablished prairie, young woodland, nonnative grassland, lawn; gentle hills, at eastern edge of Loess Hills.

Green Belt Park. 83 acres; Sioux City, Public Works Department.

Location: far southern Sioux City, along bluffline north and south of U.S. Hwy. 20; no designated public access.

Facilities: undeveloped; bluff-top trail extends along western edge of South Ravine Park south into the adjacent Green Belt Park; scenic view.

Natural assets: woodlands, hill and bluff prairies.

Green Valley Golf Course and Park. 200 acres of golf course, 60 acres of park; Sioux City, Public Works Department.

Location: far southern Sioux City; take U.S. 75 south, turn east onto Donner Ave.

Facilities: golf course, rest rooms; scenic view and foot paths in the undeveloped park area.

Natural assets: lawn (golf course); hill prairies, woodland (park).

Sioux City Prairie (Northern Tour). 150 acres; owned by the Nature Conservancy; managed jointly by the conservancy and the Woodbury County Conservation Board.

Location: northwestern Sioux City; access from Briar Cliff College parking lot, at northeast corner of prairie, or Talbot Rd., which runs along west side of prairie.

Facilities and permitted activities: walking trails, guided nature walks.

Natural assets: hill prairies; good birding.

South Ravine Park. 120 acres; Sioux City, Public Works Department.

Location: far southern Sioux City, access via Lincoln Way just east of U.S. 75 (also known as South Lewis Blvd.).

Facilities and permitted activities: bluff-top and other hiking trails, picnic area, playground equipment; First Bride's Monument, at far northern end of bluff-top trail, grave site of first white bride in Sioux City.

Natural assets: woodland, bluff prairie, lawn, creek; scenic view (adjacent urban developments).

Southwood Conservation Area. 463 acres; Woodbury County Conservation Board.

Location: just south and west of Smithland, adjacent to southern edge of Fowler Forest Preserve; entrance off marked gravel road—turn south off Iowa Hwy. 141 about 1 mile west of Smithland, or turn west off County L-12 south of Smithland.

Facilities and permitted activities: hiking and cross-country ski trails, self-guided nature trail, bridle trails, picnic area, primitive camping, fishing, hunting.

Natural assets: forest, small native hill and ridgetop prairies, reconstructed prairie, retired agricultural land, nonnative grasslands, farm ponds; gentle hills, at eastern edge of Loess Hills.

Stone State Park (Northern Tour). 1,069 acres; Iowa Department of Natural Resources.

Location: northwest corner of Sioux City, bordered by Iowa Hwy. 12 (on west) and Talbot Rd. (on east).

Facilities and permitted activities: hiking and bridle trails, two self-guided nature trails, picnic areas, stream fishing, modern campground, Bur Oak Nature Center.

Natural assets: ridgetop and upper hillside prairies, forested areas; view from bluff top.

War Eagle Park. 23 acres; Sioux City, Public Works Department.

Location: central Sioux City, access via West Fourth St. at War Eagle Drive.

Facilities and permitted activities: hiking trails, picnic area, shelter and rest room; War Eagle Monument (marking Chief War Eagle's grave) was removed temporarily in Spring 1988 because of a major landslide.

Natural assets: bluff prairie, woodland, lawn; scenic view of confluence of Big Sioux and Missouri rivers, looking across floodplain into Nebraska and South Dakota.

Note: Within Sioux City, a number of additional privately and publicly owned sites contain native prairie or woodland. The listings here omit city-owned parks with small native communities.

NEARBY ATTRACTIONS

Ponca State Park. See Dixon County, Nebraska.

EDUCATIONAL RESOURCES

Woodbury County Conservation Board. Phone (712) 279-6488; write Courthouse, Eighth Floor, Sioux City, Iowa 51101.

Full-time naturalist gives scheduled nature walks during summer in Sioux City Prairie and other County Conservation Board areas; walks and slide presentations also given on request for small groups, school classes, and organizations.

Friends of the Sioux City Prairie. Contact Woodbury County Conservation Board or call Dianne Blankenship at (712) 255-3447.

Gives guided nature walks on Sioux City Prairie, usually on the second Saturday of each month (May through September); expanded schedule during Prairie Heritage Week (early September).

Bur Oak Nature Center, Stone State Park. Open to public noon to 5 Saturday and Sunday, Memorial Day to Labor Day; open by appointment throughout the year to school and other groups.

Houses nature displays, auditorium for environmental education programs; quarter-mile nature trail nearby; summer part-time naturalist offers trail tours and other programs on request. Park naturalist also presents programs throughout year to school classes and other groups on request.

Sioux City Public Museum. 2901 Jackson St., Sioux City, Iowa 51104; open 9 to 5 Monday through Saturday, 2 to 5 Sunday; closed holidays.

Displays of early Sioux City history and of prehistoric life (fossils) of western Iowa; general displays on natural history, minerals and rocks, American Indians, Civil War history. Classes for children and adults in science and history; sales desk, craft displays, research library.

Monona County

Loess Hills National Natural Landmark (Central Tour). 10,720 acres; landmark designation does not change land ownership, so parcels previously in private ownership remain as such.

Location: in the most rugged Loess Hills, from Turin approximately 7 miles northward, including the Loess Hills Wildlife Area and surrounding private lands; also includes land in Harrison County.

Facilities and permitted activities: no public use outside the Loess Hills Wildlife Area.

Natural assets: designated nationally significant by the National Park Service, Department of the Interior, illustrating the ecological and geological natural heritage of the United States.

Loess Hills Pioneer State Forest (Central Tour). Eventually 17,190 acres (in Monona and Harrison counties), to be purchased from willing sellers over several years; Iowa Department of Natural Resources.

Location: slated eventually to include land surrounding Preparation Canyon State Park, extending west and south to the Harrison County border, and land in Harrison County; some segments near the park were purchased by 1987.

Facilities and permitted activities: will include a wide variety of activities, such as hiking and other trail uses, camping, nature study, and hunting.

Natural assets: will include forest and prairie; will be managed to maintain forest, prairie, and wildlife resources.

Loess Hills Wildlife Area (Central Tour). 2,504 acres (largest publicly owned parcel in Loess Hills); Iowa Department of Natural Resources.

Location: northeast of Onawa; take County L-12 north, turning east off County L-12 to follow "Public Access" signs for 2.5 miles. Or, from Castana (Iowa Hwy. 175), follow signs 3.5 miles to west.

Facilities and permitted activities: hiking trails, primitive camping and hunting allowed; Loess Hills Prairie Seminar held annually, guided nature talks.

Natural assets: prairies and woodlands of various types and ages; some cropland planted for wildlife; hiking along ridges allows excellent opportunities for observing extensive prairies; scenic views of floodplain from bluffs.

Preparation Canyon State Park (Central Tour). 344 acres; Iowa Department of Natural Resources.

Location: approximately 5 miles southwest of Moorhead; follow signs from Iowa Hwy. 183 westward. Or, from Blencoe, take County E-60 east and follow "State Park" signs.

Facilities and permitted activities: hiking trails, picnic areas; no camping; guided nature talks.

Natural assets: woodlands of various types and ages, some nonprairie grasslands, lawn; historical interest, site of early Mormon settlement.

Turin Loess Hills Nature Preserve (Central Tour). 220 acres; Iowa Department of Natural Resources, dedicated into State Preserve System; southern portion of Loess Hills Wildlife Area.

Location: 1.5 miles north of Turin on County L-14.

Facilities and permitted activities: same as Loess Hills Wildlife Area (no established hiking trails).

Natural assets: bluff, hillside, and ridgetop prairies; woodlands; some cropland planted for wildlife.

Whiting Woods. 80 acres; Monona County Conservation Board.

Location: approximately 4 miles west and south of Mapleton; follow signs west from Iowa Hwy. 175.

Facilities and permitted activities: hiking trail, pond fishing, picnic area, shelter and rest room.

Natural assets: in eastern rolling Loess Hills; woodland, lawn, pond; surrounded by agricultural land.

NEARBY ATTRACTIONS

Lewis and Clark State Park. 286 acres; on the Missouri River floodplain 4 miles west of Onawa, with a modern campground and opportunities for a variety of water sports.

EDUCATIONAL RESOURCES

Loess Hills Prairie Seminar. Held annually since 1977 on a weekend in early June, at the Loess Hills Wildlife Area. Nature walks and talks on geology, ecology, organisms, and species of the Hills. Open without cost to the general public; no previous training required. Participants range from infants to the elderly; they typically camp in the wildlife area and share minimal-cost catered meals. A must for anyone seriously interested in Iowa's natural history or in the Loess Hills. Preregistration required. Contact the Western Hills Area Education Agency, 1520 Morningside Ave., Sioux City, Iowa 51106.

Monona County Conservation Board. Phone (712) 423-2400; write Box 209, Onawa, Iowa 51040.

A ranger-naturalist conducts nature hikes for the general public in the Loess Hills Wildlife Area and at Preparation Canyon State Park at least once a month, also for school and other groups upon request. Talks and slide presentations on the Loess Hills, Turin Man archaeological discovery, and prairies scheduled regularly and given on request.

Harrison County

Gleason-Hubel Wildlife Area (Central Tour). 165 acres; Harrison County Conservation Board.

Location: 1 mile southeast of Little Sioux on small county road; consult Central Tour for directions and map.

Facilities and permitted activities: hiking trails; hunting permitted.

Natural assets: primarily woodland, some ridgetop prairies.

Loess Hills National Natural Landmark (Central Tour). See description under Monona County (above). The Harrison County unit includes land approximately from the Gleason-Hubel Wildlife Area northward to Murray Hill (County F-20) and east (to a maximum width of 2 miles), for a total area of 2,980 acres.

Loess Hills Pioneer State Forest (Central Tour). See description under Monona County (above). Three management units in Harrison County will include one to the east and south of Pisgah, a second in the bluffs to the east of Little Sioux, and a third along the east side of Iowa Hwy. 183 just north of Iowa Hwy. 127.

Murray Hill Scenic Area (Central Tour). 3 acres; Harrison County Conservation Board.

Location: on County F-20, 2 miles northeast of Little Sioux or 4 miles west of Pisgah.

Facilities and permitted activities: parking area, trail to top of bluff; only western bluff face crossed by a major highway.

Natural assets: bluff prairie, wonderful view from bluff top.

Niles Historical Village. 2 acres; Harrison County Conservation Board.

Location: on U.S. 30, 2 miles northeast of Missouri Valley.

Facilities and permitted activities: reconstructed pioneer buildings (log house, general store, schoolhouse) containing artifacts of early settlement; open May 1 to October 1.

Natural assets: lawn.

Sawmill Hollow Wildlife Area. 155 acres; Harrison County Conservation Board.

Location: 0.5 mile off Iowa Hwy. 183, 6.5 miles north of Missouri Valley; access via dirt road to the east, impassable when wet.

Facilities and permitted activities: hiking trails, lake fishing and boating; hunting permitted.

Natural assets: primarily woodland, some cropland planted for wildlife, some reconstructed prairie; scenic view of floodplain from bluff top.

NEARBY ATTRACTIONS

DeSoto National Wildlife Refuge (Central Tour). 7,823 acres; Fish and Wildlife Service, U.S. Department of the Interior.

Location: on the Missouri River floodplain, on U.S. 30, 5 miles west of Interstate 29; partially in Washington County, Nebraska. Phone (712) 642-4121. Write Route 1, Box 114, Missouri Valley, Iowa 51555.

Facilities and permitted activities: visitors' center with regularly shown wildlife film, museum containing items recovered from Civil War–era sunken steamboat (the *Bertrand*), displays of refuge wildlife, desk selling interpretive materials and guidebooks; 12-mile self-guided auto tour with stations describing local ecology, observation tower, nature trails for walking; boating, fishing, picnicking, wading, photography, limited hunting. Visitors' center open 9 to 4:30 361 days each year; refuge open 6 A.M. to 10 P.M. April 15 to September 30; road through refuge open mid-October into early November.

Natural assets: stopping point for hundreds of thousands of migrating waterfowl; fall peak of snow goose migration (up to 200,000 birds) in mid-November, spring peak in late March; call refuge to check migrational status. Iowa Department of Natural Resources also monitors the number and location of geese; call the wildlife division at (515) 281-5918. Wintering ground for dozens of bald eagles. Abundant additional wildlife, including 240 bird species. Floodplain forests, reconstructed native grasslands, croplands, wetlands. Seven-mile-long former oxbow of the Missouri River, now a lake.

Sioux Dam Fishing Access. 10 acres; on County L-14 just south of the Harrison-Monona county line (a bit more than 2 miles north of Murray Hill); a pleasant place to stop and picnic or camp while driving along the base of the bluffs.

EDUCATIONAL RESOURCES

Harrison County Conservation Board. Phone (712) 647-2785; write RR 1, Box 113, Woodbine, Iowa 51579.
Educational programs on request, either indoors or in the field, for small groups, schools, and organizations, as time permits.

DeSoto National Wildlife Refuge. In addition to the many educational aids described above, environmental education programs offered for school groups on request.

Pottawattamie County

Fairmount Park. 45 acres; city of Council Bluffs.
Location: east-central Council Bluffs.
Facilities and permitted activities: city park with playground, shelters, rest rooms, ice skating rink.
Natural assets: mostly woodland, some bluff prairies, lawn and flower gardens; excellent bluff-top view of city and floodplain.

Lewis and Clark Monument. 40 acres; city of Council Bluffs.
Location: north side of Council Bluffs, just east of Interstate 29.
Facilities and permitted activities: historic monument; site commemorat-

ing the meeting along the Missouri River of Lewis and Clark with Oto and Missouri Indians on August 3, 1804.

Natural assets: lawn and flower gardens, mostly oak-dominated forests, some ridgetop and upper hillside prairies; excellent bluff-top view of Missouri River floodplain, Council Bluffs abutting the forested hills to the south and relict prairies on tops of steepest slopes to the north.

Smith Area. 201 acres; Iowa Department of Natural Resources.

Location: north side of Iowa Hwy. 191, 1.5 miles north of junction with U.S. 6.

Facilities and permitted activities: wildlife preserve; no public access.

Natural assets: woodland, cropland.

NEARBY ATTRACTIONS

See listings for Washington, Douglas, and Sarpy counties, Nebraska.

EDUCATIONAL RESOURCES

Pottawattamie County Conservation Board. Phone (712) 328-5638; write County Courthouse Annex, Council Bluffs, Iowa 51501.

No educational programs on the Loess Hills.

Fontenelle Forest and Neale Woods Nature Centers. See Washington, Douglas, and Sarpy counties, Nebraska.

Mills County

Mile Hill Recreation Area. 39 acres; Mills County Conservation Board.

Location: south of U.S. 34, approximately 2 miles west of Glenwood.

Facilities and permitted activities: undeveloped.

Natural assets: woodlands, old fields (no native prairie), lake.

Pony Creek Park. 53 acres; Mills County Conservation Board.

Location: follow U.S. 34 approximately 2 miles west from Glenwood, turn north onto gravel road at Pony Creek Conservation Area sign, proceed north nearly 2 miles, veering left at junctions.

Facilities and permitted activities: woodland nature trail, lake fishing, picnic area, camping.

Natural assets: woodland, lawn.

NEARBY ATTRACTIONS

Fontenelle Forest Nature Center. See Sarpy County, Nebraska, and Southern Tour.

EDUCATIONAL RESOURCES

Mills County Conservation Board. Phone (712) 527-9685; write RR 1, Pony Creek Park, Pacific Junction, Iowa 51561.

No educational programs on the Loess Hills.

Fontenelle Forest Nature Center. See Sarpy County, Nebraska, and Southern Tour.

Mills County Historical Museum (Southern Tour). East side of Glenwood in Glenwood Lake Park, follow Sharp St. east through the center of town. Phone (712) 527-5038; write Box 190, Glenwood, Iowa 51534. Open Sundays 2 to 5, Memorial Day to Labor Day, and by special appointment for groups and school classes.

Displays of artifacts and reconstructions of the Glenwood Indians (and earlier Indians), film on the Glenwood; collections of early settlement items from southeastern Iowa (furniture, clothing, machinery, one-room school, and the like); Pioneer Crafts Day held annually, the second Sunday in August.

Loess Hills Prehistoric Heritage Society. Write 225 W. Florence Ave., Glenwood, Iowa 51534. The society is raising funds to construct an Earthlodge Interpretive Center dedicated to educating the public about Loess Hills history and prehistory, in particular about the Glenwood prehistoric Indians. The center would offer classes for all ages.

Fremont County

O. S. Wing Area. 130 acres; recently acquired by Iowa Department of Natural Resources.

Location: 1.5 miles south of Hamburg, on east side of U.S. 275 (just north of Missouri state line).

Facilities and permitted activities: undeveloped.

Natural assets: primarily young woodland, prairie that was heavily pastured until recently, farm pond.

Pinky's Glen. 48 acres; Fremont County Conservation Board.

Location: on County J-10, 2.5 miles west of Tabor.

Facilities and permitted activities: picnicking, lake fishing, camping.

Natural assets: formerly agricultural land converted to nonnative grasslands; some woodland; lake.

Waubonsie State Park (Southern Tour). 1,209 acres; Iowa Department of Natural Resources.

Location: along Iowa Hwy. 2, entrance 2 miles west of U.S. 275 and 5 miles east of Interstate 29; enter via Iowa Hwy. 239.

Facilities and permitted activities: hiking and bridle trails, two self-guided nature trails, picnicking areas, shelters and rest rooms, modern campground.

Natural assets: mostly forest, ridgetop and upper hillside prairies, magnificent bluff prairies along County L-48; bluff-top view of four states; excellent birding.

NEARBY ATTRACTIONS

Forney Lake Wildlife Area (Southern Tour). 1,128 acres; Iowa Department of Natural Resources.

Location: on County L-44, 3 miles north of Thurman.

Facilities and permitted activities: campground, birding, hunting.

Natural assets: shallow marsh on the Missouri River floodplain adjacent to the Loess Hills, feeding and resting place for thousands of geese and other migrating waterfowl; includes 55 acres of upland timber in the Loess Hills, just east of the area headquarters.

Riverton Wildlife Area. 2,493 acres; Iowa Department of Natural Resources.

Location: just northwest of Riverton.

Facilities and permitted activities: birding, hunting, boat ramp.

Natural assets: shallow marsh along the West and East Nishnabotna

River floodplain, feeding and resting place for migrating waterfowl; some floodplain timber; prairie restoration and cropland on upland areas.

EDUCATIONAL RESOURCES

Fremont County Conservation Board. Phone (712) 374-2347; write Fremont County Golf Course, RR 1, Sidney, Iowa 51652.

No educational programs on the Loess Hills.

MISSOURI

Note: For area maps or additional information on the state-owned areas listed below, phone the Missouri Department of Conservation at (816) 233-3212 or write 3408 Ashland, St. Joseph, Missouri 64506.

Atchison County

Brickyard Hill Loess Mound Prairie Natural Area. 125 acres of the larger (1,942-acre) Brickyard Hill Wildlife Area, a strip running along the bluffs in the southwestern corner of the wildlife area; Missouri Department of Conservation.

Location: take the Watson exit (116) off Interstate 29; turn east onto County B and then immediately take a right turn onto County RA. In 0.3 mile, a small gravel road turns off to the right. The natural area lies to the east of the gravel road, extending for about a mile of the road's length. The entrance to the main parking area is 0.2 mile farther down County RA, on the left, but to reach the natural area prairies, you must park at another lot, approximately 3 miles east and south, and hike 1 mile west; obtain a map before attempting to do so.

Facilities and permitted activities, in wildlife area as a whole: hiking trails, picnicking, primitive camping in designated areas, fishing, hunting, trapping (by special permit).

Natural assets: wildlife area, mostly forest, scattered grasslands (both nonnative and small prairies), lake; natural area, mostly forest, patchy hill prairie openings along upper edge of the bluffline.

Indian Cave State Park. See Nemaha and Richardson counties, Nebraska.

Holt County

McCormack Loess Mounds Natural Area (Southern Tour). 112 acres, the western half of the 227-acre Jamerson C. McCormack Wildlife Area; the Nature Conservancy and Missouri Department of Conservation.

Location: on the east side of U.S. 159, 1.5 miles south of the Squaw Creek National Wildlife Refuge headquarters. Watch for marked parking area; must hike 0.5 mile uphill to reach prairies.

Facilities and permitted activities, in wildlife area as a whole: hiking trails, picnicking, primitive camping, limited hunting, observation tower overlooking prairie.

Natural assets: mostly forest, ridgetop and hillside prairies forming interconnected and fairly extensive prairie units, rugged loess topography that is quite unusual for the region; wonderful view of Squaw Creek wetlands from bluff tops.

Riverbreaks State Forest. 1,838 acres; Missouri Department of Conservation.

Location: entrance on County T, 4 miles south of Forest City; also on County O, 1.5 miles north of County T, and on surrounding gravel roads.

Facilities and permitted activities: hiking and bridle trails, back-country camping, fishing, hunting.

Natural assets: mostly forest, nonnative grasslands; a few tiny prairie patches high on bluff faces may well be the southernmost bluff prairies remaining in the Loess Hills; some manipulation for wildlife (cropland, creation of ponds).

Squaw Creek National Wildlife Refuge (Southern Tour). 6,886 acres, 100 acres of which form the Loess Hills Research Natural Area; Fish and Wildlife Service, U.S. Department of the Interior.

Location: just south of Mound City; take the Rulo exit (79) off Interstate 29, proceed west on U.S. 159 for 2.5 miles to refuge headquarters (on east side of the refuge). Phone (816) 442-3187; write Box 101, Mound City, Missouri 64470.

Facilities and permitted activities: 10-mile looping road with observation towers, foot trails, wayside exhibits; picnicking; fishing; photo blind available. Loess Bluff Trail extends from refuge headquarters into the Loess Hills. Refuge open daily sunrise to sunset, headquarters 7:30 to 4 weekdays.

Natural assets: mostly wetlands on the Missouri River floodplain managed to provide feeding and resting grounds for migrating waterfowl and other wildlife; human-made marshes, croplands, floodplain woodlands, and native wet grasslands. Phone refuge for status of migrating birds. Excellent birding, 268 species of birds, large populations of ducks, geese, bald eagles in season; other wildlife abundant. A small section east of the refuge headquarters is in Loess Hills—mostly woodland, ridgetop prairie openings, abandoned cropland.

NEARBY ATTRACTIONS

Big Lake State Park. Due west of Squaw Creek; has a pleasant year-round campground and modern motel and cabin accommodations with a dining room.

Indian Cave State Park. See Nemaha and Richardson counties, Nebraska.

NEBRASKA

Dixon County

Ponca State Park. 892 acres; Nebraska Game and Parks Commission.

Location: 2 miles north of Ponca on County Spur 26E.

Facilities and permitted activities: hiking and cross-country ski trails, horseback trail rides, playground, picnicking, shelters and rest rooms, boating, river fishing, swimming pool, primitive camping, complete modern camping facilities, housekeeping cabins.

Natural assets: woodlands of various types and ages, primarily bur oak (at ridgetops especially), which are approaching the edge of their range and are often dwarfed by the harsh climate; basswood and other communities in moister sites; woodlands more limited in diversity and extent than those in southern Nebraska; small prairie remnants within woodlands and at tops of bluffs. A region of rolling Cretaceous bedrock unevenly coated by loess, sometimes deep and other times shallow—note bedrock underlying large bluffs facing the Missouri River's floodplain, at northeastern edge of park. View across South Dakota to Loess Hills of Plymouth County, Iowa, looking across the Missouri and Big Sioux river valleys.

NEARBY ATTRACTIONS

See listings for Plymouth and Woodbury counties, Iowa.

Washington County

Cuming City Cemetery and Nature Preserve. 11 acres; Dana College in Blair, Nebraska.

Location: 4 miles north of downtown Blair, 0.2 mile west of U.S. 75 on County P-214, which intersects U.S. 75 just south of the Stuart Creek crossing and 0.5 mile north of the Blair Country Club.

Facilities and permitted activities: observation of nineteenth century gravestones, nature appreciation.

Natural assets: native tall-grass prairie.

DeSoto National Wildlife Refuge. See description under Harrison County, Iowa.

Fort Atkinson State Historical Park. 154 acres; Nebraska Game and Parks Commission.

Location: approximately 15 miles north of downtown Omaha, on the eastern edge of the city of Fort Calhoun; follow signs east from U.S. 75.

Facilities and permitted activities: primarily a reconstruction (in progress) of the first military outpost west of the Missouri River, a major fort in operation from 1820 to 1827, built to regulate the region's burgeoning fur trade and to maintain peace between traders and Indians. Walking trails, rest rooms, interpretive center depicting the region's early nineteenth-century history. Open 9 to 5 daily in summertime, grounds open year-round; living history demonstrations on weekends throughout the summer.

Natural assets: reconstructed upland and floodplain prairies, upland and floodplain woodlands, some lawn.

Neale Woods Nature Center. See Douglas County, Nebraska.

See listings for Harrison County, Iowa.

Douglas and Sarpy Counties

Fontenelle Forest Nature Center (Southern Tour). 1,300 acres; privately owned by Fontenelle Forest Association.

Location: just south of Omaha in Bellevue; follow signs east from U.S. 75. Phone (402) 731-3140, or write 1111 Bellevue Blvd. North, Bellevue, Nebraska 68005.

Facilities and permitted activities: great variety of natural science educational programs for all ages offered year-round—hiking trails, guided nature and astronomy walks, films, lectures, slide programs, classroom programs and teaching aids, programs for groups, speaker's bureau, short courses on natural history topics, workshops, nature camps, field trips, special seasonal events. Interpretive center with displays, library, large shop. Monthly newsletter, plant guide, bird list, booklets for self-guided nature and history trails. Open 362 days a year 8 to 5, till 6 on weekends from April 1 to October 31.

Natural assets: mature and younger upland and floodplain forests, marsh, diversity of birds and other wildlife, archaeological and historical relics, rugged loess bluff topography bordering Missouri River's floodplain.

Hummel Park. 202 acres; city of Omaha, Parks, Recreation, and Public Property Department.

Location: far northeastern Omaha, north of Interstate 680 along Pershing Dr.

Facilities and permitted activities: hiking and nature trails, children's summer day camp, picnic areas, play equipment, shelter, scenic overlook, historical marker.

Natural assets: loess bluffs with mature forests bordering Missouri River's floodplain, some lawn, stream.

Neale Woods Nature Center (Southern Tour). 300 acres; privately owned by Fontenelle Forest Association.

Location: just north of Omaha on the Douglas-Washington county line; follow signs west from Pershing Dr./North River Rd. Phone (402) 453-5615, or write 14323 Edith Marie Ave., Omaha, Nebraska 68112.

Facilities and permitted activities: a variety of natural science educational programs, activities, and facilities similar to those offered at Fontenelle Forest, including interpretive center with displays and shop. Self-guided nature trail. Open 362 days a year 8 to 5, except Sundays noon to 5. Open till 6 on weekends from April 1 to October 31.

Natural assets: upland forests of various ages and types, restored tallgrass prairie, nonnative grasslands, diversity of birds and other wildlife, rolling loess topography bordering Missouri River's floodplain.

NEARBY ATTRACTIONS

See listings for Harrison and Pottawattamie counties, Iowa.

EDUCATIONAL RESOURCES

See Fontenelle Forest and Neale Woods nature centers, above.

Otoe County

Arbor Lodge State Historical Park and Arboretum (Southern Tour). 65 acres; Nebraska Game and Parks Commission.

Location: western Nebraska City; follow Centennial Ave. south from U.S. 75, or take Second Ave. west from downtown Nebraska City.

Facilities and permitted activities: walking trails, picnicking, playground, rest rooms; furnished mansion and carriage house with coach collection of J. S. Morton, founder of Arbor Day. Grounds open 8 to sunset daily, year-round; mansion open 1 to 5 from April 20 to November 1, with expanded hours (9 to 5) in summer, guided tours.

Natural assets: no natural ecosystems; diverse and beautiful arboretum with Italian terraced flower garden, trail with labeled trees, prairie plants garden.

NEARBY ATTRACTIONS

See listings for Fremont County, Iowa.

Nemaha and Richardson Counties

Indian Cave State Park (Southern Tour). 3,000-plus acres; Nebraska Game and Parks Commission.

Location: on Nemaha-Richardson county line adjacent to the Missouri River, 5 miles east of Nebraska Hwy. 67 (enter on Spur 64E).

Facilities and permitted activities: hiking and cross-country ski trails, picnicking, shelters and rest rooms, river fishing, horseback trail rides, backpacking (primitive camping and simple shelters), complete modern camping facilities (including laundromats), group camping; reconstruction of mid-nineteenth-century river settlement, American Heritage Program (re-enactment of old-time crafts) in summer.

Natural assets: primarily forests (upland and floodplain) of various ages and types, mostly young; linear remnants of tall-grass ridgetop prairies in extreme southeastern corner of park; reconstructed prairie; marsh; pasture and lawn; diverse birdlife and other wildlife; loess-topped, fairly rugged bluffs irregularly underlain by Pennsylvanian bedrock (note bedrock under loess on road to Indian Cave); huge sandstone cave with ancient petroglyphs; borders the Missouri River.

NEARBY ATTRACTIONS

See listings for Atchison and Holt counties, Missouri.

TEN

NORTHERN TOUR

Sioux City Area and
North into Plymouth County

This 33-mile loop (map 3) follows paved roads except in the northernmost section, which is graveled. Even though the tour leads through Sioux City, where restaurants are readily available, picnicking is a highly recommended alternative, and hiking is a must for maximum enjoyment. The tour is easily completed in a few hours but could fill a pleasurable day, depending on the amount of time you spend outside your car. Overnight accommodations are not necessary, although campsites are available in Stone State Park. Guided nature hikes are given regularly at Sioux City Prairie and Five-Ridge Prairie. For dates and times, call the educational resources listed under Plymouth and Woodbury counties. The tour may be extended by visiting Ponca State Park, across the Missouri River in Nebraska, which is described in the listings under Dixon County, Nebraska.

SIOUX CITY AREA (5 MILES)

When entering Sioux City and driving to or from tour sites, notice the large loess bluffs, many of which are covered by prairie, that intermittently form the western and southern boundaries of much of Sioux City. The bluffs can be readily viewed from Interstate 29 and Riverside Blvd. (Iowa Hwy. 12), Sioux City being one of the few places where such bluffs are bordered by major highways. A number of public use areas are located along the bluffs, beginning in the south with the rolling Green Valley Golf Course and Park (near Sergeant Bluff) and proceeding north to South Ravine Park, Floyd Monument Park, and War Eagle Park. Most other bluffs

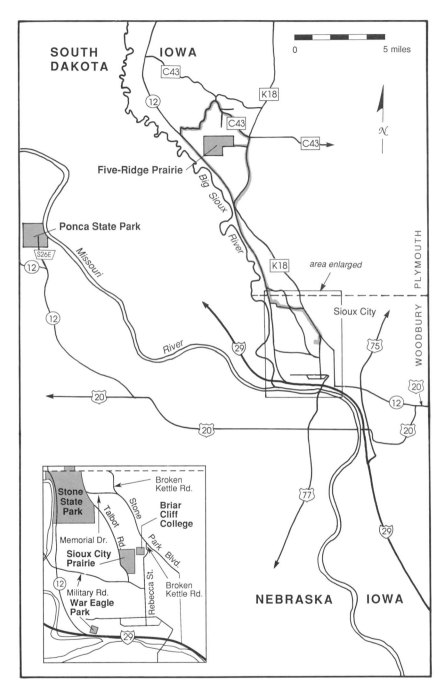

Map 3. *Northern Tour. Heidi Perry.*

Figure 75. *The Northern Tour travels through the largest prairies that remain in the Loess Hills, which contain the greatest diversity of prairie plants. The landscape here is more gently rolling than to the south. Photo by the author.*

are privately owned. Although you could hike in the public areas or stop to enjoy their overlooks, many opportunities in remoter and wilder terrain are available later in the tour.

Sioux City Prairie. Start at the Sioux City Prairie: take Rebecca St. north, turning west into the Briar Cliff College entrance drive. Drive to the parking area at the top of the hill. The marked entrance point at the northeastern corner of the prairie is just beyond and above the maintenance shed.

A prairie of this size within a metropolitan area is a major educational asset, and Sioux City Prairie is used as such, being sought out regularly by the city's amateur naturalists and by biology students at the adjacent college. Rolling over 150 acres that lie east of the first rows of bluffs, the prairie is moister and thus denser with more tall-grass species than the dry, sparse, bluffside prairies you have just been observing. Although trees are invading some drainages, the prairie is burned regularly in an attempt to discourage invasion of woody species. Walking the windblown ridgetop trails here is a must, both for enjoyment of the great diversity of plants and birds and for the view of the distant city. Notice too the typical loess landforms: the irregular skyline, long and narrow ridge crests, and intricate, angular terrain with numerous drainages.

Stone State Park. Proceed north on Rebecca St. and Broken Kettle Rd., which leads into Stone Park Blvd.; turn left onto Memorial Dr., which leads into the east entrance of Stone State Park. When you stop to pay the park entrance fee, note the small demonstration prairie immediately across the road from the fee booth. The park brochure, with a map of roads and trails, and a visitor's guide, which lists flowers in bloom each month, can be picked up at the nearby ranger station.

Stone State Park contains fine examples of prairies and woodlands, including rare species from each. Examples are Keen's myotis and the evening bat in woodlands and tumblegrass, pawnee skipper, and the ottoe skipper in prairies. Much of the park appears to be forested, especially those lowlands that can be seen from the road. Although some woodlands are fairly mature, many are the result of the recent woody invasion of prairies, a process that continues to the present. Bands of invading shrubs extending upslope from woodlands into grasslands threaten to complete the invasion process, obliterating prairies if steps are not taken to prevent it. Whatever their age, the woodlands contain many fewer woodland species than those farther south, where woodland diversity is maximal. Prairies survive primarily as strips along ridgetops and on upper slopes of the driest hillsides.

The tour leads through the park, exiting to the west. You may choose simply to drive the loop, but stops and walks along the road are highly recommended. The Carolyn Benne Nature Trail, located to the north in Coon Hollow, leads first through a fairly mature woodland that probably was once an oak savanna. Note the broad, open-grown shapes of the bur oaks. The trail proceeds upslope to a prairie-covered ridge and back downslope again. Do walk along the ridgetop and examine its vegetation. The trail was named after a Sioux City environmental educator, now deceased, whose work left its mark on local residents and environmental programs to the present day. Brochures available at the trailhead elaborate on the trail's species and features. A second nature trail leaves from the Bur Oak Nature Center, which is open most summer weekend afternoons.

A stop at Dakota Point affords a panoramic view of the Big Sioux River, which like the Missouri River carried substantial amounts of glacial outwash that was, in turn, sorted and lifted by the wind and deposited to form the Loess Hills. Observe here the combined wide valley of the Big Sioux and Missouri rivers, the latter being visible in the distance to the west. The contact point between the flat floodplain, which is dominated by the processes of erosion and alluvial deposition, and the sharply rising hills is quite dramatic. Try to picture clouds of dust rising up out of the valley to form the hills on which you now stand.

Leaving Dakota Point and proceeding straight eastward, notice the fairly rapid upslope invasion of woodlands, a process accelerated by the numerous ravines typical of the Loess Hills. The ravines are slightly moister than adjacent ridges, giving first shrubs and then trees an easy route along which to move upslope.

(If weather and roads are dry, you may wish to exit on the east side of the park and travel north along the unmarked Talbot Rd., which leads into the dirt road that goes east to Iowa Hwy. 12. That route offers good views of the open prairies just north of the park.)

Exiting the park onto Iowa Hwy. 12, turn south to look at the first road-cut east of the road, just outside the park entrance. Notice the horizontal layers of rock underlying the loess. That bedrock dates from the age of the dinosaurs, the Cretaceous Period 90 million years ago. Sediments that formed the rock were deposited in and along the coasts of shallow seas that then were invading the region. Hidden within the rocks are fossils of numerous marine organisms, as well as those of land-dwelling flowering-plant leaves (e.g., forerunners of magnolia, poplar, sassafras, and willow). Flowering plants had only recently come into dominance. In the Loess Hills, Cretaceous bedrock can be seen only in the Sioux City area, where the Missouri River was propelled around a major bend and thus cut deeply into the hills and cliffs bordering the river. Rock exposures also are obvious across the river in Ponca State Park, Nebraska. In the roadcut you are observing, black bands of lignite, reddish stains from oxidized iron, shale, sandstone, and limestone are all present.

From that point north, for approximately 14 miles, a nearly continuous outcrop of Cretaceous bedrock (in particular Dakota sandstone) is exposed along the east side of Iowa Hwy. 12.

SIOUX CITY NORTH TO FIVE-RIDGE PRAIRIE AND BACK SOUTH TO STONE STATE PARK (28 MILES)

From Sioux City, take Iowa Hwy. 12 north into Plymouth County and the far northern Loess Hills. The area differs from the Hills to the south in many ways. Large vertical prairies are absent. The topography in general is more subdued and less sharp-featured. The Cretaceous bedrock is closer to the surface and thus has greater control over the land's shape. The uneven depth of the loess coating the bedrock is obvious in the bluffs of Ponca State Park and surrounding areas across the Missouri River, in Nebraska.

Plymouth County is the heartland of the Loess Hills prairies that remain today. Woodlands, invading shrublands, and croplands are all present, but they are less evident than elsewhere in the Hills. Conversely, prairies that elsewhere have been relegated to the steepest, driest bluffs here roll inland for miles, dominating large sections of the landscape as they probably did throughout the Hills before settlement. Some of those prairies remain remarkably large and open, perhaps because the north's drier climate is more conducive to grasses than trees, or because tree seeds are not abundant, or because land-use practices have emphasized haying and large cattle operations rather than conversion to cropland.

The prairies themselves look different from those to the south, having a greater number of species and in particular more tall-grass species such as switchgrass, Indiangrass, and big bluestem. The large northern grasslands offer refuge for a number of rare species: the plains pocket mouse, prairie rattlesnake, and ottoe skipper, along with buffalo berry, cowboy's delight, and tumblegrass, among other rare plants. Open-country birds find the region especially attractive. The horned lark, killdeer, and upland sandpiper are found in Iowa's native Loess Hills ecosystems only here, along with other more common open-country species. The prairies derive importance as the welcoming ground for Great Plains species that over the past several thousand years migrated eastward along the Missouri River valley and spread from Plymouth County to points farther south in the Loess Hills.

Driving along Iowa Hwy. 12, paralleling the Big Sioux River on your west, you will be passing near the site where the vertebrae of a gigantic marine reptile, a plesiosaur, were excavated in the late 1800s. Those remains from the age of dinosaurs are evidence of the ancient seas that covered the region 90 million years ago. The vertebrae now are on display in the Sioux City Public Museum.

You also will pass near a number of archaeological sites where Great Oasis and Mill Creek prehistoric cultural remains were excavated. The two Indian cultures simultaneously occupied sites in the northeastern Loess

Hills and other nearby regions beginning in approximately A.D. 900. The Indians built substantial and permanent homes, which were clustered together to form villages. Communities raised corn and squash, supplementing their horticultural diet by hunting game and gathering wild plant foods. The Mill Creek culture appears to have been especially structured and socially complex, displaying evidence of close ties with Cahokia, a large political and religious urban center on the Mississippi River. The Great Oasis and Mill Creek cultures had disappeared by 1300, possibly because of the effects of climatic change or increasing pressures from other Indian groups. The fate of the lost cultures remains unknown.

Approximately 6 miles north of Stone State Park, turn north onto County K-18 (at the second K-18 turnoff). Notice catsteps on the dry grassland north of the road. The long, narrow, parallel terraces cutting horizontally across the hillsides were probably formed by the repeated slippage and downslope movement of shelves of loess. Woodlands fill some ravines, leaving upland ridges as grasslands. The valley floors are all cropland. Some hillside land has been converted to cropland, although prairies (sometimes overgrazed) do remain. Some prairies have been hayed rather than grazed, a practice that preserves many of their natural qualities.

A bit more than 3 miles from Iowa Hwy. 12, turn onto the mile-long entrance road into the Five-Ridge Prairie. The road becomes dirt, which is impassable when wet. Once you park, you must hike 0.5 mile to reach the upland prairies and the major segment of this large, L-shaped preserve. Grazing has been intensive in the past. Research on prairie preservation through intensive burning is in progress here. Invading woodlands have claimed two-thirds of the land. Long, narrow prairies remain on uplands, providing habitat for several rare species. A hike into the preserve allows ample opportunity for botanizing, excellent bird-watching, general appreciation of the wild and remote, and a good workout.

Leaving the preserve, turn north again on County K-18; in 0.5 mile, turn west (left) onto graveled County C-43 and follow the signs to Joy Hollow Camp. Note how most of the prairie here has been converted to cropland or planted pasture, and terraces have been installed to control erosion, a major problem in the Hills. Although native Loess Hills communities are not obvious, you still can appreciate the knobs of loess protruding skyward. Proceed 3 miles, passing first a county road to the left and then a county road to the right, until you come to a crossroad. Again following the Joy Hollow Camp sign, turn left onto the road that immediately goes downhill. The curving gravel road will lead you back to Iowa Hwy. 12.

Along the way, you will travel 0.7 mile to the top of the hill. Below you to the northwest and extending along the road for more than a mile lies one of the largest remaining prairies in Iowa, a privately owned (no public access) prairie referred to as the Bowl. It is nestled in one of the largest roadless areas left in the state. Although a bit of the area is tied up in cropland and a water impoundment, the vast majority has been grazed only in moderation. Notice the catsteps on hillsides close to the road. The uneven, deep, nonparallel cuts across distant hillsides have been formed by cattle. Dogwood is beginning to invade the ravines. The Loess Hills end abruptly just north of the Bowl.

As you continue westward and descend from the Hills, you may notice several farm ponds, all of which have been constructed. Deep loess soil is too well drained to form natural lakes. Constructed ponds today provide habitat for some species that previously inhabited Missouri River floodplain wetlands. Watch also for colonies of bank swallows inhabiting vertical loess banks along the road. Soon you cross gentler, lower hills, and then neatly sectioned agricultural land emerges on the flat floodplain below you. Turn south on Iowa Hwy. 12 and return to Sioux City.

ELEVEN

CENTRAL TOUR

DeSoto National Wildlife Refuge to Loess Hills Wildlife Area

This tour (map 4) is 57 miles long, or 81 miles total with the DeSoto auto tour, the two detours, and their returns. The roads are primarily paved, although there are some gravel sections. The tour can be easily driven in a few hours, but allow at least half a day or preferably more so that you can get out of your car and enjoy firsthand the many excellent public use areas. Sections of the tour are fairly isolated. Be sure to fill your gas tank in Missouri Valley. Motel accommodations are available in Missouri Valley near the beginning of the tour and in Onawa near the tour's end. Camping is allowed at the Sioux Dam Fishing Area and in the Loess Hills Wildlife Area. Restaurants, gas stations, and grocery stores are located in Missouri Valley, Pisgah, and Onawa. Sites for picnicking and hiking are scattered throughout the route. (Additional information on tour sites can be found in the listings for Harrison and Monona counties, Iowa.)

If you are driving to DeSoto from Omaha, you may want to plan a stop at one of Omaha's fine nature centers or at Fort Atkinson State Historical Park. The latter is an excellent reconstruction of an 1820s fort, which gives you a feeling for life there in the early historic period. (See the listings for Washington, Douglas, and Sarpy counties, Nebraska, and the first leg of the Southern Tour for details.)

DESOTO NATIONAL WILDLIFE REFUGE EAST TO MISSOURI VALLEY (8 MILES, PLUS 12 MILES FOR DESOTO AUTO TOUR LOOP)

DeSoto is some way from the Loess Hills in both distance and natural characteristics. Yet a tour to this area of the state would not be complete

239

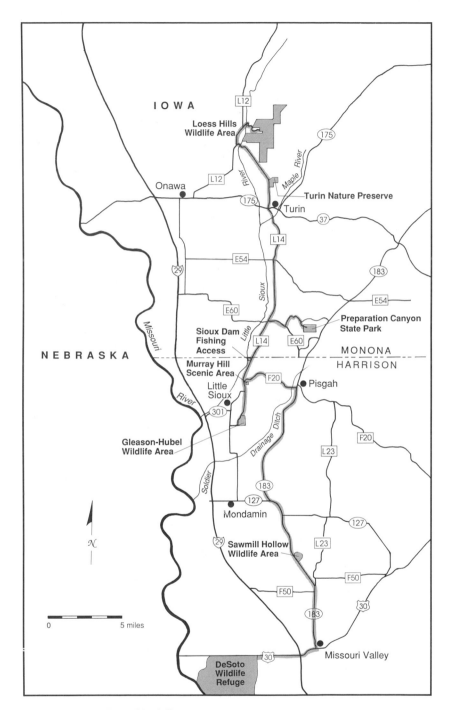

Map 4. *Central Tour. Heidi Perry.*

Figure 76. *The Central Tour leads through the best developed sections of the Loess Hills. It terminates in the Loess Hills Wildlife Area, shown here, which offers ample opportunities for hiking and exploration of both prairies and woodlands. Don Poggensee.*

without a stop at DeSoto to view a seasonally spectacular event of major import. Although waterfowl numbers and habitat along the Missouri River have decreased substantially since the 1800s, hundreds of thousands of ducks and geese still migrate along the corridor from their Gulf Coast wintering grounds to subarctic breeding grounds and back again. En route, the birds assemble at the few remaining protected habitats. In mid-November you may see congregations of more than 200,000 snow geese and large numbers of other geese and duck species at DeSoto. Bald eagles gather in early winter, feeding on the abundant waterfowl. Be sure to consult the Harrison County listings for dates that the refuge is open and for phone numbers to call for information on the status of waterfowl migration.

Start your tour at the refuge visitors' center, where you can observe wildlife displays and the remains of the Civil War–era steamboat, the *Bertrand.*

Driving the self-guided auto tour through the refuge, you will see flood-tolerant forests of cottonwood and willow, which are far different from the upland Loess Hills woodlands you will see later, and plantings of tall prairie grasses. Remember the grasses' size and lush, dense growth so that you can mentally compare them with the shorter, sparser prairie species in the Hills. At one time, river oxbows such as the one constituting the refuge's wetlands were common across the broad Missouri River valley.

Turn east onto U.S. 30 when leaving the refuge. While driving toward the Loess Hills, reflect on differences in pattern and texture between the flat floodplain you are crossing and the rugged bluffs you are approaching. The floodplain, once as wild as the Hills, is now rich agricultural land sliced into neat rectangles by roads, dikes, and fence lines. Except for the few native inhabitants remaining in refuges and roadside wildlands, floodplain animals and plants are exotics that were brought to the area by Euro-American settlers. Many of the nonnative species survive here only because of continued human use of the land.

In contrast, the Loess Hills that rise dramatically ahead of you are patterned by nature's curving lines, the forces of the wind and sun, and the muted colors and sounds of species present for thousands of years. Communities are dominated by wild things—native prairie grasses, bur oak woodlands, migrating hawks, and many more. The change in landforms, type of land use, and dominant species is razor-sharp, occurring within a few feet along the base of the Loess Hills. The change is even more dramatic near the north end of the refuge tour, where the western bluffline is higher and more pristine.

Proceed into Missouri Valley and turn north onto Iowa Hwy. 183.

MISSOURI VALLEY NORTH TO PISGAH (22 MILES)

Leaving Missouri Valley and proceeding north, you will be tracing the boundary between a cultivated floodplain (to the west) and the wilder, more natural Loess Hills (to the east). The picturesque road skirts some high-quality prairie-dominated bluff faces. However, some of the bluffs are far less dramatic than those farther north on the car tour. Here they may be no more than 20 feet high and intensely grazed to the point that planes of loess have slipped downslope and now form large, bare-faced steps in the loess. Massive invasion of eastern red cedar is also a problem. Where terrain becomes more rugged, agricultural use of the land is less intense and, as a result, greater amounts of forest or prairie remain.

While driving along the western edge of the Hills, note how the land was settled. Many small farmsteads were tucked into valleys at the base of the bluffs, often at the northern edge of the valleys where homes would be most sheltered and would best receive the winter's sparse sunlight. The sites were protected from the ravages of the free-flowing Missouri River, yet they offered easy access to wood, water, and potential pasture and cropland. Crops were grown in the Hills rather than the valley until the Missouri River floodplain was drained and cultivated. Watch for small, old cabins tucked in next to larger, modern houses occupied by today's farmers.

Elderly apple trees may attest to the pioneer's recognition of the fruit-growing qualities of loess soil. Reportedly, every homestead had its own apple orchard. From time to time, you also may notice old-time excavations into the loess. Early residents constructed stables, storage caves, kilns, and the like in the dry, structurally stable loess hillsides.

A glance westward onto the Missouri River's floodplain forms an impression of extreme human manipulation and control of the environment. Notice the numerous narrow dikes separating neatly squared fields. Those dikes may hold ditches that confine streams and attempt to prevent flooding, or they may form roadways that provide transportation into valley fields when standing water accumulates in the spring. Gazing back at the Hills, you may notice other attempts to control flooding by slowing runoff. Look for basin terraces that skirt lower grazed slopes and for siltation structures at the base of drainages. Runoff and erosion are major problems in the Hills.

Only one public use area, Sawmill Hollow Wildlife Area (6.5 miles north of U.S. 30, on the east side of the road), lies along this entire stretch. *Do not attempt to drive the dirt entrance road in wet weather.* You can always hike the half-mile, fairly level entrance road.

Toward the north, in the vicinity of Mondamin, you will be traversing a region famous for its apple crops from the time of settlement. A mile beyond the junction with Iowa Hwy. 127 West, for 3 miles northward, Iowa Hwy. 183 skirts the western edge of the southernmost segment of Iowa's proposed Loess Hills Pioneer State Forest, which will include management for prairies as well as woodlands. Sections of the forest have already been purchased from private landowners. Signs indicating public land ownership mark such sections, and other signs designate the route as part of the Lewis and Clark Trail, a reference to Lewis and Clark's expedition up the Missouri River in 1804. It was the white people's first expedition to the area, and its journals provide our first written descriptions of the Hills.

Iowa Hwy. 183 then turns into the Soldier River valley. Throughout the

Hills, the river's water is confined to a straight channel, appropriately named the Soldier Drainage Ditch, to prevent flooding. Before the river was channelized, it meandered back and forth, carving the wide valley you see before you. Note the remnants of old, flat-topped, loess-mantled alluvial terraces, some of which are crossed by the road, along both sides of the valley. Those terraces and remnants of river oxbows seen along the road are signs of the river's earlier wanderings. The hills to the east of the valley are much less rugged than the hills to the west, which are closer to the Missouri River. Soils in the valley are thicker, richer, and better developed than those in the Hills. Approaching Pisgah, to your east, you pass a second section of the proposed Loess Hills Pioneer State Forest.

Just after entering Pisgah, take the first turn to the left (west), onto an unmarked paved road, County F-20.

PISGAH WEST TO MURRAY HILL (4.7 MILES)

Construction of a major highway west from Pisgah was possible because of the area's relatively gently rolling topography. Many sections of the westernmost Loess Hills are too rugged to allow such east-west traffic. After traversing a few miles of cropland and fairly open prairie or planted pasture, the road cuts sharply downhill across the face of a major bluff (Murray Hill), the only highway to do so in the Hills.

Before starting the decline, pull into the marked parking area (Murray Hill Scenic Area) on the south side of the road. The hike from there to the top of Murray Hill is a worthwhile effort, for the hilltop provides an unforgettable view in all directions. Go straight up the slope south of the parking area, veering to the right to pass around the barbed wire fence at the top of the first rise. A footpath then leads to the top of Murray Hill. As you proceed upslope, compare the ungrazed, native prairie underfoot with the grazed prairie across the fence. Also, notice characteristics of the native prairie that will help you differentiate prairie grasslands from human-planted grasslands elsewhere (see the prairies section of chapter 5). The sharp demarcation between the natural Loess Hills ecosystems and the agricultural land on the floodplain below is obvious from Murray Hill.

You might try identifying some of the plants in the Murray Hill prairie, using the sketches in this book. One easy candidate is yucca, found here on the steepest, driest slopes. The dominant Loess Hills grasses, little bluestem and side-oats grama, are also abundant. Consider the harsh environment in which the prairie plants survive—the excessively well-drained soil and steep slopes with extreme exposures to sun and wind. That desertlike environment fosters growth of the Great Plains species that make Loess Hills prairies so unusual.

Driving down the face of Murray Hill, you are traversing successively deeper, older layers of loess. Murray Hill is one of the best sites to observe the phenomenal depth of the fine-textured, uniform accumulation built of wind-lifted silt over thousands of years. Other roadcut features include loess kindchen, whitish knobs of calcium carbonate formed within the loess, and exposed shapes carved into the loess by tree roots. Vertical loess banks are one of the few places where tree roots deep in the soil can be regularly observed. In the roadcut at the base of Murray Hill, note the change in soil texture. It marks the point where the earliest deposits of loess come into contact with underlying, older geological materials.

When County F-20 meets County L-14, look back to the northeast at the southern slope of Murray Hill. The large, vertical, eroded bluff face gives you another glimpse of the depth of the loess. Catsteps—small, naturally forming terraces—are easily seen on upper hillsides nearby.

Within the last few miles, you have viewed all of the region's major landscape types: the flat Missouri River floodplain, the rugged western bluff faces, and the gently sloping inland agricultural lands, which yield to the flat floodplains of the Missouri River's tributaries.

DETOUR: GLEASON-HUBEL WILDLIFE AREA
(5.5 MILES ROUND TRIP)

At the base of Murray Hill, before you proceed northward, consider detouring a few miles south to Gleason-Hubel. Go south for about a quarter of a mile on County F-20 until you meet a dirt road to the east. Look back up into the valley and observe the small, ancient cemetery on the south-facing hillside. It is the burying place of one of the most colorful early settlers of the area, Charles Larpenteur, who died in 1872. Larpenteur worked for the American Fur Company in the upper Missouri River basin until 1851, when he returned to the Loess Hills with his Assiniboine Indian wife and growing family. He joined a group of Mormon pioneers who had dropped out of the migration to Utah and staked out the now-abandoned town of Fontainebleau at the base of Murray Hill. The site flourished as a supply point, stage stop, and post office for several years. With its decline,

Larpenteur went back to fur trading in the Indian country, returning to Iowa a year before his death. The part of County F-20 that you are driving on has been named in memory of Larpenteur.

Pass the dirt-road turnoff and proceed due south, continuing straight onto the gravel road where the paved County F-20 veers to the west. Stay on the road marked Larpenteur Memorial Road, which skirts the base of the bluffs. About halfway to Gleason-Hubel, you will pass another old cemetery with settlement-era gravestones on the east side of the road.

The road borders the western edge of the third segment of the proposed Loess Hills Pioneer State Forest. The area also was designated in 1986 as the southern portion of the Loess Hills National Natural Landmark. Together with a segment north of Turin, the landmark constitutes 10,720 acres and recognizes prime examples of the Loess Hills landform region as nationally significant geological and ecological features worthy of preservation as part of our natural heritage.

Nearly 3 miles after you leave County F-20 you will arrive at rugged Gleason-Hubel, a delightful area where you can hike through woodlands and small ridgetop prairies. When your visit to the area is completed, retrace your steps to the base of Murray Hill.

MURRAY HILL NORTH TO TURIN (13.7 MILES)

At the base of Murray Hill, take County L-14 north. The road is gravel until it intersects County E-54. This especially pictureque section takes you once again along the edge of a rugged section of the Hills, with landform shapes typical of deep loess. Examples are the knobby bumps that jut skyward on your east. Steep loess slopes tend to stand up well, forming cliffs of towering height for fine-textured soil. If chunks of loess sheer off from hillsides, they separate as vertical slabs; stream erosion in side valleys produces deep, vertical-walled gullies.

If you are lucky, you may see bank swallows flitting in and out of holes excavated into cliffs of loess. Colonies of bank swallows frequently select loess roadcuts for nesting sites. You are much less likely to see any of the several rare species found in the area, which include prairie species (such as the dusted skipper) and woodland species (the evening bat and butterflies such as the spicebush swallowtail and hickory hairstreak).

Catsteps often are accentuated on upper slopes but may be difficult to see from the tree-covered bases of hills you are traversing. Near the road,

cottonwood and other floodplain species creep upward from valley terraces. Trees may be invading slopes to their summits, although often
ridgetops remain at least partially covered by prairie. Presumably many of
the bluffs were solid prairie in presettlement times.

Stop to examine the roadcut on your east that lies 1.8 miles north of the
turn onto County L-14 at the base of Murray Hill (or 0.5 mile south of the
entrance to the Sioux Dam Fishing Access). About 10 feet up, notice a
whitish horizontal layer approximately 1 foot thick that contrasts with surrounding, darker glacial-age deposits (see fig. 6). It is volcanic ash, blown
across the Great Plains from major eruptions of now-extinct volcanoes in
today's Yellowstone National Park. Volcanic ash deposits, present in widely
scattered western Iowa sites, have been dated at 610,000 to 2 million years
old. High in the roadcut, in overlying loess, good-sized loess kindchen
once again can be seen.

Once you pass into Monona County, just beyond the Sioux Dam Fishing Access, you are driving along the western edge of the fourth and final
segment of the proposed Loess Hills Pioneer State Forest. It extends north
to County E-60 (the county road to Preparation Canyon State Park) and
east to encompass the park. Consider taking the detour to Preparation
Canyon, which is described in the following section.

About 6 miles beyond County E-60, as you start to cross the flat Maple
River valley, reflect on patterns formed by the region's mixing of hills and
valleys. If you study your state map, you can see that major tributaries to
the Missouri River enter its floodplain at an angle from the northeast. They
are typically paralleled by major highways and thus can be easily identified
on your map. The tributaries cut through the Loess Hills long ago, carving
wide valleys that have since become major agricultural areas. Thus the hills
of loess are discontinuous, chopped into a series of south-facing points
bordered on either side by major valleys. Their topography is often dramatic—look straight north at the rugged bluffs near Turin, carved on either side by major rivers. The deepest loess and the most dramatic landforms border the Missouri River valley.

At Turin, cross Iowa Hwy. 175 and continue straight ahead into town.
Across the road from the old schoolhouse, excavation of sand and gravel
has removed much of the hill. The pit is well known as a source of prehistoric animal fossils: Ice Age fossils of mammoth and mastodon, dire
wolf, musk-ox, Jefferson's ground sloth, river otter, and other animals now
either extinct or no longer present in the region. Perhaps the most famous

fossils found there are those of four human skeletons collectively called Turin man, which at the time of their discovery (1955) received national attention as Ice Age relics thought to be the oldest American human skeletons on record. Later research demonstrated that the skeletons were only approximately 5,000 years old. They had been excavated from burial pits of Middle Archaic Indians. The burials, with their shallow pits containing flexed bodies, red ocher, and grave offerings, provided insight into cultural burial practices of the period.

DETOUR: PREPARATION CANYON STATE PARK (6.6 MILES ROUND TRIP)

When County L-14 crosses County E-60, consider detouring to Preparation Canyon State Park. Following the State Park sign east, you will be skirting the northern border of the fourth segment of the proposed Loess Hills Pioneer State Forest. Notice how once you cross the westernmost, rugged bluffs the landscape gradually opens up, as the hills become more gently rounded and the valleys widen. Although native prairie and forest can be seen along much of the route, some of the wider valleys have been cultivated.

The park itself, approximately half a square mile of primarily bur oak forest (much of which is fairly young), is best explored by foot. Hiking the lovely trails, you will witness firsthand the steep slopes typical of deep loess. Hikers to the easternmost ridge of the park, which is covered by exotic grasses, will be rewarded by a panorama of the Soldier River valley.

The wild, isolated sense of the park reflects its atypical settlement in 1853 by Mormons who left the westward migration to follow the spiritual callings of Charles Thompson. When the settlers, mostly farmers, realized that Thompson was swindling them out of their worldy possessions, Thompson fled in fear for his life. He left behind a town that died by the turn of the century and today has completely disappeared.

Return from the park to County L-14.

TURIN NORTH TO THE LOESS HILLS WILDLIFE AREA (9.5 MILES)

Driving north on the gravel road of County L-14 along the edge of the Missouri River valley, you will be passing some of the most beautiful and rugged bluffs of the Loess Hills. Prairies increase in dominance in the north-

ern Hills, and their increase is visible here. As you look upward at the irregular skyline, notice the fairly expansive prairies that persist on some of
the south- and west-facing hillsides, the driest sites that are most exposed
to sun and wind. If you stop your car and look backward at the north-
facing hillsides, your impression will be totally different, for those moister
slopes have been invaded by trees and are covered by woodlands.

The massive west-facing bluff faces you are passing are called truncated
spurs by geologists. If you had been following this route several thousand
years ago, you would have been going constantly upslope and down over
a series of ridges (or spurs) reaching westward out onto the Missouri River
floodplain. Slowly, the waters of the meandering Missouri River truncated
the extended ridges by washing them away, leaving the steep bluff faces
that you see today.

This entire tour segment is within the northern section of the Loess Hills
National Natural Landmark. In addition to containing ecological and geological features of national significance, the area is home to several rare
prairie species, including the plains pocket mouse, northern grasshopper
mouse, prairie racerunner, ottoe skipper (a small butterfly), Engelmann's
milkweed, and prairie tea. Here a tiny fern unknown to science, prairie
moonwort (see fig. 60), was discovered in 1982.

About a mile north of Turin, start watching for large stones, pebbles,
and cobbles along the base of the roadcuts. The coarse, ancient, much-
weathered materials that underlie the loess were deposited by glaciers at
least half a million years ago.

At 1.7 miles north of Turin, you will see the parking area for the Turin
Loess Hills Nature Preserve, the southern portion of the Loess Hills Wildlife Area. It is one of two areas in the Loess Hills that have been dedicated
into Iowa's State Preserves System. The designation signifies that noteworthy natural features have been given the highest degree of legal protection available in Iowa. Although invasion of prairies by red cedar and
rough-leaved dogwood is evident from the road, upper hillsides contain
fine representatives of mixed-grass prairies. Please observe them from the
roadside. No hiking trails have been constructed to the bluff tops, and
walking up the steep slopes can damage plant cover and increase erosion.

Four miles beyond, you will meet County L-12, which is paved. Proceed
north 1.5 miles and then leave County L-12, turning right onto a gravel
road marked "Public Access." Follow the road 0.4 mile and then, just over
the ditched river, turn right onto another gravel road marked "Loess Hills
Public Access." Continue on this winding road (staying on the main road

and avoiding any turns onto smaller roads) until, in 2 miles, you arrive at the central parking lot of the Loess Hills Wildlife Area, which will be to your right.

The Loess Hills Wildlife Area is the largest protected area in the Loess Hills, containing significant quantities of native woodland and prairie. Woodlands are especially extensive on the moister north- and east-facing slopes. Bands of shrubs (mostly rough-leaved dogwood and smooth sumac) mark the invasion of woody species into prairies. The shrubs also are creeping upslope in prairie ravines. Although invasion of red cedar, shrubs, and trees is evident on many prairie slopes, large prairies remain on higher hillsides facing west and south. A burn program has been established to slow woodland invasion of those areas. Wildlife-area prairies, protected from cattle for more than a decade, look different from the grazed prairies and grasslands you have been seeing on private land. Some valleys of the refuge are farmed, in part to provide food for wildlife.

Leave your car to picnic, hike, or camp. Examine the excellent example of deep gully erosion just across the road from the parking area. Consider following trails along ridges reaching upslope north and east from the parking area, where you can sense what the Loess Hills' original expansive prairies must have been like. (You may wish to review the prairie features and species described in chapter 5, in preparation for your walk.)

If you plan to spend much time in the wildlife area, you may wish to get the small map and lists of plant and animal species available from the Wildlife Management Biologist's office (Department of Natural Resources) in Onawa. You also might consider returning in spring to attend the annual Loess Hills Prairie Seminar, an enjoyable three-day educational program open to anyone interested in the Loess Hills.

TWELVE

SOUTHERN TOUR

Southern Loess Hills in Iowa and
Missouri and Southeastern Nebraska

This tour (map 5) consists of four widely spaced major sites, connecting roads between the four sites, and suggested stops along the connecting roads. The sites and their connecting roads form a loop starting at Omaha's two excellent nature centers, extending south to Indian Cave State Park and then on to the southeastern corner of Nebraska, crossing the Missouri River to reach the southern Loess Hills near Squaw Creek National Wildlife Refuge in Missouri, and then extending northward along the Loess Hills to Iowa's Waubonsie State Park and back to Council Bluffs. Public access sites are fewer in the southern Loess Hills than in the north, so the tour suggests stops at sites of general or historic interest even though they may not exemplify the natural characteristics of deep loess landforms. (Additional information on some of the tour sites can be found in the listings for Nebraska from Douglas and Sarpy counties south, for Missouri, and for Fremont and Mills counties in Iowa.)

The entire tour involves considerable driving. The distance of the loop itself is 250 miles. When all suggested detours and their returns are included, the total will exceed 300 miles. Because of the distances involved, the tour could easily take a long day and, with anything more than brief stops at each site, may require spending the night away from home.

Distances between the major sites are great, and suggested additional stops along the route, although enjoyable, may not be worthy of a separate trip. For those reasons, the tour has been divided into four segments, each centered on one of the major sites and including connecting roads to the following site. Persons wanting a shorter tour can explore a single segment or connect a few segments into a shorter loop. Some visitors may

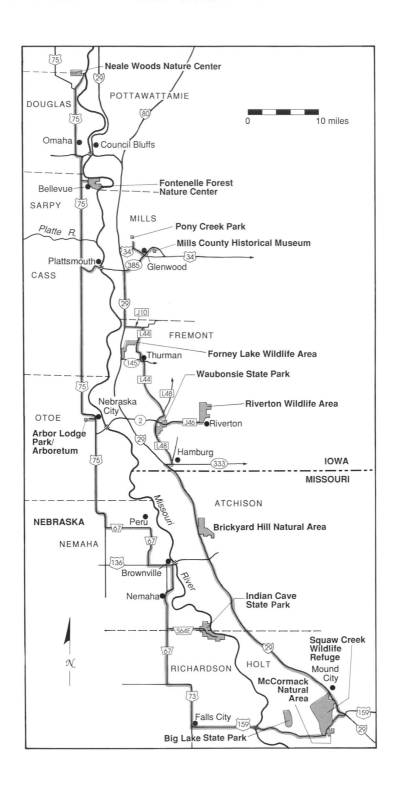

Figure 77. *The southern Loess Hills are narrow and heavily wooded. However, some dramatic prairies remain on the steepest, driest sites. The "vertical prairies" shown here are in Missouri's Atchison County. Don Kurz, Missouri Department of Conservation.*

want to explore sites on only one side of the Missouri River; others may want to cross the Missouri River at Nebraska City or Brownville and explore only sites north of those crossings.

Roads are paved for all but a few miles of the tour, and nearly all of the suggested roads are highways. Restaurants and motels may be widely spaced but can be found along all sections of the tour. Camping facilities are available at or near all the sites outside Omaha.

SEGMENT 1. NEALE WOODS AND FONTENELLE FOREST NATURE CENTERS, AND CONNECTING ROADS SOUTH TO INDIAN CAVE STATE PARK (NEALE WOODS TO INDIAN CAVE, 103 MILES; WITH DETOURS, 111 MILES)

Start at either Neale Woods Nature Center (just north of Omaha) or at Fontenelle Forest Nature Center (in Bellevue). Anyone interested in natural history will enjoy visiting either or both of those model nature centers, with their well-developed and diverse educational programs offered year-round for all ages. Beginners can ask questions and enjoy a naturalist's introduction to the area's features, while more-experienced natural historians can browse the shop's bookshelves or take off alone along miles of trails.

Both nature centers are located on large tracts of primarily wooded land in Nebraska's easternmost bluffs, directly adjacent to and including some of the Missouri River's floodplain. Although you will not see the prairies or drought-tolerant communities that make Iowa's and Missouri's Loess Hills famous, you can enjoy the mixture of forest types typical of the west side of the Missouri River. You will get a feeling for rugged, steep loess terrain as you hike Fontenelle Forest's bluffs. Drop in anytime for a casual walk or self-guided nature hike or to enjoy the interpretive centers. Call ahead for information on guided tours and scheduled programs. (See listings under Douglas and Sarpy counties, Nebraska, for phone numbers.)

Leave Omaha on U.S. 75 south. Features characteristic of deep loess are best found on the east side of the Missouri River, but a few interesting stops are possible on the Nebraska side as well. Rolling agricultural land with few, if any, typical loess features dominates the view along all major north-south highways in eastern Nebraska. In western Iowa and Missouri, north-south highways follow the Missouri River's floodplain, giving a clear view of loess bluffs that rise to the east. But Nebraska's highways lie above and to the west of the floodplain. To see the narrow band of loess-dominated features found in Nebraska, you have to turn east off the highway onto a secondary road. When you reach the bluff's edge, you typically find a narrow wooded strip bordered on top and bottom by intensively used agricultural land. Sometimes the bluff is rugged and steep, but more commonly height and slope are moderate. Agricultural use takes precedence along segments of the bluffline, and woodlands disappear. In spots, the loess is deep. In a very few sites (such as Indian Cave State Park, south of Brownville in Nemaha County, and in southern Thurston County), rugged terrain extends westward from the bluff face, and forests cover the bluff top. Prairies are absent. For all effective purposes, they have disappeared from the bluffs, bowing to the plow and presumably to invading woodlands. A few small prairies remain on ridgetops in Indian Cave State Park, but they are tallgrass prairies rather than the mixed-grass prairies that make the Loess Hills grasslands so special. Prairie or savanna ecosystems once covered at least some of the now-forested lands. Where forests have been studied in detail, prairie plants have been found scattered through the understory.

From Omaha to Plattsmouth, you frequently have excellent views of the Loess Hills bluffline across the Missouri River to the east. Because the floodplain is narrow there, the bluffs are fairly close. You also cross the Platte River valley, which historically has been important as a village site for Indians and a travel route for the pioneers.

When you reach Plattsmouth, stop to examine the spectacular vertical banks of loess bordering the sunken railroad grade just west of the toll bridge to Iowa. Turn east onto U.S. 34 at Plattsmouth, following the highway about 3 miles through town. When you start down the hill toward the Missouri River floodplain and toll bridge, park your car and walk over to the fence line on the north side of the road. From there you can peer down into the deep cuts through the loess bluffs, carved as a passageway for trains. Banks such as those demonstrate the stability and cohesion of loess. Nearly vertical cuts into loess can stand unsupported for many years. Retrace your steps back out of town.

Proceeding south once again on U.S. 75, the route for the most part is uneventful. Distant views of the Loess Hills decrease in frequency.

Just before U.S. 75 reaches downtown Nebraska City, turn west onto Second Ave. and follow it 0.7 mile to Arbor Lodge State Historical Park and Arboretum. The large, elderly trees and sedate atmosphere of the manicured park make it an excellent site for relaxing and picnicking after a long drive. Tour the mansion to appreciate the history of the homestead. Use the tagged trees and prairie-plants garden to brush up on your plant identification, but remember that tree plantings include species introduced to the region as well as native species of local woodlands. The founders of the mansion and arboretum loved trees and thoroughly appreciated the beauty of gardens. Contemplate the richness created by the sensitive propagation of trees, but keep in mind that many thousands of acres of prairies have been destroyed throughout the Midwest by human-planted and naturally spreading woodlands.

Return to U.S. 75 and proceed south. Just south of Nebraska City, the stepped loess banks bordering Nebraska Hwy. 2 a short distance east of U.S. 75 offer another demonstration of loess's inherent stability.

Continue south from Nebraska City for 15 miles, to the intersection of Nebraska Hwy. 67. Take Hwy. 67 east past Peru and then south to U.S. 136, where you turn east toward Brownville. Persons eager to reach Indian Cave State Park may continue south on Hwy. 67; those with more time may want to stay on U.S. 136 to the charming town of Brownville, which lies just north of the highway. Tucked into the hills next to the Missouri

River, Brownville is one of Nebraska's oldest towns. Although it offers little insight into the nature of loess communities, the town does boast a number of historic buildings, several museums, a summer repertory theater, Missouri River boat cruises in season, and the restored dredge *Captain Meriwether Lewis,* which helped channelize the Missouri River in the thirties and today houses a historical museum. Call the Brownville Historical Society (402-825-6001) to inquire about the calendar of events; most are concentrated in the summer season. Events and local services are offered with a pleasantly relaxed, small-town friendliness. If you want to gaze at Missouri's distant Loess Hills while picnicking, climb Fourth St. to the hilltop Capitol Square Park. Brownville State Recreation Area, just south of the bridge, offers picnic areas and campsites.

When leaving Brownville, take advantage of one of your few chances to drive along the Missouri River valley at the base of Nebraska's bluffs. Take the paved turn to the south just before (west of) the bridge. The road is marked as leading to the Brownville State Recreation Area. Continue south past the nuclear power station, where the road becomes well-maintained gravel. Compared with Iowa's Loess Hills, Nebraska's bluffs are much lower, far more heavily forested, and less steep, with fewer exposures of bare loess. In places bedrock is pronounced and overlain by loess. Occasionally, you can glimpse the cropland that commences at the tops of the bluffs. The road you are following reconnects with Nebraska Hwy. 67 at Nemaha, 5 miles south of Brownville. Proceed south to Indian Cave State Park, entering on Spur 64E. Note the prairie grasses planted along much of the entrance road.

SEGMENT 2. INDIAN CAVE STATE PARK AND CONNECTING ROADS SOUTH AND EAST TO MISSOURI'S SOUTHERN LOESS HILLS (INDIAN CAVE TO MCCORMACK NATURAL AREA, 43 MILES; WITH PARK DRIVING, ABOUT 55 MILES)

Stop at the park office to pick up a visitor's guide and map. Indian Cave State Park encompasses nearly 5 square miles of primarily wooded bluff lands. The park's natural features are best appreciated by hiking the numerous foot trails. Forests are young; many are second growth. At one time a sawmill operated at St. Deroin, the settlement-era town partially reconstructed at the north end of the park. Timber growing nearby helped power the steamboats that traveled up and down the Missouri River. The diversity of forest plants and animals is greater here in the southern corner of the state than it is farther to the north. Individual trees are larger and more robust and woodland communities are more extensive than those to the north, where moisture is limited. (Nebraska's native woodland communities are described in sidebar 8.)

At one time, prairies undoubtedly were more extensive here than they are now. Most prairies have been replaced by woodland, cropland, and nonnative grassland. The park contains the only native bluff prairies of significance in eastern Nebraska's public ownership. Watch for native prairies in the southeastern corner of the park as you drive along the road to Indian Cave. Just before you enter the river bottomland, look up to the bluff tops on either side of the road. There you will see narrow upland prairies that run northwest and southeast along ridgetops and out onto a few spurs. Hiking trails 8 and 10 lead through those prairies. If you hike either trail, notice the lush tall grasses (big bluestem, Indiangrass, and others) and plants such as the brilliant orange butterfly milkweed. They are more characteristic of the moist tall-grass prairies than of the dry, sparse, mixed-grass prairies in the Loess Hills. The Nebraskan prairies are destined to disappear soon unless the state begins controlled burns or other prairie management programs. Shrubs and young oak are invading the prairies rapidly.

As you drive other park roads, some of which are sunken into loess hill sides, you can see that in places loess is deep and highly dissected, resembling Iowa's corrugated landscape. That is a rarity in Nebraska, where loess is not uniformly deep enough to control the appearance of the landscape as it does in the Loess Hills east of the river. If you drive south along the Missouri River to Indian Cave, you will see a thin covering of loess over massive exposures of Pennsylvanian bedrock.

Leaving the park, take note of the reconstructed prairie just south of the park entrance. Take Spur 64E back to the highway junction, and proceed south on Nebraska Hwy. 67 and east and south U.S. 73 to Falls City. Turn east on U.S. 159, which crosses the Missouri River at Rulo and then leads across the broad river valley to the McCormack Natural Area. Watch for raptors and waterfowl along the valley crossing. As you approach the knobby, dissected loess bluffs, note the stark contrast between their rugged form and the absolutely flat plain shaped by the Missouri River. When U.S. 159 veers to the north, you will be driving along the eastern edge of the Squaw Creek Refuge. Watch the east side of the road for the McCormack Natural Area entrance.

SEGMENT 3. MCCORMACK LOESS MOUNDS NATURAL AREA
AND SQUAW CREEK NATIONAL WILDLIFE REFUGE, WITH
CONNECTING ROADS NORTH TO WAUBONSIE STATE PARK
(MCCORMACK TO WAUBONSIE, 60 MILES; WITH THE
WILDLIFE REFUGE LOOP, 70 MILES)

Rugged loess bluffs with good-sized prairies prevail just south of Mound
City, especially between Squaw Creek National Wildlife Refuge and the
McCormack Natural Area. Stop at the latter and hike 0.5 mile uphill to the
top of the bluffs. Take the trail eastward from the parking area; when you
approach the ridgetop, double back toward the road, going west on the
spur trail. As you approach the bluff's edge, you will have a magnificent
view of the Squaw Creek wetlands immediately below you and of distant
Kansas. Climb the observation tower for an excellent view of surrounding
prairies and woodlands.

Notice that prairies survive on the bluffs on the hottest, driest sites: hilltops and slopes facing south and west. The driest prairies contain many
Great Plains plant species now endangered in Missouri. Note also the cut
stumps and signs of burning, attempts to control the aggressive invasion of
forests. Several management techniques are being tested here: cutting,
cutting combined with herbicide treatment of stumps, and burns in various
seasons. In some cleared areas, you will see the relict catsteps, evidence
that preforest ecosystems were prairie. The preserve contains the southernmost Loess Hills prairies of any size and is close to the southern limit of
today's Loess Hills prairies.

A shorter tour into the Hills can be made by hiking the Loess Bluff Trail
behind the Squaw Creek visitors' center, 1.5 miles farther down the highway. The trail leads uphill to extremely narrow ridgetops, which are characteristic of the Loess Hills. The view is just as spectacular as in the McCormack area, but prairies along the Loess Bluff Trail are not as extensive or
diverse, lacking many of the Great Plains species found elsewhere.

While climbing the Loess Bluff Trail, you pass through a fairly mature
woodland with a diversity of tree and understory species. Many Loess Hills
woodlands are significantly younger and less diverse. Diverse woodlands
such as Squaw Creek's will become more prevalent as Loess Hills forests
mature. You may notice a few trees common along the trail that are not
abundant in Iowa: chinquapin oak (a tree with acorns but lacking the
deeply lobed leaves of other oaks) and pawpaw (with smooth-edged, large

leaves, 6 to 12 inches long). They are more typical of forests farther to the south and east, extending their range only into the most southeastern Loess Hills. That distributional pattern is true of several woody species. As a result, southern Loess Hills forests in general are far more diversified than woodlands of the northern Hills.

Be sure to bring your binoculars along to this delightfully rich birding area. In addition to watching for upland songbirds while hiking in the Hills, you will want to drive the 10-mile loop through the Squaw Creek Refuge, observing the diversity and abundance of resident and migrating birdlife. Up to 300 bald eagles can be present from mid-November to early January. Eagles often can be seen from the visitors' center and the loop road. More than a thousand mammoth white pelicans typically spiral over the refuge in September and April. Around Thanksgiving, at the peak of migration, more than 200,000 snow geese and more ducks can be present at one time. Call the refuge in advance (816-442-3187) to check the status of migrating waterfowl.

While touring the refuge, imagine the natural richness of the Missouri River floodplain before the river's flow was constricted to a narrow channel. The refuge contains several wetland plant communities, including stands of wetland grasses such as cordgrass (*Spartina*), bluejoint (*Calamagrostis*), and slough grass (*Beckmannia*), counterparts to the dry Loess Hills prairies. The loop road gives a good overview of the well developed Loess Hills bluffs and prairies found near the wildlife refuge.

Leaving Squaw Creek, take U.S. 159 to Interstate 29 North. The approach to I-29 and the interstate itself, just north of your entrance point, lie in deep cuts through the loess bluffs. Note once again the apparent cohesiveness of the nearly vertical loess bluffs.

Driving north along the interstate from Squaw Creek to Iowa, you will be skirting the western edge of the Loess Hills, but you may wonder in places what happened to the landforms. Low, rolling hills without any sign of rugged topography or native plant communities are heavily used as pasture for cattle. The Loess Hills become more prominent in Atchison County, Missouri, where in some areas they rise as sizable bluffs, some of which retain good-sized prairies. Although the steepest bluffs are inaccessible to agricultural use, many have become heavily wooded since fire's cessation. Look toward the tops of the bluffs and you can still see knobs of prairie-covered loess, impressive with their catsteps, yucca, and sparse vegetation. They are the last remnants of Missouri's once extensive loess prairies, a harbinger of what will become of Iowa's prairies if forest invasion is not checked. Invasion of the southern Loess Hills has proceeded more rapidly than in the north because the moister climate favors tree growth and because trees have always been more prevalent in the south, providing an abundant seed source for invasion.

Just south of the Watson exit (116), you will pass Brickyard Hill Loess Mound Prairie Natural Area on your east. The ridgetop prairies you can see from the interstate and those you just visited near Squaw Creek are the only Loess Hills prairies in public ownership in Missouri.

Exit Interstate 29 at Hamburg, just across the Iowa border, and take Iowa Hwy. 333 east a mile into Hamburg. Turn left (north) on Main St. and then left again (west) onto E St., which becomes County L-48. The road winds to the north and proceeds along the base of the bluffs toward Waubonsie State Park.

Approaching the park from the south, you will see some exceptionally large and undisturbed vertical prairies covering bluffs facing the Missouri River valley. They are the largest such prairies remaining in the Loess Hills, sometimes exceeding 20 acres in size and free of woody vegetation from bluff top to bottom. They inhabit truncated spurs—the edges of ridges that at one time extended out into the river valley but were partially washed away long ago by the meandering Missouri. When hiking in Waubonsie, you can examine some of those prairies and bluff faces from above.

When you reach Iowa Hwy. 2, turn east and travel 1 mile to the entrance road to Waubonsie.

SEGMENT 4. WAUBONSIE STATE PARK AND CONNECTING ROADS NORTH TO COUNCIL BLUFFS (WAUBONSIE TO COUNCIL BLUFFS, 44 MILES; WITH PARK DRIVING AND DETOURS, 70 MILES)

Enter Waubonsie State Park on Iowa Hwy. 239S. Come equipped with plant and bird guidebooks and a pair of binoculars, because you will see some of the most extensive and best-developed woodlands in the Loess Hills. More species of trees are present, and trees often are larger and older than their northern counterparts. One of the park's bur oaks has been aged at more than 300 years.

The relatively large number of woodland plants is matched by a diversity of birds and other animals. Waubonsie has been called one of the state's most interesting birding spots and an important habitat for rare butterflies. In the park you may see southern birds such as the Louisiana water thrush, forest animals such as the gray squirrel and gray fox, and any of several rare woodland animals: the zebra swallowtail, woodland vole, Keen's myotis, and hickory hairstreak or other butterflies, all species that are rare or absent farther north.

Prairie openings in the park are not devoid of such treasures; they contain biscuit-root, a plant endangered in Iowa, and the western Great Plains skink, another endangered species making its last stand on rugged, minuscule prairies at the edge of bur oak woodlands.

Natural features can be enjoyed along any of the hiking or bridle trails, but be sure to walk the Sunset Ridge Interpretive Trail at the western edge of the park. The self-guided nature trail leads through prairie-speckled woodlands to bluff-top prairies with a spectacular view of the Missouri River floodplain and glimpses of distant Nebraska, Missouri, and Kansas. Along the trail, you will see broad-crowned bur oaks. Their wide growth form indicates that the oaks matured in a savanna, where widely spaced trees grew among prairie grasses. From the high vantage at the bluff top, observe how the woodlands below you cover the moister sites (the lower hillsides, north- and east-facing hillsides) to the ridgetop, while prairies persist on the drier south- and west-facing upper ridges. Prairies on ridgetops and upper hillsides also can be seen near the picnic area at the southern end of the park.

When leaving Waubonsie, if you are touring in spring or fall during waterfowl migration, you may wish to turn east on Iowa Hwy. 2 and proceed 5 miles to Riverton Wildlife Area. You also can turn west on Hwy. 2 and then north on County L-48, which in 1.5 miles leads into County L-44. Continue on County L-44 along the base of the bluffs to Forney Lake Wildlife Area. (At Thurman, you must turn west onto Iowa Hwy. 145 and proceed to the edge of town, where you will once again pick up County L-44 north.) Both wildlife areas boast large populations of migrating ducks and geese, especially in spring when they are not hunted.

County L-48/44 from Waubonsie to Forney Lake is a picturesque road along which you will again see extensive hillside prairies, although some are heavily grazed and suffering from cedar invasion. In that section of the Hills, prairies are close to the outermost, western bluffs, and the inner hills are forested. Hillsides continue to demonstrate rugged, highly dissected topography typical of the Loess Hills, although those features extend only a few miles eastward. The Loess Hills are constricted to a narrow band south of Harrison County, Iowa. The bedrock exposed in the limestone quarry near Forney Lake dates from the Pennsylvanian Period, the age of the great coal-forming swamps, which began approximately 310 million years ago.

Proceed north from Forney Lake toward Council Bluffs by the most direct route. When County L-44 intersects County J-10, turn west and proceed to Interstate 29 North. Few public use areas exist in the Hills between Forney Lake and Council Bluffs, and the natural qualities of the Hills are subdued. Forests prevail, human disturbances increase, and in places the dramatic, dissected loess landscape is reduced to gently rolling hills. Wild character does not disappear completely, however; bobcats (endangered in the state) have been sighted in Mills County's Loess Hills, and the threatened ornate box turtle still can be found in the area.

The only stop you may want to make along this stretch is at the Mills County Historical Museum, if you are passing Glenwood when the museum is open (on summer Sunday afternoons). The area around Glenwood has been the heartland of archaeological studies in the Hills. Paleo-Indian spear points are occasionally found nearby, and a few Archaic Indian sites have been discovered in Mills County. Most significant, the Glenwood Indians, Iowa's members of the Nebraska Culture, thrived here from approximately 1000 to 1300. The Glenwood Indians, found in Iowa only in the Loess Hills, settled in horticultural communities whose residents constructed and inhabited unfortified earth-lodge houses. Excavations of Glenwood sites have left no remains for today's casual observer, but the museum displays a large Indian artifact collection and a movie on the Glenwood, as well as collections of pioneer artifacts.

You may want to picnic just west of Glenwood at Pony Creek Park on your way out of town. Return to Interstate 29 and proceed home.

FURTHER READING
AND OTHER RESOURCES

ARCHAEOLOGY AND HISTORY

Anderson, D. C. 1975. *Western Iowa Prehistory.* Ames: Iowa State University Press. An easily read summary of the development of Indian cultures in Iowa's Loess Hills region.

Chapman, C. H., and E. F. Chapman. 1983. *Indians and Archaeology of Missouri.* Columbia: University of Missouri Press. A beautifully illustrated and readable summary of the development of Indian cultures in Missouri; not related specifically to events in the Loess Hills.

Office of the State Archaeologist, Iowa. n.d. *Educational Series 1 through 7.* Concise, two- to four-page descriptions of the Paleo-Indian Period (1), Archaic Period (2), Woodland Indians (3), Mill Creek Culture (4), Nebraska Culture at Glenwood (5), Oneota Indians (6), and Great Oasis Indians (7) in Iowa. Single copies can be requested at no cost through the Office of the State Archaeologist, Eastlawn, University of Iowa, Iowa City, Iowa 52242; phone (319) 335-2389. Similar descriptions are contained in *Exploring Iowa's Past: A Guide to Prehistoric Archaeology,* by L. M. Alex, 1980, Iowa City: University of Iowa Press.

Sorensen, S., and B. P. Chicoine. 1982. *Sioux City: A Pictorial History.* Norfolk, Va.: Donning Co. The numerous photos of the settling of Sioux City provide an interesting glimpse of extensive Loess Hills prairies in the surrounding countryside; also contains a brief history of the Sioux City area.

The following films may be available at Iowa's local libraries or area education agencies; they also can be rented or purchased through the Audiovisual Center, Seashore Hall, University of Iowa, Iowa City, Iowa 52242; phone (319) 335-2567 for rental, (319) 335-2539 for purchase.

Earthlodge People, 1973, 20 minutes. Describes the lives of the Glenwood Indians (Nebraska Culture).

Iowa's Ancient Hunters: The Reconstruction of a Prehistoric Site, 1978, 28 minutes. Shows excavation of the Archaic Indian artifacts of Iowa's Cherokee Sewer site, which is just northeast of the northernmost Loess Hills.

Mill Creek Village, 1974, 27 minutes. Describes the fortified Wittrock village, an Iowa Mill Creek Culture site.

Prehistoric Cultures, 1974, 26 minutes. Gives an overview of the development of Indian cultures in Iowa.

Other films in the series describe excavations outside the Loess Hills region.

NATURAL COMMUNITIES

Great Plains Flora Association (T. M. Barkley, ed.). 1986. *Flora of the Great Plains*. Lawrence: University Press of Kansas. Definitive guide to the plants of the region.

Thom, R. H., and G. Iffrig. 1985. *Directory of Missouri Natural Areas*. Jefferson City: Missouri Natural Areas Committee, Missouri Departments of Conservation and Natural Resources. Brief descriptions and maps of the McCormack and Brickyard Hill natural areas and of other natural areas throughout Missouri.

Van Bruggen, T. 1983. *Wildflowers, Grasses, and Other Plants of the Northern Plains and Black Hills* (Third Edition). Interior, S.D.: Badlands Natural History Association. An excellent guide for the beginning botanist or for anyone not familiar with the unusual mixture of plant species in the Loess Hills; color photographs and plant descriptions.

Weaver, J. E. 1954. *North American Prairie*. Lincoln, Neb.: Johnson Publishing. Although written some time ago, this classic description of the midcontinent prairies still provides insight to amateurs and professionals. Easily readable descriptions of community types and major plant species.

MISCELLANEOUS

Iowa Conservationist: A Special Loess Hills Issue 43 (4), April 1984. Articles and illustrations of Iowa's Loess Hills geology, archaeology, fossil mammals, animals, plants, their western affinities and community associations, preservation needs, and selected public use areas. Excellent and colorful introductions for the lay public. Available in libraries throughout the state, or request a copy (while supplies last) from *Iowa Conservationist*, Department of Natural Resources, Wallace State Office Building, Des Moines, Iowa 50319-0034.

Iowa's Loess Hills: A Symposium, Part 1. 1985. *Proceedings of the Iowa Academy of Science* 92 (5). Technical articles on amphibians and reptiles, birds, mammals, fungi, rust fungi, soil lichens, bryophytes, pteridophytes, vegetation, and phytogeography of Iowa's Loess Hills.

Iowa's Loess Hills: A Symposium, Part 2. 1986. *Proceedings of the Iowa Academy of Science* 93 (3). Technical articles on geography, frontier settlement, Quaternary biostratigraphy and paleoecology of fossil mammals, Pleistocene and recent land snails, archaeological research, and preservation of Iowa's Loess Hills.

Mutel, C. F. 1989. Iowa's Loess Hills. In *Take the Next Exit*, R. Sayre, ed. Ames: Iowa State University Press. An introduction to natural features of Iowa's Loess Hills, with descriptions of sites where one can view the major features described.

CHAPTER
BIBLIOGRAPHIES

1. INTRODUCTION

Beveridge, T. R. 1980. *Geologic Wonders and Curiosities of Missouri.* Educational Series 4, Division of Geology and Land Survey. Rolla: Missouri Department of Natural Resources. Pp. 37–42.

Bush, B. F. 1895. Notes on the mound flora of Atchison County, Missouri. *Missouri Botanical Garden Annual Report* 6: 121–134.

Cassen, A. L. 1960. Surveying the first railroad across Iowa: The journal of John I. Blair. *Annals of Iowa* 3 (35): 332.

Catlin, G. 1876. *North American Indians*, Vol. 2. London: Chatto and Windus. Pp. 407–408.

Culbertson, I. A., J. F. McDermott, ed. 1952. Journal of an expedition to the Mauvaises Terres and the Upper Missouri in 1850. *Smithsonian Institution Bureau of American Ethnology* Bulletin 147: 29–31.

Prior, J. C. 1976. *A Regional Guide to Iowa Landforms.* Educational Series 3. Iowa City: Iowa Geological Survey.

Ruhe, R. V. 1969. *Quaternary Landscapes of Iowa.* Ames: Iowa State University Press. Figure 2.2.

Thom, R. H., and J. H. Wilson. 1980. The natural divisions of Missouri. *Transactions, Missouri Academy of Science* 14: 9–21.

2. ANCIENT LANDSCAPES AND COMMUNITIES

Anderson, D. C., and P. M. Williams. 1974. Western Iowa proboscidians. *Proceedings of the Iowa Academy of Science* 81: 185–191.

Anderson, W. I. 1983. *Geology of Iowa: Over Two Billion Years of Change.* Ames: Iowa State University Press.

Baker, R. G., and K. A. Waln. 1985. Quaternary pollen records from the Great Plains and Central United States. Pp. 191–203 in *Pollen Records of Late-Quaternary North American Sediments*, V. Bryant, Jr., and R. Holloway, eds. Dallas: American Association of Stratigraphic Palynologists Foundation.

Bettis, E. A., J. C. Prior, G. R. Hallberg, et al. 1986. Geology of the Loess Hills region. *Proceedings of the Iowa Academy of Science* 93: 78–85.

Brenner, R. L., R. F. Bretz, B. J. Bunker, et al. 1981. *Cretaceous Stratigraphy and Sedimentation of Northwestern Iowa, Northeastern Nebraska, and Southeastern South Dakota*. Guidebook Series 4. Iowa City: Iowa Geological Survey.

Frest, T. J., and J. R. Dickson. 1986. Land snails (Pleistocene-Recent) of the Loess Hills: A preliminary survey. *Proceedings of the Iowa Academy of Science* 93: 130–157.

Hallberg, G. R. 1986. Pre-Wisconsinan glacial stratigraphy of the Central Plains region in Iowa, Nebraska, Kansas, and Missouri. *Quaternary Science Reviews* 5: 11–15. (IGCP Project 24.)

Kurten, B., and E. Anderson. 1980. *Pleistocene Mammals of North America*. New York: Columbia University Press.

McDonald, H. G., and D. C. Anderson. 1983. A well-preserved ground sloth (*Megalonyx*) cranium from Turin, Monona County, Iowa. *Proceedings of the Iowa Academy of Science* 90: 134–140.

Rhodes, R. S., and H. A. Semken. 1986. Quaternary biostratigraphy and paleoecology of fossil mammals from the Loess Hills region of western Iowa. *Proceedings of the Iowa Academy of Science* 93: 94–129.

Shimek, B. 1895. A theory of loess. *Proceedings of the Iowa Academy of Science* 3: 82–89.

———. 1910. Geology of Harrison and Monona counties. *Iowa Geological Survey* 20, Annual Report 1909: 271–486.

White, C. A. 1870. The bluff deposit. *Report of the Geological Survey of the State of Iowa* 1: 103–117.

3. HUMANS COME TO THE HILLS

Alex, L. M. 1980. *Exploring Iowa's Past: A Guide to Prehistoric Archaeology*. Iowa City: University of Iowa Press.

Anderson, A. D. 1961. The Glenwood sequence: A local sequence for a series of archaeological manifestations in Mills County, Iowa. *Journal of the Iowa Archeological Society* 10: 1–101.

Anderson, D. C. 1973. Ioway ethnohistory: A review (parts 1 and 2). *Annals of Iowa* 41: 1228–1241 and 42: 41–59.

———. 1975. The development of archaeology in Iowa: An overview. *Proceedings of the Iowa Academy of Science* 82: 71–86.

———. 1985. Reburial: Is it reasonable? *Archaeology* 38: 48–51.

———. 1987. Toward a processual understanding of the Initial Variant of the Middle Missouri tradition: The case of the Mill Creek Culture in Iowa. *American Antiquity* 52: 522–537.

———, M. Finnegan, J. Hotopp, et al. 1978. The Lewis Central School site (13PW5): A resolution of ideological conflicts at an Archaic ossuary in western Iowa. *Plains Anthropologist* 23: 183–219.

———, J. A. Tiffany, M. Fokken, et al. 1979. The Siouxland Sand and Gravel site (13WD402): New data and the application of Iowa's new state law protecting ancient cemeteries. *Journal of the Iowa Archeological Society* 26: 121–145.

Andreas, A. T. 1875. *Illustrated Atlas of the State of Iowa*. Chicago: Andreas Atlas Co.

Baker, R. G., and K. L. Van Zant. 1980. Holocene vegetational reconstruction in northwestern Iowa. Pp. 123–138 in *The Cherokee Excavations: Holocene Ecology and Human Adaptations in Northwestern Iowa*, D. C. Anderson and H. A. Semken, eds. New York: Academic Press.

Bardwell, J. 1981. The paleoecological and social significance of zooarchaeological remains from Central Plains tradition earth lodges of the Glenwood locality, Mills County, Iowa. M.S. thesis, University of Iowa, Iowa City.

Benn, D. W., ed. 1981. Archaeological investigations at the Rainbow Site, Plymouth County, Iowa. Technical report, funded by the Interagency Archaeological Services, Denver, under Contract C3571 (78); Luther Archaeological Research Center Report, Decorah, Iowa.

Bettis, E. A., and D. M. Thompson, eds. 1982. *Interrelationships of Cultural and Fluvial Deposits in Northwest Iowa*. Ames: Association of Iowa Archaeologists.

———, J. C. Prior, G. R. Hallberg, et al. 1986. Geology of the Loess Hills region. *Proceedings of the Iowa Academy of Science* 93: 78–85.

Bonney, M. A. June 1984. Historical survey of early settlement in the Loess region of Iowa, 1803–1900. Unpublished report to the State Preserves Board, Department of Natural Resources, Des Moines.

———. 1986. Frontier settlement and community building on western

Iowa's Loess Hills. *Proceedings of the Iowa Academy of Science* 93: 86–93.

Bush, B. F. 1895. Notes on the mound flora of Atchison County, Missouri. *Missouri Botanical Garden Annual Report* 6: 121–134.

Chapman, C. H., and E. F. Chapman. 1983. *Indians and Archaeology of Missouri.* Columbia: University of Missouri Press.

Fisher, A. K., W. D. Frankforter, J. A. Tiffany, et al. 1985. Turin: A Middle Archaic burial site in western Iowa. *Plains Anthropologist* 30: 195–218.

Henning, D. R., ed. 1968. Climatic change and the Mill Creek Culture of Iowa: Part 1. *Journal of the Iowa Archeological Society* 15: 1–191.

———, ed. 1969. Climatic change and the Mill Creek Culture of Iowa: Part 2. *Journal of the Iowa Archeological Society* 16: 192–358.

———. 1980. A prehistoric cultural resource in the proposed Perry Creek Reservoir. Department of Anthropology, Division of Archaeological Research, Technical Report 80-10, University of Nebraska, Lincoln.

Horton, L. N. 1981. A forest people on the plains: The Potawatomi Indians. Pp. 24–38 in *Oklahoma's Forgotten Indians*, R. E. Smith, ed. Oklahoma City: Oklahoma Historical Society.

Hotopp, J. A. 1978. A reconsideration of settlement patterns, structures, and temporal placement of the Central Plains tradition in Iowa. Ph.D. dissertation, University of Iowa, Iowa City.

Iowa Secretary of State. Land survey records, 1836–1858. Field notes of the survey of townships and township boundaries in Iowa. State Archives, State Historical Society of Iowa, Des Moines.

Loomis, W. E., and A. L. McComb. 1944. Recent advances of the forest in Iowa. *Proceedings of the Iowa Academy of Science* 51: 217–224.

Mott, M. 1938. The relation of historic Indian tribes to archaeological manifestations in Iowa. *Iowa Journal of History and Politics* 36: 227–314.

Pammel, L. H., G. B. MacDonald, and H. B. Clark. 1915. The native and cultivated forest trees and shrubs of the Missouri River basin. *Proceedings of the Iowa Academy of Science* 22: 23–56.

Pottawattamie County Board of Supervisors. 1875. Minute books. Council Bluffs, Iowa.

Rhodes, R. S., and H. A. Semken. 1986. Quaternary biostratigraphy and paleoecology of fossil mammals from the Loess Hills region of western Iowa. *Proceedings of the Iowa Academy of Science* 93: 94–129.

Thompson, D. M., and E. A. Bettis. 1980. Archaeology and Holocene landscape evolution in the Missouri drainage of Iowa. *Journal of the Iowa Archeological Society* 27: 1–60.

Thomson, G. W. 1987. Iowa's forest area in 1832: A reevaluation. *Proceedings of the Iowa Academy of Science* 94: 116–120.

———, and H. G. Hertel. 1981. The forest resources of Iowa in 1980. *Proceedings of the Iowa Academy of Science* 88: 2–6.

Tiffany, J. A. 1986. An archaeological research design for the western Iowa Loess Hills. *Proceedings of the Iowa Academy of Science* 93: 158–162.

———, S. J. Schermer, J. L. Theler, et al. 1988. The Hanging Valley site (13HR28): A stratified Woodland burial locale in western Iowa. *Plains Anthropologist* 33: 219–260.

VanderZee, J. 1913. Episodes in the early history of the western Iowa country. *Iowa Journal of History and Politics* 11: 323–363.

Wedel, M. M. 1981. The Ioway, Oto, and Omaha Indians in 1700. *Journal of the Iowa Archeological Society* 28: 1–13.

White, C. A. 1870. The bluff deposit. *Report of the Geological Survey of the State of Iowa* 1: 103–117.

Williams, P. A. 1975. The Williams site (13PM50): A Great Oasis component in northwest Iowa. *Journal of the Iowa Archeological Society* 22: 1–33.

4. PHYSICAL CHARACTERISTICS OF TODAY'S LOESS HILLS

Bettis, E. A. 1983. Gully formation in western Iowa. *Iowa Geology* 8: 12–15.

———, J. C. Prior, G. R. Hallberg, et al. 1986. Geology of the Loess Hills region. *Proceedings of the Iowa Academy of Science* 93: 78–85.

Darwin, C. 1882. *The Formation of Vegetable Mould through the Action of Worms.* New York: International Scientific Series, Appleton and Co.

National Oceanographic and Atmospheric Administration. June 1977. Climatography of the United States No. 20: Climate of Oregon, Missouri. Environmental Data Service, National Climatic Center, Asheville, N.C.

———. July 1984. Climatography of the United States No. 20: Glenwood, Iowa. Environmental Data Service, National Climatic Center, Asheville, N.C.

———. Local climatological data—Annual summary with comparative data 1980, St. Joseph, Missouri. Environmental Data Service, National Climatic Center, Asheville, N.C.

————. Local climatological data—Annual summary with comparative data 1986, Sioux City, Iowa. Environmental Data Service, National Climatic Center, Asheville, N.C.

Oschwald, W. R., F. F. Riecken, R. I. Dideriksen, et al. 1965. Principal soils of Iowa. Special Report 42, Department of Agronomy, Iowa State University Cooperative Extension Service, Ames, Ia.

Piest, R. F., C. E. Beer, and R. G. Spomer. 1976. Entrenchment of drainage systems in western Iowa and northwestern Missouri. *Proceedings of the Third Federal Inter-agency Sedimentation Conference*, prepared by the Sedimentation Committee of Water Resources Council. Pp. 5-48 to 5-60.

————, L. S. Elliott, and R. G. Spomer. 1977. Erosion of the Tarkio drainage system, 1845–1976. *Transactions of the American Society of Agricultural Engineers* 20: 485–488.

Ruhe, R. V., J. C. Prior, T. E. Fenton, et al. 1983. Survey of potential natural landmark. Unpublished report prepared for National Park Service, U.S. Department of Interior.

Salisbury, N. E., and R. Dilamarter. 1969. *An Eolian Site in Monona County, Iowa*. Development Series Report 7, Iowa State Advisory Board for Preserves. Iowa City: Iowa Department of Natural Resources.

Shaw, R. H., and P. J. Waite. 1964. *The Climate of Iowa III. Monthly, Crop Season and Annual Temperature and Precipitation Normals for Iowa*. Department of Agronomy, Iowa State University, and the Weather Bureau, U.S. Department of Commerce, cooperating Special Report 38.

Shimek, B. 1910. Geology of Harrison and Monona counties. *Iowa Geological Survey* 20, Annual Report 1909: 271–486.

Thompson, D. M., and E. A. Bettis. 1980. Archaeology and Holocene landscape evolution in the Missouri drainage of Iowa. *Journal of the Iowa Archeological Society* 27: 1–60.

Waite, P. J. 1967. Climate of the States: Iowa. U.S. Department of Commerce, Environmental Science Services Administration, Climatography of the United States No. 60-13.

5. NATURAL COMMUNITIES OF THE LOESS HILLS TODAY

Aikman, J. M. 1926. Distribution and structures of the forests of eastern Nebraska. *University of Nebraska Studies* 26: 3–75.

————, and C. L. Gilly. 1948. A comparison of the forest floras along the

Des Moines and Missouri rivers. *Proceedings of the Iowa Academy of Science* 55: 63–73.

Barkley, T. M., ed. 1977. *Atlas of the Flora of the Great Plains.* Ames: Iowa State University Press.

Bush, B. F. 1895. Notes on the mound flora of Atchison County, Missouri. *Missouri Botanical Garden Annual Report* 6: 121–134.

Carter, J. L. 1963. Plant communities of the loess bluffs of northwestern Iowa. *Proceedings of the Iowa Academy of Science* 70: 45–50.

Christiansen, J. L., and C. M. Mabry. 1985. The amphibians and reptiles of Iowa's Loess Hills. *Proceedings of the Iowa Academy of Science* 92: 159–163.

Farrar, D. R. 1985. Pteridophytes of Iowa's Loess Hills—Adaptations to dry habitats. *Proceedings of the Iowa Academy of Science* 92: 196–198.

Frest, T. J., and J. R. Dickson. 1986. Land snails (Pleistocene-Recent) of the Loess Hills: A preliminary survey. *Proceedings of the Iowa Academy of Science* 93: 130–157.

Great Plains Flora Association (T. M. Barkley, ed.). 1986. *Flora of the Great Plains.* Lawrence: University Press of Kansas.

Heineman, P. L. 1982. Woody plant invasion of Iowa loess bluff prairies. Master's thesis, University of Nebraska at Omaha.

Howe, R. E. 1984. Animals of the Loess Hills. *Iowa Conservationist* April: 28–30.

———, D. M. Roosa, J. P. Schaufenbuel, et al. 1985. Distribution and abundance of birds in the Loess Hills of western Iowa. *Proceedings of the Iowa Academy of Science* 92: 164–175.

Iffrig, G. F. 1983. Distribution and ecology of Loess Hills prairies in Atchison and Holt counties in northwestern Missouri. Pp. 129–133 in *Proceedings of the Seventh North American Prairie Conference, August 4–6, 1980,* C. L. Kucera (ed.). Springfield, Mo.

Johnson, T. R. 1987. *The Amphibians and Reptiles of Missouri.* Jefferson City: Missouri Department of Conservation.

Lampe, R. P., and J. B. Bowles. 1985. Annotated checklist of the mammals of the Loess Hills of western Iowa. *Proceedings of the Iowa Academy of Science* 92: 176–179.

Missouri Department of Conservation. *Checklist of Rare and Endangered Species of Missouri, August 1985.* Jefferson City: Natural History Section.

Morrill, J. B., Jr. 1953. Prairie flora on the Missouri River bluffs of western Iowa. M.S. thesis, Iowa State College, Ames.

Nelson, P. W. 1985. *The Terrestrial Natural Communities of Missouri.* Jefferson City: Missouri Department of Natural Resources.

Novacek, J. M. 1985. The Loess Hills of western Iowa: A problem in phytogeography. *Proceedings of the Iowa Academy of Science* 92: 213–219.

————, D. M. Roosa, and W. P. Pusateri. 1985. The vegetation of the Loess Hills landform along the Missouri River. *Proceedings of the Iowa Academy of Science* 92: 199–212.

Oard, M., and L. H. Tiffany. 1985. Soil lichens of the Loess Hills prairies in Iowa. *Proceedings of the Iowa Academy of Science* 92: 189–192.

Pammel, L. H., G. B. MacDonald, and H. B. Clark. 1915. The native and cultivated forest trees and shrubs of the Missouri River basin. *Proceedings of the Iowa Academy of Science* 22: 23–56.

Pusateri, W. P. 1984. Special plants of the Loess Hills. *Iowa Conservationist* April: 23–26.

Schennum, W. 1984. Natural communities of the Loess Hills. *Iowa Conservationist* April: 20–22.

Shimek, B. 1910. Geology of Harrison and Monona counties. *Iowa Geological Survey* 20, Annual Report 1909: 271–486.

Tiffany, L. H., and G. Knaphus. 1985. The rust fungi (*Uredinales*) of the Loess Hills region of Iowa. *Proceedings of the Iowa Academy of Science* 92: 186–188.

————, J. E. Shearer, A. W. Gabel, et al. 1985. Fungi of the Iowa Loess Hills. *Proceedings of the Iowa Academy of Science* 92: 180–185.

Van der Linden, J. O., and D. R. Farrar. 1985. Bryophytes of the Loess Hills of western Iowa. *Proceedings of the Iowa Academy of Science* 92: 193–195.

Varland, D. 1982. Raptor banding and migration in the loess bluffs of southwest Iowa. *Iowa Bird Life* 52: 43–47.

Weaver, J. E. 1954. *North American Prairie.* Lincoln, Neb.: Johnson Publishing.

Wilson, J. H. 1984. *Rare and Endangered Species of Missouri.* Jefferson City: Missouri Department of Conservation.

6. THE LOESS HILLS OF THE FUTURE

Bettis, E. A., J. C. Prior, G. R. Hallberg, et al. 1986. Geology of the Loess Hills region. *Proceedings of the Iowa Academy of Science* 93: 78–85.

Farrar, D. R., D. M. Roosa, and J. C. Prior. 1985. Iowa's Loess Hills—A national treasure. *Proceedings of the Iowa Academy of Science* 92: 157–158.

Iowa Conservation Commission. December 1985. Loess Hills Pioneer State Forest preliminary management plan. Unpublished document, Iowa Department of Natural Resources, Des Moines.

Prior, J. C. 1987. Loess Hills: A national natural landmark. *Iowa Geology* 12: 16–19.

Roosa, D. M. 1984. Preserving the Hills and conservation update. *Iowa Conservationist* April: 15.

————, D. R. Farrar, and M. Ackelson. 1986. Preserving natural diversity in Iowa's Loess Hills: Challenges and opportunities. *Proceedings of the Iowa Academy of Science* 93: 163–165.

Ruhe, R. V., J. C. Prior, T. E. Fenton, et al. 1983. Survey of potential natural landmark. Unpublished report prepared for National Park Service, U.S. Department of Interior.

Schennum, W. 1984. Natural communities of the Loess Hills. *Iowa Conservationist* April: 20–22.

Tiffany, J. A. 1986. An archaeological research design for the western Iowa Loess Hills. *Proceedings of the Iowa Academy of Science* 93: 158–162.

INDEX

Illustrations are indicated by *italicized* numbers